ICSE 10

MATHEMATICS

12 + 1 SAMPLE PAPERS

MOHIT TRIPATHI

EDUCATOR

B.Sc. (Maths), MCA, GNIIT

BOARD SAMPLE PAPER WITH SOLUTION & ANALYSIS BASED ON LATEST CIRCULAR ISSUED IN JULY FOR 2022-23 EXAM

Title	: ICSE Class 10 Mathematics
Author Name	: Mr. Mohit Tripathi
Published By	: EduGorilla Community Pvt. Ltd.
Publishers Address	: Sector-12/651, First Floor Opp. Arvindo Park, Near Jama Masjid, Indira Nagar, Lucknow, Uttar Pradesh-226016, India

Copyright

Disclaimer

Created & Compiled by EduGorilla Publication

Printed by EduGorilla Community Pvt. Ltd.

INDEX

ICSE X MATHEMATICS

TO GET FREE ACCESS SCAN THE QR CODE

* PREVIOUS YEAR PAPERS
* TOPPERS ANSWER SHEET
* STUDY NOTES & VIDEO LECTURES
* VIDEO SOLUTION OF SELF-ASSESSMENT PAPERS
* LIVE DISCUSSION ON MEQ (MOST EXPECTED QUESTIONS)

MATHEMATICS (51)

CLASS X

There will be **one** written paper of **two and a half** hours duration carrying **80 marks** and an Internal Assessment of **20 marks**.

Certain questions may require the use of Mathematical tables (Logarithmic and Trigonometric tables).

1. Commercial Mathematics
   (i) Goods and Services Tax (GST)
   Computation of tax including problems involving discounts, list price, profit, loss, and basic/cost price including inverse cases. Candidates are also expected to find the price paid by the consumer after paying State Goods and Service Tax (SGST) and Central Goods and Service Tax (CGST) - the different rates as in vogue on different types of items will be provided. Problems based on corresponding inverse cases are also included.
   (ii) Banking
   Recurring Deposit Accounts: computation of interest and maturity value using the formula:

$$I = P \frac{n(n+1)}{2 \times 12} \times \frac{r}{100}$$

$$MV = P \times n + I$$

2. Algebra
   (i) Linear Inequations
   Linear Inequations in one unknown for x $\in$ N, W, Z, R. Solving:
   - Algebraically and writing the solution in set notation form.
   - Representation of solution on the number line.
   (ii) Quadratic Equations in one variable
   (a) Nature of roots
   - Two distinct real roots if $b - 4ac > = 0$
   - Two equal real roots if $b - 4ac = 0$
   - No real roots if $b^2 - 4ac < 0$
     (b) Solving Quadratic Equations by:
     - Factorization
     - Using Formula.
   (c) Solving simple quadratic equation problems.
   (iii) Ratio and Proportion
   (a) Proportion, Continued proportion, the mean proportion
   (b) Componendo, dividendo, alternendo, invertendo properties and their combinations.
   (iv) Factorization of polynomials:
   (a) Factor Theorem.
   (b) Remainder Theorem.
   (c) Factorizing a polynomial completely after obtaining one factor-by-factor theorem.
   Note: f (x) not to exceed degree 3.
   (v) Matrices
   (a) Order of a matrix. Row and column matrices.
   (b) Compatibility for addition and multiplication.
   (c) Null and Identity matrices.
   (d) Addition and subtraction of 2×2 matrices.
   (e) Multiplication of a 2×2 matrix by a non-zero rational number ⊚ a matrix.
   (vi) Arithmetic Progression
   - Finding the General term of an A.P.

- Finding the Sum of the first 'n' terms of an A.P.

(vii) Co-ordinate Geometry

(a) Reflection

i. Reflection of a point in a line: x=0, y =0, x= a, y=a, the origin.

ii. Reflection of a point in the origin.

iii. Invariant points.

(b) Co-ordinates expressed as (x, y), Section formula, Midpoint formula, Concept of a slope, equation of a line, and Various forms of straight lines.

i. Section and Mid-point formula (Internal section only, coordinates of the centroid of a triangle included).

ii. Equation of a line:

- Slope –intercept form $y = mx + c$
- Two-point form $(y - y_1) = m(x - x_1)$ Geometric understanding of 'm' as slope/ gradient/ $\tan\theta$ where θ is the angle the line makes with the positive direction of the x-axis.
  Geometric understanding of 'c' as the y-intercept/the ordinate of the point where the line intercepts the y-axis/
  the point on the line where x=0.
- Conditions for two lines to be parallel or perpendicular.

3. Geometry

(a) Similarity

Similarity, conditions of similar triangles.

i. Comparison with congruency, keyword being proportionality.

ii. Three conditions: SSS, SAS, AA. Simple applications (proof not included).

iii. Applications of Basic Proportionality Theorem.

(b) Circles

i. Angle Properties

- The angle that an arc of a circle subtends at the center is double that which it subtends at any point on the remaining part of the circle.
  - Angles in the same segment of a circle are equal.
  - The angle in a semi-circle is a right angle.

ii. Cyclic Properties:

- Opposite angles of a cyclic quadrilateral are supplementary.
- The exterior angle of a cyclic quadrilateral is equal to the opposite interior angle.

iii. Tangent and Secant Properties:

- The tangent at any point of a circle and the radius through the point are perpendicular to each other.
- If two circles touch, the point of contact lies on the straight line joining their centers.
- From any point outside a circle, two tangents can be drawn, and they are equal in length.
- If two chords intersect internally or externally then the product of the lengths of the segments are equal.
- If a chord and a tangent intersect externally, then the product of the lengths of segments of the chord is equal to the square of the length of the tangent from the point of contact to the point of intersection.
- If a line touches a circle and from the point of contact, a chord is drawn, the angles between the tangent and the chord are respectively equal to the angles in the corresponding alternate segments.

Note: Proofs of the theorems are not required.
Applications of all Circle Theorems in solving numerical and theoretical problems are included.

iv. Constructions
   (a) Construction of tangents to a circle from an external point.
   (b) Circumscribing and inscribing a circle on a triangle and a regular hexagon.

4. Mensuration
   Area and volume of solids – Cylinder, Cone, and Sphere.
   Three-dimensional solids - right circular cylinder, right circular cone, and sphere: Area (total surface and curved surface) and Volume. Direct application problems include cost, Inner and Outer volume, and melting and recasting methods to find the volume or surface area of a new solid. Combination of solids included.
   Note: Problems on Frustum are not included.

5. Trigonometry
   (a) Using Identities to prove simple algebraic trigonometric expressions
   $\sin^2 A + \cos^2 A = 1$
   $1 + \tan^2 A = \sec^2 A$
   $1 + \cot^2 A = \operatorname{cosec}^2 A; \ 0 \le A \le 90°$
   (b) Heights and distances: Solving 2-D problems involving angles of elevation and depression using trigonometric tables.
   Note: Cases involving more than two right-angled triangles are excluded.

6. Statistics
   Statistics – basic concepts, Mean, Median, Mode. Histograms and Ogive.
   (a) Computation of:

◉ Measures of Central Tendency: Mean*, median class, and modal class for grouped data (only continuous data).
* Mean by all 3 methods included:

Direct $\qquad : \quad \dfrac{\Sigma fx}{\Sigma f}$

Short-cut $\quad : \quad A + \dfrac{\Sigma fd}{\Sigma f}$ where $d = x - A$

Step-deviation:
$A + \dfrac{\Sigma ft}{\Sigma f} \times i$ where $t + \dfrac{x - A}{i}$

(b) Graphical Representation. Histograms and Less than Ogive.
   ▪ Finding the mode from the histogram, the upper quartile, lower Quartile, and median, etc. from the ogive.
   ▪ Calculation of inter Quartile range.

7. Probability
   Random experiments, Sample space, Events, the definition of probability, and Simple problems on single events.
   SI UNITS, SIGNS, SYMBOLS AND ABBRVIATIONS (1) Agreed conventions
   (a) Units may be written in full or using the agreed symbols, but no other abbreviation may be used.
   (b) The letter 's' is never added to symbols to indicate the plural form.
   (c) A full stop is not written after symbols for units unless it occurs at the end of a sentence.
   (d) When unit symbols are combined as a quotient, e.g., meter per second, it is recommended that it should be written as m/s, or as m s^{-1}.
   (e) Three decimal signs are in common international use: the full point, the mid-point, and the comma. Since the full point is sometimes used for multiplication and the comma for spacing

digits in large numbers, it is recommended that the mid-point be used for decimals.

(2) Names and symbols

In general			
Implies that	$\Rightarrow$	is logically equivalent to is approximately equal to	$\Leftrightarrow$
Identically equal to $\equiv$			$>>$

In set language			
Belongs to	$\in$	does not belong to is not equivalent to	$\notin$
is equivalent to	$\leftrightarrow$		$\nleftrightarrow$
union	$\cup$ universal set ξ	the intersection is contained in the empty set whole numbers real numbers	$\cap \subset$
natural (counting) N numbers			$\varnothing$ W R
integers Z			

In measures			
Kilometer	km	Meter	m
Centimeter	cm	Millimeter	mm
Kilogram	kg L	Gram	g
Liter square kilometer	km²	Centiliter	cL
square centimeter	cm²	Square meter	m2
meter cubic meter	m³	Hectare	ha
kilometers per hour	km/h	Cubic centimeter	cm³
		Meters per second	m/s

INTERNAL ASSESSMENT

The minimum number of assignments: Two assignments as prescribed by the teacher.

Suggested Assignments

- Comparative newspaper coverage of different items.
- Survey of various types of Bank accounts, and rates of interest offered.
- Planning a home budget.
- Conduct a survey in your locality to study the mode of conveyance / Price of various essential commodities / favorite sports. Represent the data using a bar graph/histogram and estimate the mode.
- To use a newspaper to study and report on shares and dividends.
- Set up a dropper with ink in it vertically at a height say 20 cm above a horizontally placed sheet of plain paper. Release one ink drop; observe the pattern, if any, on the paper. Vary the vertical distance and repeat. Discover any pattern of relationship between the vertical height and the ink drop observed.
- You are provided (or you construct a model as shown) - three vertical sticks (the size of a pencil) stuck to a horizontal board. You should also have discs of varying sizes with holes (like a doughnut). Start with one disc; place it on (in) stick A. Transfer it to another stick (B or C); this is one move (m). Now try with two discs placed in A such that the large disc is below, and the smaller disc is above (number of discs = n=2 now). Now transfer them one at a time in B or C to obtain a similar situation (larger disc below). How many moves? Try with more discs (n = 1, 2, 3, etc.) and generalize.

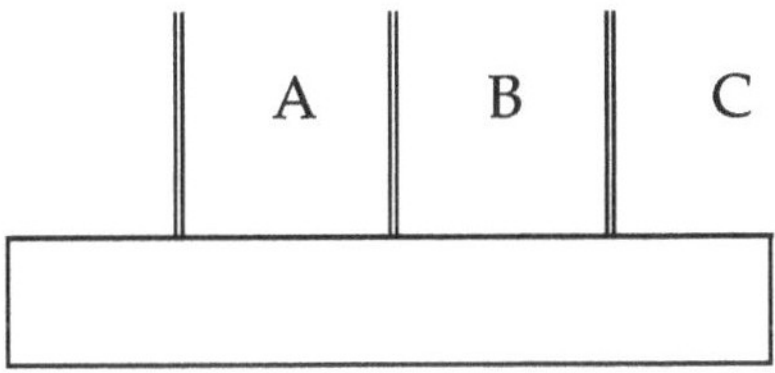

- The board has some holes to hold marbles, red on one side and blue on the other. Start with one pair. Interchange the positions by making one move at a time. A marble can jump over another to fill the hole behind it. The move (m) equals 3. Try with 2 (n=2) and more. Find the relationship between n and m.

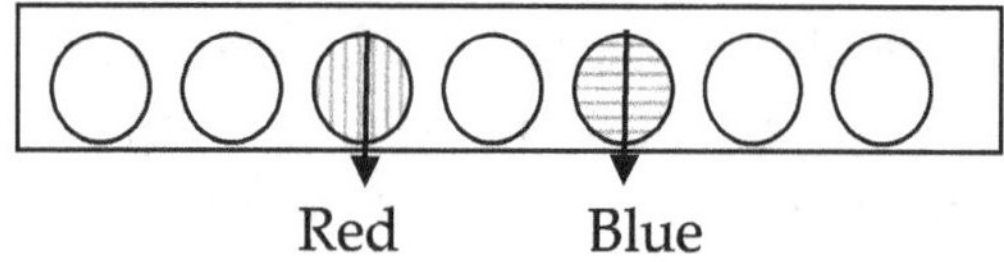

- Take a square sheet of paper side 10 cm. Four small squares are to be cut from the corners of the square sheet and then the paper is folded at the cuts to form an open box. What should be the size of the squares cut so that the volume of the open box is maximum?
- Take an open box, four sets of marbles (ensuring that the marbles in each set are of the same size), and some water. By placing the marbles and water in the box, attempt to answer the question: do larger marbles or smaller marbles occupy more volume in a given space?
- An eccentric artist says that the best paintings have the same area as their perimeter (numerically). Let us not argue whether such sizes increase the viewer's appreciation, but only try and find what sides (in integers only) a rectangle must have if its area and perimeter are to be equal (Note: there are only two such rectangles).
- Find by constructing the center of a circle, using only a 60-30 set square and a pencil.
- Various types of "cryptarithms".

EVALUATION

The assignments/project work is to be evaluated by the subject teacher and by an External Examiner. (The External Examiner may be a teacher nominated by the Head of the school, who could be from the faculty **but not teaching the subject in the section/class**. For example, a teacher of Mathematics of Class VIII may be deputed to be an External Examiner for Class X, Mathematics projects.)

The Internal Examiner and the External Examiner will assess the assignments independently.

Award of Marks   (20 Marks)
Subject Teacher (Internal Examiner)
                                      10 marks
External Examiner   10 marks

The total marks obtained out of 20 are to be sent to the Council by the Head of the school. The Head of the school will be responsible for the online entry of marks on the Council's CAREERS portal by the due date.

Mind Map : Quadratic Equation

Trace the Mind Map
- First Level
- Second Level
- Third Level

Quadratic Equations

Definition

- Standard form of quadratic equation is $ax^2+bx+c = 0$, where a, b and c are all real numbers and $a \neq 0$.
- Equation with one variable, having power two e.g., $3x^2+4x+7 = 0$.

Discriminant

- For quadratic equation $ax^2+bx+c = 0$, $a \neq 0$ the expression $b^2 - 4ac$ is called discriminant and it is denoted by 'D'.
- $D = b^2 - 4ac$.

Simple work problems

Based on quadratic equations are follows
(i) Problems based on time and work
(ii) Problems based on speed, distance, and time
(iii) Problems based on geometrical figure

Methods

Factorization

- Factorise expression on left hand side. Put each factor equal to zero and solve.

e.g., $x^2+x-6=0 \Rightarrow$
$(x+3)\,(x-2) = 0$
Either $x+3 = 0$ or $x - 2 = 0$
$\Rightarrow x = -3$ or $x = 2$

Completing Square

Any quadratic equation can be converted into the form $(x + a)^2 \pm b^2 = 0$ by adding and subtracting same terms

Factorize :
$x^2+6x+9=0$
$(x+3)^2=0$
$x=-3, -3$

Method of solving by using formula

If the quadratic equation is $ax^2+bx+c=0$, $a \neq 0$

$$x = \frac{-b \pm \sqrt{b^2 - 4ac}}{2a}$$

here $b^2 - 4ac$ is discriminant (D)
If D $= 0$, then the roots are real and equal
If D > 0, then the roots are real and unequal
If D < 0, then the roots are imaginary.

Mind Map : Ratio and Proportion

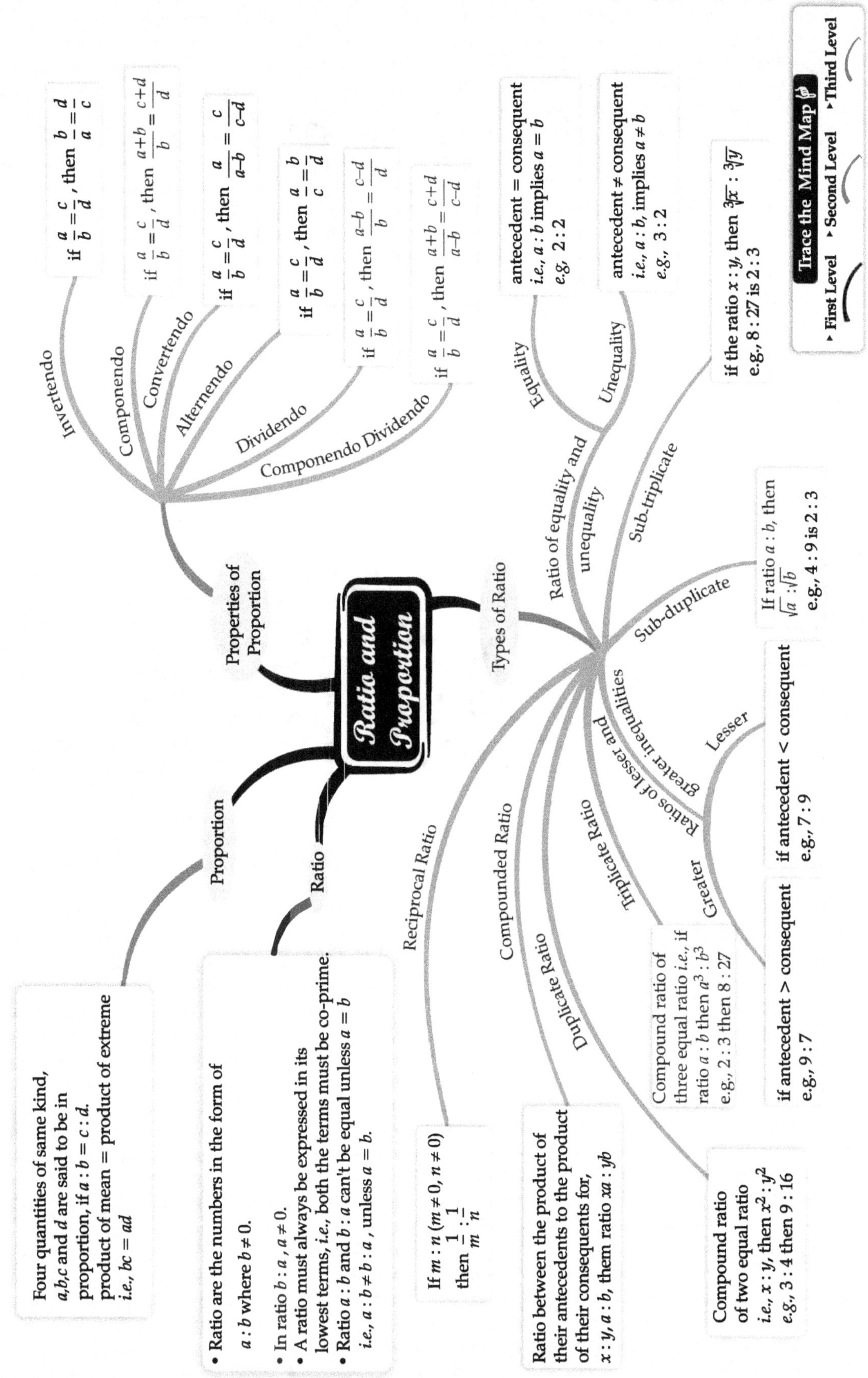

Mind Map : Remainder and factor Theorem

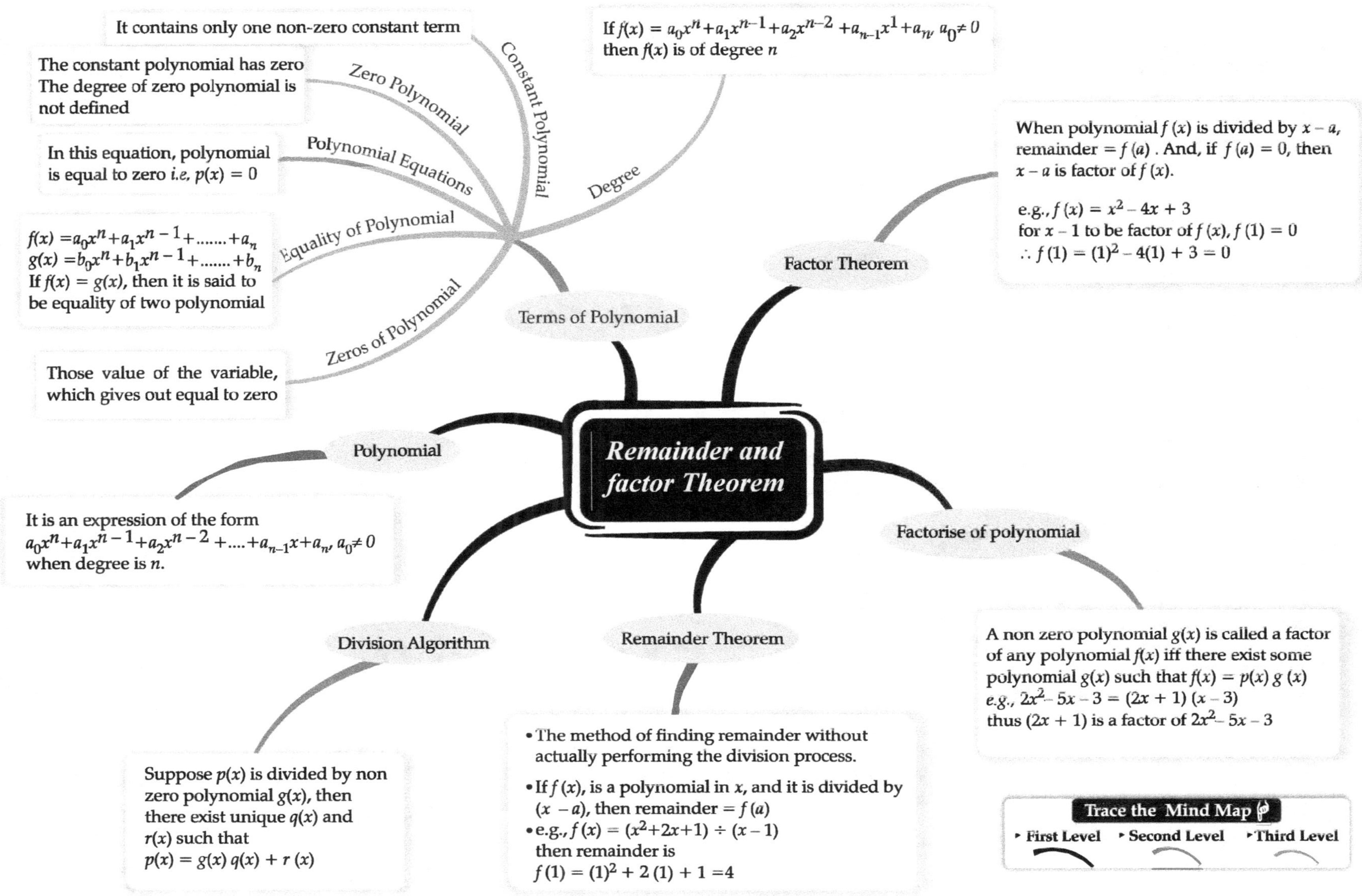

Remainder and factor Theorem

Factor Theorem

When polynomial $f(x)$ is divided by $x - a$, remainder $= f(a)$. And, if $f(a) = 0$, then $x - a$ is factor of $f(x)$.

e.g., $f(x) = x^2 - 4x + 3$
for $x - 1$ to be factor of $f(x)$, $f(1) = 0$
$\therefore f(1) = (1)^2 - 4(1) + 3 = 0$

Factorise of polynomial

A non zero polynomial $g(x)$ is called a factor of any polynomial $f(x)$ iff there exist some polynomial $g(x)$ such that $f(x) = p(x)\, g(x)$
e.g., $2x^2 - 5x - 3 = (2x + 1)(x - 3)$
thus $(2x + 1)$ is a factor of $2x^2 - 5x - 3$

Remainder Theorem

- The method of finding remainder without actually performing the division process.
- If $f(x)$, is a polynomial in x, and it is divided by $(x - a)$, then remainder $= f(a)$
- e.g., $f(x) = (x^2 + 2x + 1) \div (x - 1)$
  then remainder is
  $f(1) = (1)^2 + 2(1) + 1 = 4$

Division Algorithm

Suppose $p(x)$ is divided by non zero polynomial $g(x)$, then there exist unique $q(x)$ and $r(x)$ such that
$p(x) = g(x)\, q(x) + r(x)$

Terms of Polynomial

Degree

If $f(x) = a_0 x^n + a_1 x^{n-1} + a_2 x^{n-2} + \ldots + a_{n-1} x^1 + a_n,\ a_0 \neq 0$
then $f(x)$ is of degree n

Constant Polynomial

It contains only one non-zero constant term

Zero Polynomial

The constant polynomial has zero
The degree of zero polynomial is not defined

Polynomial Equations

In this equation, polynomial is equal to zero i.e, $p(x) = 0$

Equality of Polynomial

$f(x) = a_0 x^n + a_1 x^{n-1} + \ldots + a_n$
$g(x) = b_0 x^n + b_1 x^{n-1} + \ldots + b_n$
If $f(x) = g(x)$, then it is said to be equality of two polynomial

Zeros of polynomial

Those value of the variable, which gives out equal to zero

Polynomial

It is an expression of the form
$a_0 x^n + a_1 x^{n-1} + a_2 x^{n-2} + \ldots + a_{n-1} x^1 + a_n,\ a_0 \neq 0$
when degree is n.

Mind Map : Matrix

Matrix

Order

- Order of matrix = No. or rows × No. of columns
- e.g., $A = \begin{bmatrix} 2 & 1 & 5 \\ 3 & -2 & 7 \end{bmatrix}$ ← 1st row, ← 2nd row (1st column, 2nd column, 3rd column)
- It is an order of 2×3

Matrix

- Rectangular arrangement of numbers, arranged in rows and columns.
- e.g. $[5]$, $\begin{bmatrix} 5 & 3 \\ 1 & 2 \end{bmatrix}$, etc
- Plural of matrix is matrices.
- Each number in a matrix is called its element.
- Horizontal lines are rows, whereas vertical lines are columns.

Operations

Addition in Matrices
e.g., $\begin{bmatrix} 2 & 1 \\ 5 & 6 \end{bmatrix} + \begin{bmatrix} 3 & 2 \\ 1 & 4 \end{bmatrix} = \begin{bmatrix} 5 & 3 \\ 6 & 10 \end{bmatrix}$

Subtraction in Matrices
e.g., $\begin{bmatrix} 5 & 4 \\ 2 & 1 \end{bmatrix} - \begin{bmatrix} 3 & 0 \\ 4 & 2 \end{bmatrix} = \begin{bmatrix} 2 & 4 \\ -2 & -1 \end{bmatrix}$

Additive Inverse
If zero is added to any number or no. is added to zero then we get the same number
e.g., $3 + 0 = 0 + 3 = 3$

Multiplication in Matrix
Product of two matrices is possible only if and only if number of columns in first matrix is equal to the number of rows in second matrix.
e.g., $\begin{bmatrix} 2 & 3 \\ -1 & 2 \end{bmatrix} \begin{bmatrix} 4 & -1 \\ 0 & -2 \end{bmatrix} = \begin{bmatrix} 8+0 & -2-6 \\ -4+0 & 1-4 \end{bmatrix} = \begin{bmatrix} 8 & -8 \\ -4 & -3 \end{bmatrix}$

Matrix multiplication by a number
e.g. If $A = \begin{bmatrix} 1 & -3 \\ 2 & -1 \end{bmatrix}$, then $6A = \begin{bmatrix} 6 & -18 \\ 12 & -6 \end{bmatrix}$

Transpose of Matrices
Interchanging of rows and columns.
e.g. $A = \begin{bmatrix} 2 & 3 & 1 \\ 0 & 4 & 7 \end{bmatrix}$ or $A' = \begin{bmatrix} 2 & 0 \\ 3 & 4 \\ 1 & 7 \end{bmatrix}$

Equality of Matrices
- Both have same order and elements of both matrices are equal.
- e.g. $A = \begin{bmatrix} 2 & 3 \\ 1 & 5 \end{bmatrix}$ and $B = \begin{bmatrix} 2 & 3 \\ 1 & 5 \end{bmatrix}$, $A = B$

Types

Unit or Identity Matrix
Each element of its leading diagonal is unity and other elements are zero
e.g. $\begin{bmatrix} 1 & 0 & 0 \\ 0 & 1 & 0 \\ 0 & 0 & 1 \end{bmatrix}$

Zero or Null Matrix
Each element of matrix is zero.
e.g. $[0 \ 0]$, $\begin{bmatrix} 0 \\ 0 \end{bmatrix}$

Rectangular Matrix
Matrix in which no. of rows and columns aren't equal
e.g. $\begin{bmatrix} 2 & 4 & 7 \\ 1 & 0 & 5 \end{bmatrix}_{2 \times 3}$

Diagonal Matrix
Matrix having diagonal element are non zero and others are zero
e.g. $\begin{bmatrix} 1 & 0 \\ 0 & 4 \end{bmatrix}$

Row Matrix
Matrix which has only one row
e.g., $[a \ b]$ ← single row (1st column, 2nd column)

Column Matrix
Matrix which has only one column
e.g. $\begin{bmatrix} a \\ b \end{bmatrix}$ ← 1st row, ← 2nd row (Single column)

Square Matrix
Matrix which has an equal no. of rows and columns
e.g. $\begin{bmatrix} a & b \\ c & d \end{bmatrix}$ ← 1st row, ← 2nd row (1st column, 2nd column)

Mind Map : Arithmetic Progression

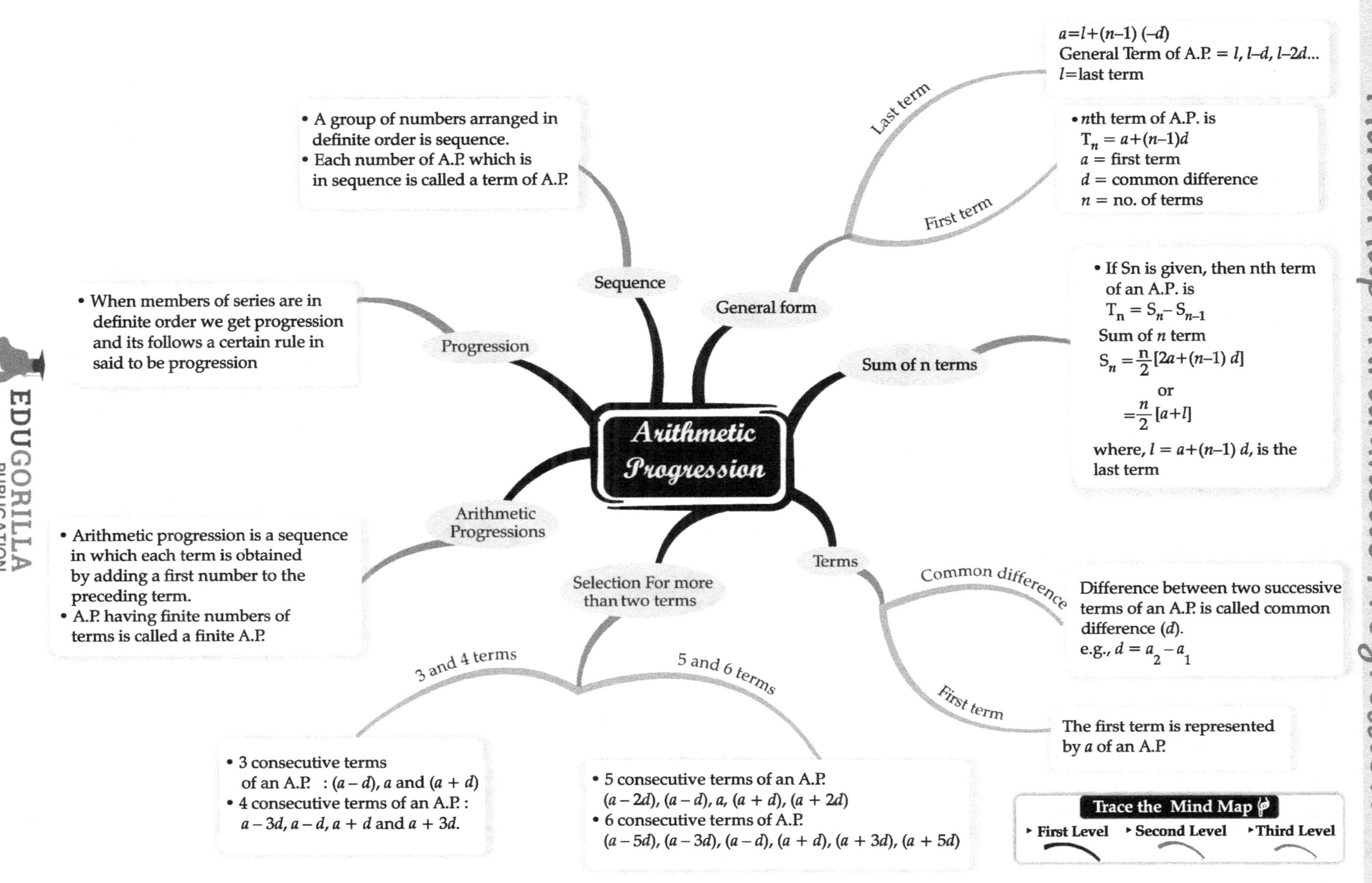

Mind Map : Reflection

Definition

It is a kind of transformation. It is a 'flip' of a shape over the line of reflection.

Co-ordinate Axes

Two mutually perpendicular number lines intersecting each other at origin. It is also called rectangular axes or axes of reference.

Co-ordinates

- Co-ordinate of origin $= (0, 0)$
- Position of a point in a expressed by a pair of two numbers e.g. $P(4, 3)$

x-co-ordinate

First number x in pair (x, y) is the distance of point P from y-axis i.e., x-co-ordinate or abscissa.

y-co-ordinate

Second number y in pair (x, y) is the distance of point P from x-axis i.e., y-co-ordinate or ordinate.

Invariant point

- When the point lies of the lines then image of that point is itself
- Invariant point remains unchanged after a reflection.

About x-axis

P' is the image of P in x axis such that $P' = (x, -y)$

$M_x(x, y) = (x, -y)$

when a point is reflected in x axis, sign of its ordinate changes

About y-axis

P' is the image of P in y-axis such that $P' = (-x, y)$.

$M_x(x, y) = (-x, y)$

when a point is reflected in y-axis, sign of its cissa changes.

About origin

When a point $P(x, y)$ is reflected in origin, sign of its abscissa and ordinate both changes. P' is the image of $P(x, y)$ in the origin, such as $P' = (-x, -y)$.

$M_0(x, y) = (-x, -y)$

Trace the Mind Map

- First Level
- Second Level
- Third Level

Mind Map : Section and Mid-Point Formula

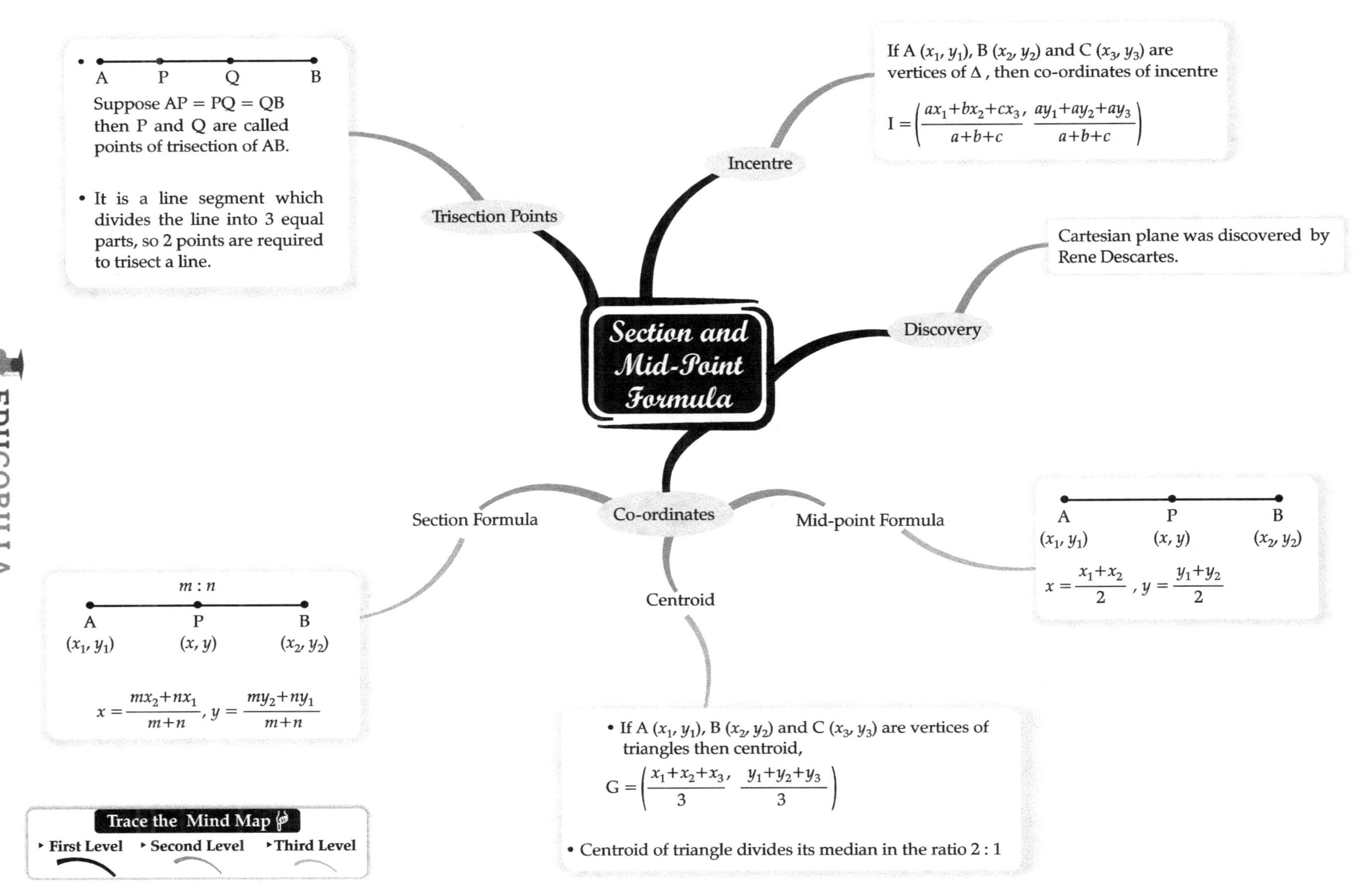

Mind Map : Equation of a lines

Equation of a lines

Concept of Slope

Slope is also known as gradient and it is represented by m.

$$m = \tan\theta = \frac{y_1 - y_2}{x_1 - x_2} \text{ or } \frac{y_2 - y_1}{x_2 - x_1}$$

Equally Inclined Lines

Lines which makes equal angles with both the axes.

Parallelism Condition

If two lines having slopes m_1 and m_2 are parallel, then angle θ between them is $0°$.

$$\tan\theta = \tan 0° = \frac{m_1 - m_2}{1 + m_1 m_2} = 0$$

$$m_2 - m_1 = 0 \Rightarrow m_1 = m_2$$

so, two lines are parallel, if their slopes are equal.

Intercept of axes

x–Intercept

If a line meets x–axis at a point then distance from origin is called x–intercept.

y–Intercept

If a line meets at y–axis then distance from origin is called y – intercept.

Intercept form

$$\frac{x}{a} + \frac{y}{b} = 1$$

Angle between two lines

- Let θ be angle between l_1 and l_2, then

$$\tan\theta = \left| \frac{\tan\alpha_2 - \tan\alpha_1}{1 + \tan\alpha_2 \tan\alpha_1} \right|$$

if $\tan\alpha_1 = m_1$ and $\tan\alpha_2 = m_2$

then $\tan\theta = \dfrac{(m_2 - m_1)}{1 + m_1 m_2}$

- If ϕ be exterior angle between the lines

then $\tan\phi = \tan(\pi - \theta) = -\tan\theta = \dfrac{-(m_2 - m_1)}{1 + m_1 m_2}$

$$\tan\theta = \frac{\pm(m_2 - m_1)}{1 + m_1 m_2}$$

Different forms of equations

Slope intercept form

- Equation having slope m and making an intercept c on y–axis, is $y = mx + c$
- If passes through origin, then equation will be $y = mx$

With One point slope

Equation of line passes through (x_1, y_1) and slope m is given by $(y - y_1) = m(x - x_1)$

With Two points

Equations of line passing through the points (x_1, y_1) and (x_2, y_2) is given by

$$(y - y_1) = \left| \frac{y_2 - y_1}{x_2 - x_1} \right| (x - x_1)$$

Perpendicularity

- If two lines having slopes m_1 and m_2 are perpendicular, then angle θ between them is $90°$.

$$\tan\theta = \tan 90°$$
$$1 + m_1 \times m_2 = 0$$
$$m_1 . m_2 = -1$$

Trace the Mind Map

- First Level
- Second Level
- Third Level

Mind Map : Similarity

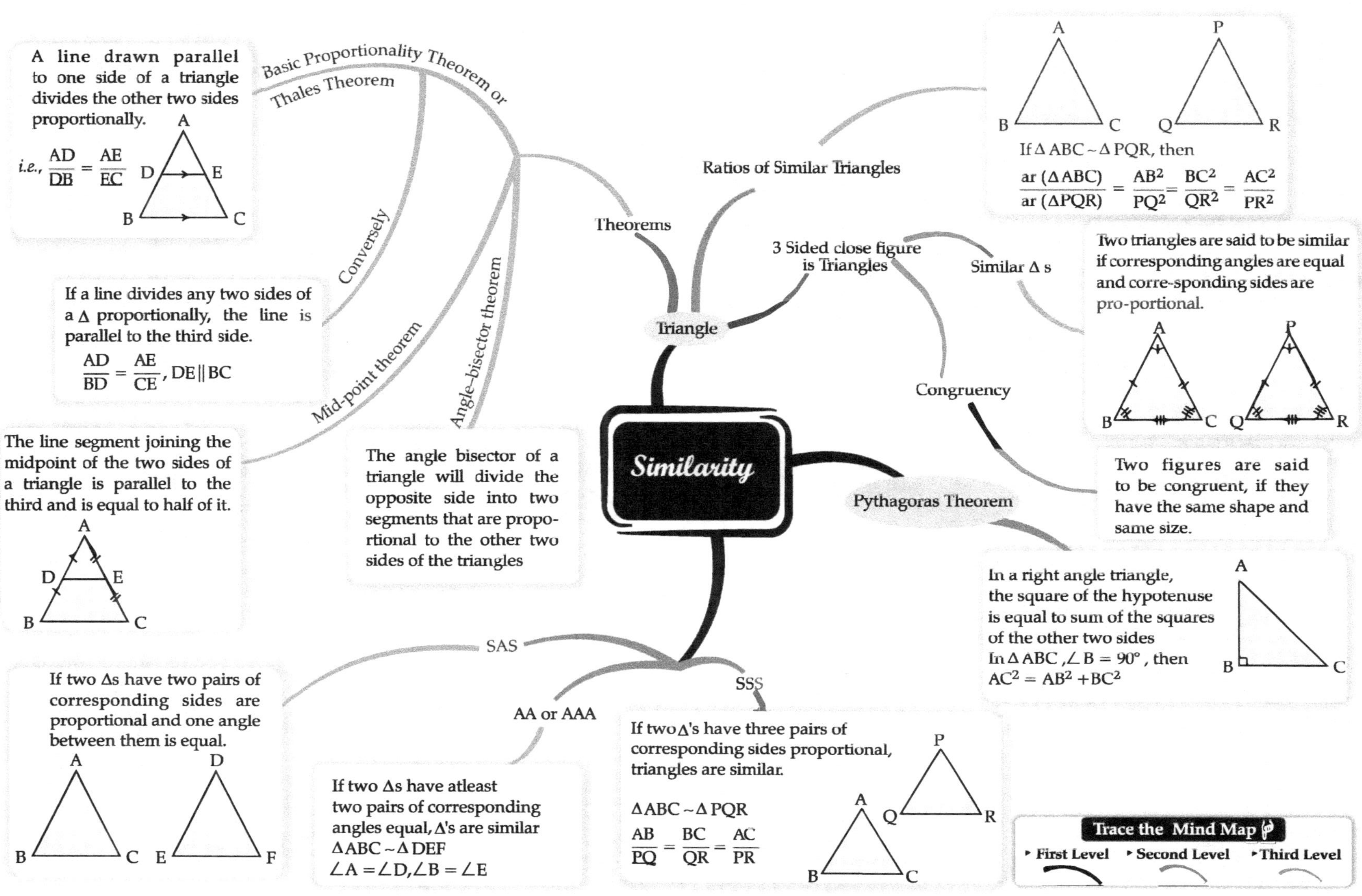

Similarity

Triangle

3 Sided close figure is Triangles

Ratios of Similar Triangles

If $\triangle ABC \sim \triangle PQR$, then
$$\frac{ar(\triangle ABC)}{ar(\triangle PQR)} = \frac{AB^2}{PQ^2} = \frac{BC^2}{QR^2} = \frac{AC^2}{PR^2}$$

Similar $\triangle$ s

Two triangles are said to be similar if corresponding angles are equal and corre-sponding sides are pro-portional.

Congruency

Two figures are said to be congruent, if they have the same shape and same size.

Pythagoras Theorem

In a right angle triangle, the square of the hypotenuse is equal to sum of the squares of the other two sides
In $\triangle ABC$, $\angle B = 90°$, then
$AC^2 = AB^2 + BC^2$

Theorems

Basic Proportionality Theorem or Thales Theorem

A line drawn parallel to one side of a triangle divides the other two sides proportionally.
i.e., $\dfrac{AD}{DB} = \dfrac{AE}{EC}$

Conversely

If a line divides any two sides of a $\triangle$ proportionally, the line is parallel to the third side.
$$\frac{AD}{BD} = \frac{AE}{CE}, DE \| BC$$

Mid-point theorem

The line segment joining the midpoint of the two sides of a triangle is parallel to the third and is equal to half of it.

Angle–bisector theorem

The angle bisector of a triangle will divide the opposite side into two segments that are propo-rtional to the other two sides of the triangles

SSS

If two$\triangle$'s have three pairs of corresponding sides proportional, triangles are similar.
$\triangle ABC \sim \triangle PQR$
$$\frac{AB}{PQ} = \frac{BC}{QR} = \frac{AC}{PR}$$

AA or AAA

If two $\triangle$s have atleast two pairs of corresponding angles equal, $\triangle$'s are similar
$\triangle ABC \sim \triangle DEF$
$\angle A = \angle D, \angle B = \angle E$

SAS

If two $\triangle$s have two pairs of corresponding sides are proportional and one angle between them is equal.

Trace the Mind Map

- First Level
- Second Level
- Third Level

Mind Map : Circle

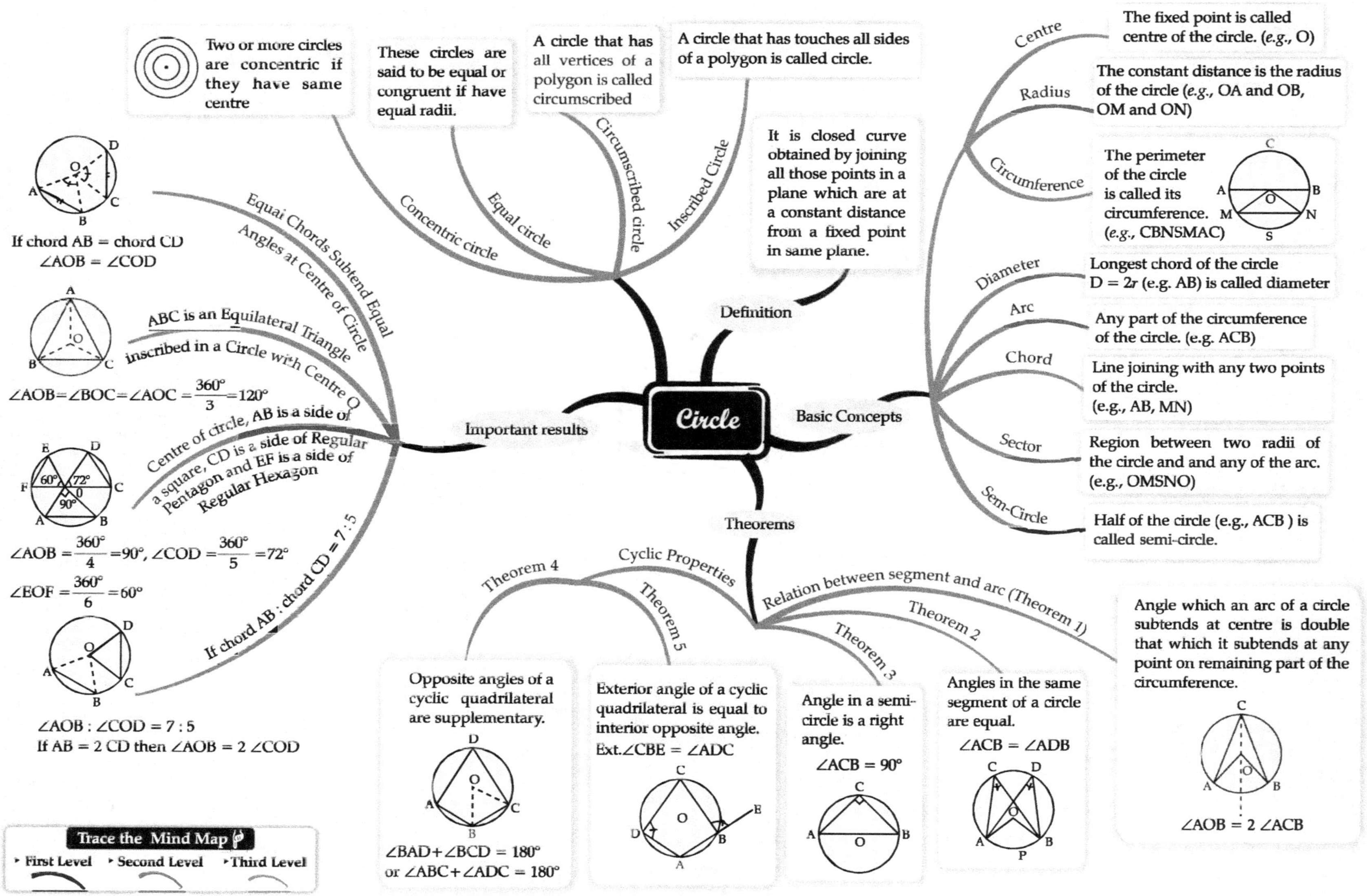

Circle

Basic Concepts

- **Centre** — The fixed point is called centre of the circle. (e.g., O)
- **Radius** — The constant distance is the radius of the circle (e.g., OA and OB, OM and ON)
- **Circumference** — The perimeter of the circle is called its circumference. (e.g., CBNSMAC)
- **Diameter** — Longest chord of the circle $D = 2r$ (e.g. AB) is called diameter
- **Arc** — Any part of the circumference of the circle. (e.g. ACB)
- **Chord** — Line joining with any two points of the circle. (e.g., AB, MN)
- **Sector** — Region between two radii of the circle and any of the arc. (e.g., OMSNO)
- **Sem-Circle** — Half of circle (e.g., ACB) is called semi-circle.

Definition

It is closed curve obtained by joining all those points in a plane which are at a constant distance from a fixed point in same plane.

Inscribed Circle

A circle that has touches all sides of a polygon is called circle.

Circumscribed circle

A circle that has all vertices of a polygon is called circumscribed

Equal circle

These circles are said to be equal or congruent if have equal radii

Concentric circle

Two or more circles are concentric if they have same centre

Theorems

Relation between segment and arc (Theorem 1)

Angle which an arc of a circle subtends at centre is double that which it subtends at any point on remaining part of the circumference.

$\angle AOB = 2\angle ACB$

Theorem 2 — Angles in the same segment of a circle are equal.

$\angle ACB = \angle ADB$

Theorem 3 — Angle in a semi-circle is a right angle.

$\angle ACB = 90°$

Cyclic Properties

Theorem 5 — Exterior angle of a cyclic quadrilateral is equal to interior opposite angle.

Ext.$\angle CBE = \angle ADC$

Theorem 4 — Opposite angles of a cyclic quadrilateral are supplementary.

$\angle BAD + \angle BCD = 180°$
or $\angle ABC + \angle ADC = 180°$

Important results

Equal Chords Subtend Equal Angles at Centre of Circle

If chord AB = chord CD
$\angle AOB = \angle COD$

ABC is an Equilateral Triangle inscribed in a Circle with Centre O

$\angle AOB = \angle BOC = \angle AOC = \dfrac{360°}{3} = 120°$

Centre of circle, CD is a side of Regular Square, and EF is a side of a Pentagon a Regular Hexagon

$\angle AOB = \dfrac{360°}{4} = 90°, \ \angle COD = \dfrac{360°}{5} = 72°$

$\angle EOF = \dfrac{360°}{6} = 60°$

If chord AB : chord CD = 7 : 5

$\angle AOB : \angle COD = 7 : 5$
If AB = 2 CD then $\angle AOB = 2 \angle COD$

Mind Map : Mensuration

Combination of Solids

When we combine two solids together, they form a new type of solid.

$$\triangle + \text{(hemisphere)} = \text{Combination of 2 solids}$$

Cone + hemisphere

Conversion of Solids

When we convert a solid shape to another solid given shape, surface area usually changes. but, the volume is preserved.

Hemisphere

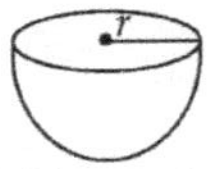

- A hemisphere is half part of a sphere.
- Volume $= \frac{2}{3}\pi r^3$ cube unit
- Total surface area $= 3\pi r^2$ sq.unit
- Curved surface area $= 2\pi r^2$ sq.unit

Spherical shell

- It is the solid enclosed between two concentric spheres
- Volume $= \frac{4}{3}\pi(R^3 - r^3)$

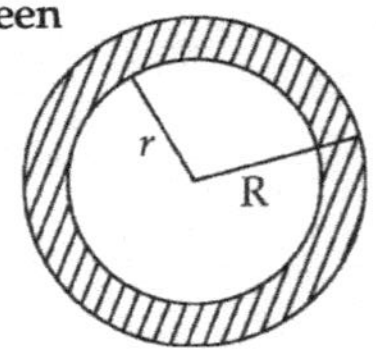

Trace the Mind Map
- First Level
- Second Level
- Third Level

Mensuration

Solids

Sphere

- A solid obtained on revolving a circle about any diameter of it.
- Volume $= \frac{4}{3}\pi r^3$ cube unit
- Surface area $= 4\pi r^2$ sq.unit

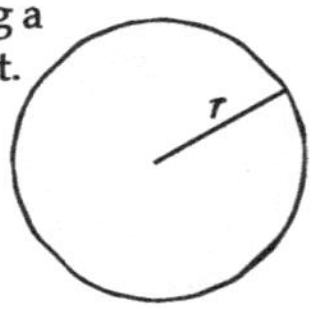

Cylinder

Hollow

- The solid obtained on revolving a rectangle about one of its side.
- Thickness of wall $= (R - r)$ unit
- Area of cross section $= \pi(R^2 - \pi r^2)$ unit^2 $= \pi(R^2 - r^2)$ unit^2 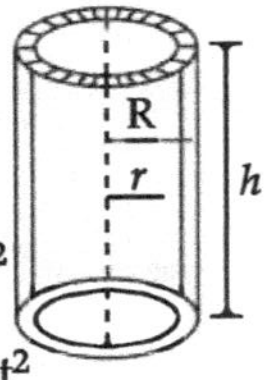
- External curved surface area $= 2\pi Rh$
- Internal curved surface area $= 2\pi rh$ unit^2
- Curved surface area $= 2\pi(R+r)h$
- Total surface area $= 2\pi(R+r)(h+R-r)$ unit^2
- Volume $= \pi h(R^2 - r^2)$ unit^3

Solid

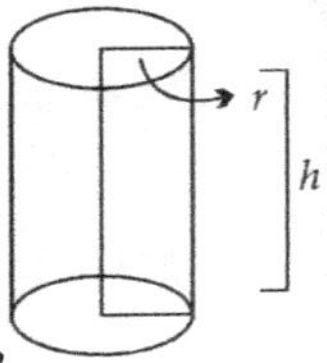

- A solid which has uniform circular cross-section.
- Area of cross section $= \pi r^2$ unit^2
- Perimeter of cross section $= 2\pi r$
- Curved surface area $= 2\pi rh$ unit^2
- Total surface area $= 2\pi r\,(h+r)$ unit^2
- Volume $= \pi r^2 h$.

Here $\pi = \frac{22}{7}$, $r =$ radius
$h =$ height

Cone

- The solid obtained on revolving a right-angled triangle about one of its side.

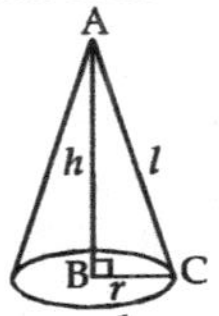

where, $l^2 = h^2 + r^2$
- Volume $= \frac{1}{3}\pi r^2 h$ cube unit
- Curved or lateral surface area $= \pi r l$ sq.unit
- Total surface area $= \pi r(l+r)$ sq.unit

here, $r =$ radius
$l =$ slant height
$h =$ height

Mind Map : Trigonometry

Trigonometric Ratios

$$\sin \theta = \frac{\text{Perpendicular}}{\text{Hypotenuse}} = \frac{P}{H}$$

$$\cos \theta = \frac{\text{Base}}{\text{Hypotenuse}} = \frac{B}{H}$$

$$\tan \theta = \frac{\text{Perpendicular}}{\text{Base}} = \frac{P}{B}$$

$$\operatorname{cosec} \theta = \frac{\text{Hypotenuse}}{\text{Perpendicular}} = \frac{H}{P}$$

$$\sec \theta = \frac{\text{Hypotenuse}}{\text{Base}} = \frac{H}{B}$$

$$\cot \theta = \frac{\text{Base}}{\text{Perpendicular}} = \frac{B}{P}$$

sin θ, cos θ, tan θ, cosec θ, sec θ, cot θ

Trace the Mind Map

▸ First Level ▸ Second Level ▸ Third Level

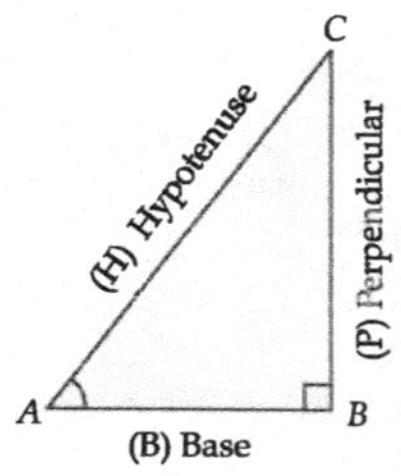

Pythagoras Theorem

In right angled triangle ABC
$$(AC)^2 = (AB)^2 + (BC)^2$$
$$(H)^2 = (B)^2 + (P)^2$$

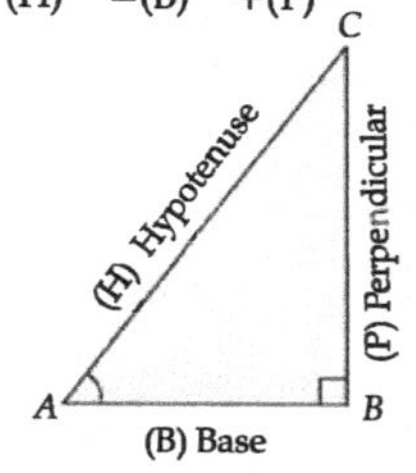

Trigonometric Ratio Table

θ	0°	30°	45°	60°	90°
sin θ	0	$\frac{1}{2}$	$\frac{1}{\sqrt{2}}$	$\frac{\sqrt{3}}{2}$	1
cos θ	1	$\frac{\sqrt{3}}{2}$	$\frac{1}{\sqrt{2}}$	$\frac{1}{2}$	0
tan θ	0	$\frac{1}{\sqrt{3}}$	1	$\sqrt{3}$	∞
cosec θ	∞	2	$\sqrt{2}$	$\frac{2}{\sqrt{3}}$	1
sec θ	1	$\frac{2}{\sqrt{3}}$	$\sqrt{2}$	2	∞
cot θ	∞	$\sqrt{3}$	1	$\frac{1}{\sqrt{3}}$	0

Angle of Elevation

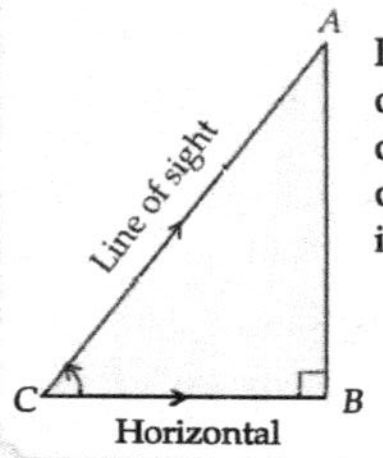

If a man standing at any point C on the level ground, is viewing an object at A. The angle, which the line of sight AC makes with the horizontal is an angle of elevation.

Angles of Depression

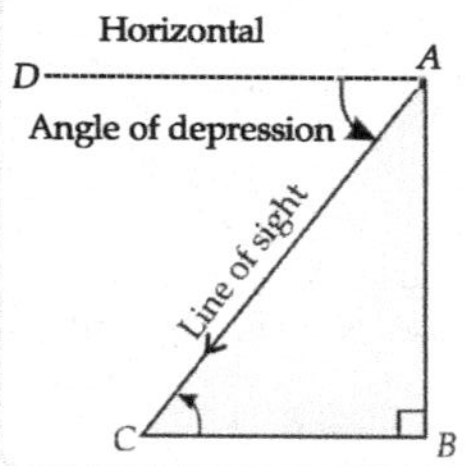

If a man is standing at A and is viewing an object C at level ground. The angle, which the line of sight (AC) makes with horizontal (AD) is an angle of depression.

$\angle ACB = \angle DAC.$

Mind Map : Statistics

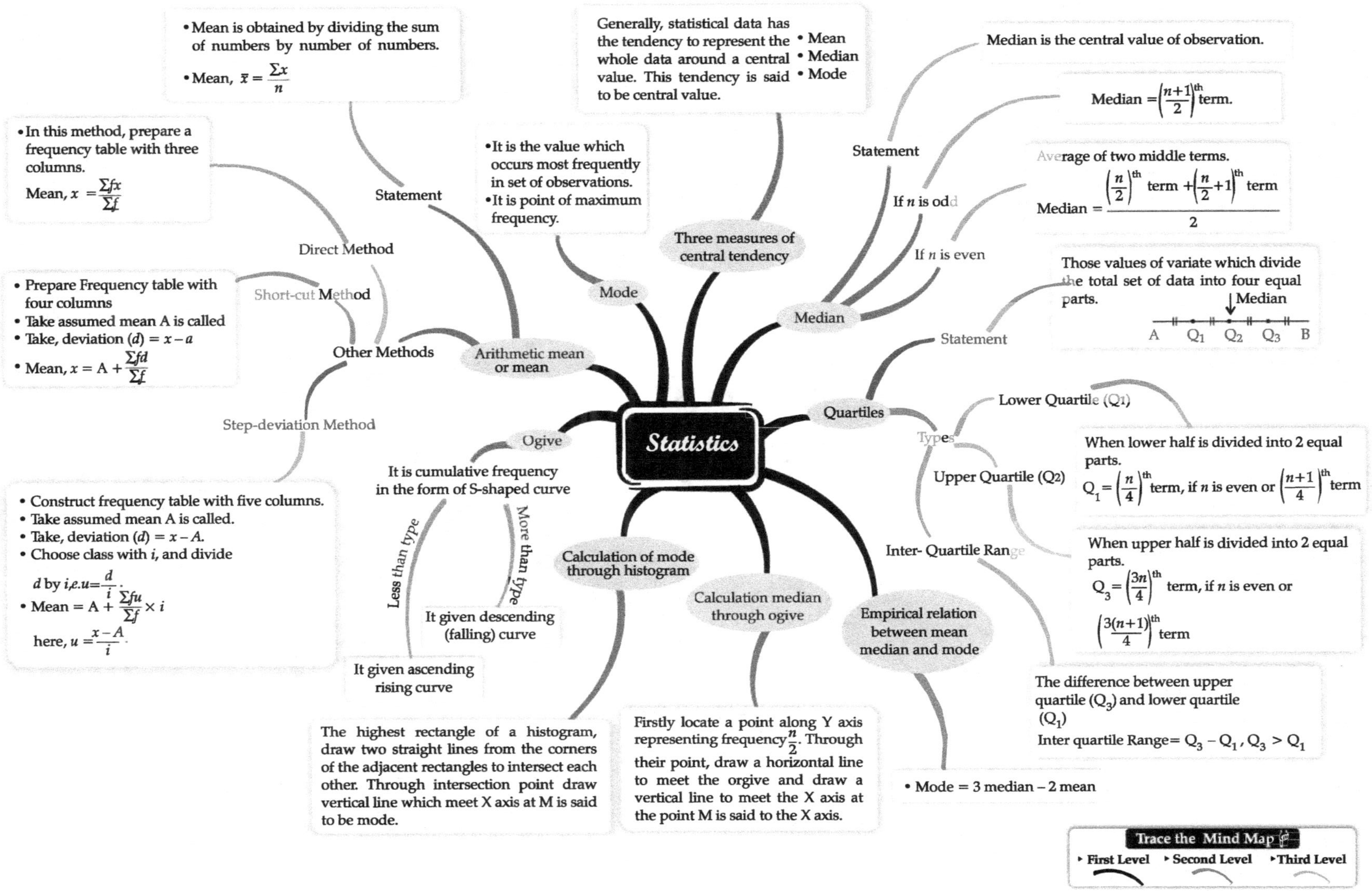

Statistics

Three measures of central tendency

Generally, statistical data has the tendency to represent the whole data around a central value. This tendency is said to be central value.
- Mean
- Median
- Mode

Median

Statement

Median is the central value of observation.

If n is odd

$$\text{Median} = \left(\frac{n+1}{2}\right)^{th} \text{term.}$$

If n is even

Average of two middle terms.

$$\text{Median} = \frac{\left(\frac{n}{2}\right)^{th} \text{term} + \left(\frac{n}{2}+1\right)^{th} \text{term}}{2}$$

Quartiles

Statement

Those values of variate which divide the total set of data into four equal parts.

A Q_1 Q_2 Q_3 B |Median

Types

Lower Quartile (Q_1)

When lower half is divided into 2 equal parts.
$$Q_1 = \left(\frac{n}{4}\right)^{th} \text{term, if } n \text{ is even or } \left(\frac{n+1}{4}\right)^{th} \text{term}$$

Upper Quartile (Q_2)

When upper half is divided into 2 equal parts.
$$Q_3 = \left(\frac{3n}{4}\right)^{th} \text{term, if } n \text{ is even or } \left(\frac{3(n+1)}{4}\right)^{th} \text{term}$$

Inter- Quartile Range

The difference between upper quartile (Q_3) and lower quartile (Q_1)

Inter quartile Range= $Q_3 - Q_1$, $Q_3 > Q_1$

Empirical relation between mean median and mode

- Mode = 3 median – 2 mean

Calculation median through ogive

Firstly locate a point along Y axis representing frequency $\frac{n}{2}$. Through their point, draw a horizontal line to meet the orgive and draw a vertical line to meet the X axis at the point M is said to the X axis.

Calculation of mode through histogram

The highest rectangle of a histogram, draw two straight lines from the corners of the adjacent rectangles to intersect each other. Through intersection point draw vertical line which meet X axis at M is said to be mode.

Ogive

It is cumulative frequency in the form of S-shaped curve.

More than type

It given descending (falling) curve

Less than type

It given ascending rising curve

Mode

- It is the value which occurs most frequently in set of observations.
- It is point of maximum frequency.

Arithmetic mean or mean

Statement

- Mean is obtained by dividing the sum of numbers by number of numbers.
- Mean, $\bar{x} = \dfrac{\sum x}{n}$

Direct Method

- In this method, prepare a frequency table with three columns.

Mean, $x = \dfrac{\sum fx}{\sum f}$

Short-cut Method

- Prepare Frequency table with four columns
- Take assumed mean A is called.
- Take, deviation (d) = $x - a$
- Mean, $x = A + \dfrac{\sum fd}{\sum f}$

Step-deviation Method

- Construct frequency table with five columns.
- Take assumed mean A is called.
- Take, deviation (d) = $x - A$.
- Choose class with i, and divide d by i.e. $u = \dfrac{d}{i}$

$$\text{Mean} = A + \frac{i}{\sum f} \cdot \frac{\sum fu}{\sum f} \times i$$

here, $u = \dfrac{x - A}{i}$.

Other Methods

Mind Map : Probability

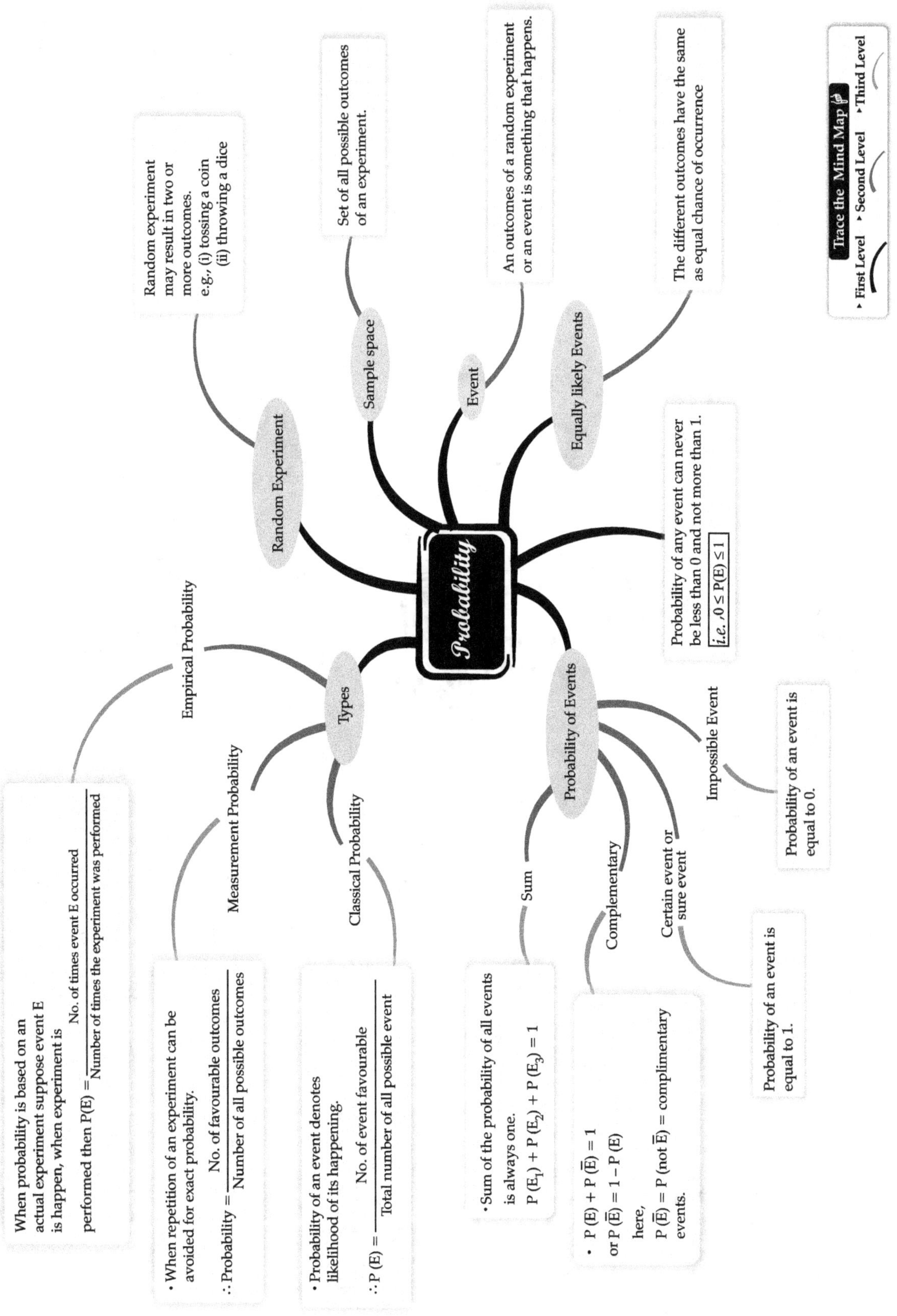

Trace the Mind Map
▸ First Level ▸ Second Level ▸ Third Level

Probability

Random Experiment
Random experiment may result in two or more outcomes.
e.g., (i) tossing a coin (ii) throwing a dice

Sample space
Set of all possible outcomes of an experiment.

Event
An outcomes of a random experiment or an event is something that happens.

Equally likely Events
The different outcomes have the same as equal chance of occurrence

Probability of any event can never be less than 0 and not more than 1.
i.e., $0 \leq P(E) \leq 1$

Types

Empirical Probability
When probability is based on an actual experiment suppose event E is happen, when experiment is performed then $P(E) = \dfrac{\text{No. of times event E occurred}}{\text{Number of times the experiment was performed}}$

Measurement Probability
- When repetition of an experiment can be avoided for exact probability.
- $\therefore$ Probability $= \dfrac{\text{No. of favourable outcomes}}{\text{Number of all possible outcomes}}$

Classical Probability
- Probability of an event denotes likelihood of its happening.
- $\therefore P(E) = \dfrac{\text{No. of event favourable}}{\text{Total number of all possible event}}$

Probability of Events

Impossible Event
Probability of an event is equal to 0.

Sum
- Sum of the probability of all events is always one.
  $P(E_1) + P(E_2) + P(E_3) = 1$

Complementary
- $P(E) + P(\bar{E}) = 1$
  or $P(\bar{E}) = 1 - P(E)$
  here,
  $P(\bar{E}) = P(\text{not } \bar{E}) =$ complimentary events.

Certain event or sure event
Probability of an event is equal to 1.

EDUGORILLA
PUBLICATION

SOLVED SAMPLE PAPER

MATHEMATICS

Maximum Marks: 80
Time allowed: Two and a half hours
Answers to this Paper must be written on the paper provided separately.
You will not be allowed to write during the first 15 minutes.
This time is to be spent reading the question paper.
The time given at the head of this Paper is the time allowed for writing the answers.

Attempt all questions from Section *A* and any four questions from Section *B*.
The intended marks for questions or parts of questions are given in brackets [].

SECTION A (40 Marks)

Question 1.
Choose the correct answers to the questions from the given options: [15]
(i) The SGST paid by a customer to the shopkeeper for an article that is priced at Rs 500 is Rs 15.
The rate of GST charged is:
(a) 1.5%
(b) 3%
(c) 5%
(d) 6%
Solution: Option (d)
SGST = Rs. 15 so total GST = Rs. 30

$$\text{rate of GST} = \frac{\text{Total GST}}{\text{MP}} \times 100$$
$$= \frac{30}{500} \times 100$$
$$= \frac{30}{500} \times 100 => 6\%$$

(ii) When the roots of a quadratic equation are real and equal then the discriminant of the quadratic equation is:
(a) Infinite
(b) Positive
(c) Zero
(d) Negative
Solution: Option (c)

(iii) If $(x - 1)$ is a factor of $2x^2 - ax - 1$, then the value of ' a ' is:
(a) -1
(b) 1

(c) 3

(d) -3

Solution: Option (b)

$$\text{let } x - 1 = 0 \text{ so } x = 1$$
$$2x^2 - ax - 1 = 0$$
$$2(1)^2 - a(1) - 1 = 0$$
$$2 - a - 1 = 0$$
$$-a = -1$$
$$a = 1$$

(iv) Given $\begin{bmatrix} a & b \\ c & d \end{bmatrix} \times X = \begin{bmatrix} p \\ q \end{bmatrix}$. The order of matrix X is:

    (a) 2×2

    (b) 1×2

    (c) 2×1

    (d) 1×1

    Solution: Option (c)

$$2 \times 2 \times r \times c = 2 \times 1$$
$$2 \times c = 2 \times 1$$
$$\therefore r = 2, c = 1$$
$$\therefore \qquad \text{order} = 2 \times 1$$

(v) $57, 54, 51, 48, \ldots\ldots\ldots$ are in Arithmetic Progression. The value of the 8th term is:

    (a) 36

    (b) 78

    (c) -36

    (d) -78

    Solution: Option (a)

$$a = 57$$
$$d = 54 - 57 \Rightarrow -3$$
$$a_8 = a + 7d$$
$$= 57 + 7 \times (-3)$$
$$= 57 - 21$$
$$= 36$$

(vi) The point $A(p, q)$ is invariant about $x = p$ under reflection. The coordinates of its image A' is:

    (a) $A'(p - q)$

    (b) $A'(-p, q)$

    (c) $A'(p, q)$ss

    (d) $A'(-p, -q)$

    Solution: Option (c)

    Since the point is invariant

(vii) In the given diagram the $\triangle$ ABC is similar to $\triangle$ DEF by the axiom:

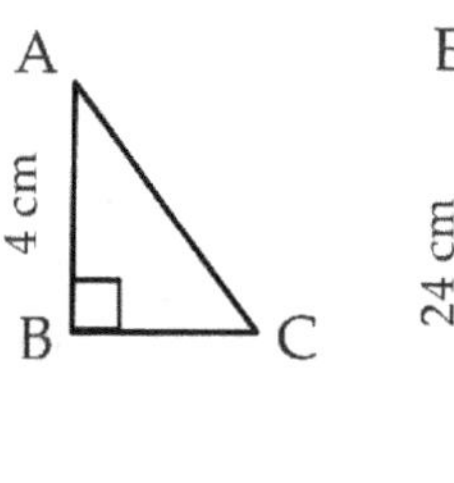
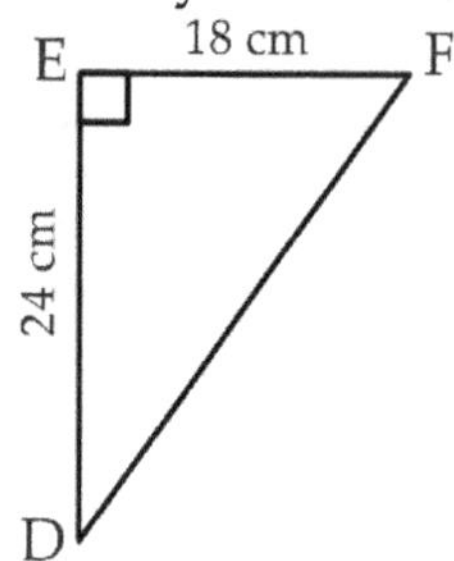

(a) SSS

(b) SAS

(c) AAA

(d) RHS

Solution: Option (b)

$$\frac{4}{24} = \frac{3}{18} \Rightarrow \frac{1}{6} \text{ and } \angle ABC = \angle DEF = 90°$$

$$\therefore SAS$$

(viii) The volume of a right circular cone with the same base radius and height as that of a right circular cylinder is $120cm^3$. The volume of the cylinder is:

(a) $240cm^3$

(b) $60cm^3$

(c) $360cm^3$

(d) $480cm^3$

Solution: Option (c)

$\because$ radius (r) and height (h) of the cone is the same as a cylinder

the volume of the cone $\qquad = \frac{1}{3}\pi r^2 h$

the volume of the cylinder $\quad = \pi r^2 h$

$$\frac{1}{3}\pi r^2 h = 120\pi r^2 h \quad = 120 \times 3 \Rightarrow 360cm^3$$

(ix) The solution set for the given inequation is:

$$-8 \leq 2x < 8, x \in W$$

(a) $\{-4, -3, -2, -1, 0, 1, 2, 3, 4\}$

(b) $-4, -3, -2, -1\}$

(c) $\{0, 1, 2, 3\}$

(d) $\{-8, -7, -6, -5, -4, -3, -2, -1, 0, 1, 2, 3, 4, 5, 6, 7, 8\}$

Solution: Option (c)

$-8 \leq 2x < 8, x \in w$

$-8 \leq 2x$ and $2x < 8$

$-\frac{8}{2} \leq x$ and $x < \frac{8}{2}$

$-4 \leq x$ and $x < 4$

$\therefore -4 \leq x < 4, x \in W$

Solution Set is: $\{0,1,2,3\}$

(x) The probability of the Sun rising from the east is P(S). The value of P(S) is:

(a) $P(S) = 0$

(b) $P(S) < 0$

(c) $P(S) = 1$

(d) $P(S) > 1$

Solution: Option (c)

As the statement is a universal truth or sure event.

(xi) If $\begin{bmatrix} 2 & x \\ 0 & 1 \end{bmatrix} + 3 \begin{bmatrix} 2 & 1 \\ 4 & 0 \end{bmatrix} = \begin{bmatrix} 8 & 8 \\ 12 & 1 \end{bmatrix}$ The value of x is:

(a) 2

(b) 3

(c) 4

(d) 5

Solution: Option (d)

$$\begin{bmatrix} 2 & x \\ 0 & 1 \end{bmatrix} + \begin{bmatrix} 6 & 3 \\ 12 & 0 \end{bmatrix} = \begin{bmatrix} 8 & 8 \\ 12 & 1 \end{bmatrix}$$
$$x + 3 = 8$$
$$x = 8 - 3 = 5 \textbf{ Ans.}$$

(xii) The centroid of an $\triangle$ ABC is G(6,7). If the coordinates of the vertices A, B, and C are (a, 5), (7,9), and (5,7) respectively.

The value of a is

(a) 9

(b) 6

(c) 3

(d) 7

Solution: Option (b)

$$(x, y) = \left\{ \frac{x_1 + x_2 + x_3}{3}, \frac{y_1 + y_2 + y_3}{3} \right\}$$
$$6 = \frac{a + 7 + 5}{3}$$
$$a + 12 = 18$$
$$a = 18 - 12 = 6$$

(xiii) In the given diagram AC is the diameter of the circle and $\angle ADB = 35°$

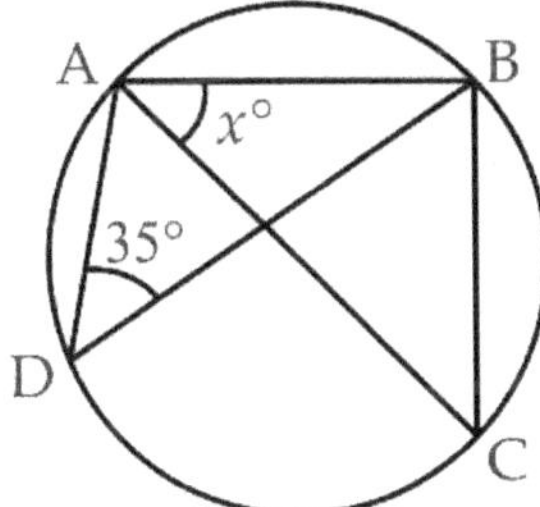

The degree measure of x is:

(a) 55°

(b) 35°

(c) $45°$

(d) $70°$

Solution: Option (a)

$$\angle ABC = 90° \quad \text{[angle on diameter]}$$
$$\angle ACB = 35° \quad \text{[angles in the same segment]}$$
$$\therefore x + 90 + 35 = 180$$
$$x = 180 - 125$$
$$= 55°$$

(xiv) If the nth term of an Arithmetic Progression (A.P.) is $(n + 3)$, then the first three terms of the A.P. are:

(a) $1, 2, 3$

(b) $2, 4, 6$

(c) $4, 5, 6$

(d) $7, 8, 9$

Solution: Option (c)

$$(a_n) = n + 3$$
$$\text{let} \quad n = 1 => a_1 = 1 + 3 \Rightarrow 4$$
$$n = 2 => a_2 = 2 + 3 \Rightarrow 5$$
$$n = 3 => a_3 = 3 + 3 \Rightarrow 6$$
$$\therefore \quad = 4,5,6$$

(xv) The median of a grouped frequency distribution is found graphically by drawing:

(a) A linear graph

(b) A histogram

(c) A frequency polygon

(d) A cumulative frequency curves

Solution: Option (d)

Question 2.

(i) Salman deposits Rs. 1200 every month in a recurring deposit account for $2\frac{1}{2}$ years. If the rate of interest is 6% per annum, find the amount he will receive on maturity. **[4]**

Solution:

Per month installment $(P) =$ Rs. 1200

$$\text{time} \quad n = \frac{5}{2} \times 12 \Rightarrow 30 \text{ months}$$
$$\text{rate} = 6\%$$
$$\text{Maturity Amount} = p \times n + \frac{p \times n(n+1) \times r}{2400}$$
$$= 1200 \times 30 + \frac{1200 \times 30 \times 31 \times 6}{2400}$$
$$= 36000 + 2790$$
$$= \text{Rs. } 38790$$

(ii) $3, 9, m, 81$, and n are in continued proportion. Find the values of m and n, **[4]**

Solution:

$3, 9, m, 81$ and n ax in continued Proportion

$$\therefore \quad \frac{3}{9} = \frac{9}{m} = \frac{m}{81} = \frac{81}{n}$$

$$\frac{1}{3} = \frac{9}{m} = \frac{m}{81} = \frac{81}{h}$$

$$\therefore \quad \frac{1}{3} = \frac{9}{m}$$

$$m = 27 \qquad\qquad \textbf{Ans.}$$

and
$$\frac{1}{3} = \frac{81}{n}$$

$$n = 81 \times 3$$

$$= 243$$

(iii) Prove that: $\dfrac{\cos A}{1+\sin A} + \dfrac{1+\sin A}{\cos A} = 2\sec A$ **[4]**

Solution:

LHS

$$= \frac{\cos A}{1 + \sin A} + \frac{1 + \sin A}{\cos A}$$

$$= \frac{\cos^2 A + (1 + \sin A)^2}{(1 - \sin A)\cos A}$$

$$= \frac{\cos^2 A + 1 + \sin^2 A + 2\sin A}{(1 + \sin A)\cos A}$$

$$= \frac{1 + 1 + 2\sin A .}{(1 + \sin A)\cos A} \qquad [\sin^2 A + \cos^2 A = 1]$$

$$= \frac{(2 + 2\sin A)}{(1 + \sin A)\cos A}$$

$$= \frac{2(1 + \sin A)}{1 + \sin A} \times \sec A$$

$$= 2\sec A \qquad \text{RHS}$$

Question 3.

(i) The inner circumference of the rim of a circular metal tub is 44cm. **[4]**

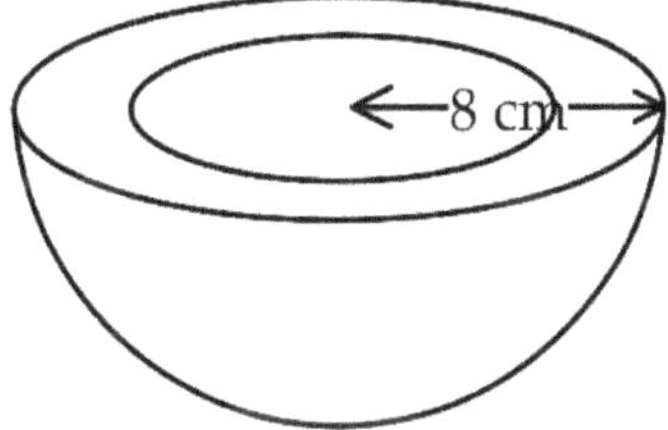

Find:

(a) The inner radius of the tub

(b) The volume of the material of the tub if it's outer radius is 8cm.

Use $\pi = \dfrac{22}{7}$

Give your answer correct to three significant figures

Solution:

(a) let inner radius $= r \; cm$

$$2\pi r = 44$$

$$r = \frac{244}{x \times 22} \times 7$$

$$= 7cm \; \text{Ans.}$$

outer radius $= 8cm.$

(b) Volume of material = Outer Volume−inner Volume

$$= \frac{2}{3}\pi R^3 - \frac{2}{3}\pi r^3$$

$$= \frac{2}{3} \times \frac{22}{7}[8^3 - 7^3]$$

$$= \frac{2}{3} \times \frac{22}{7} \times [512 - 343]$$

$$= \frac{2}{3} \times \frac{22}{7} \times 169 \Rightarrow \frac{7436}{21}$$

$$= 354.09$$

$$= 354cm^3$$

From the given figure: [4]

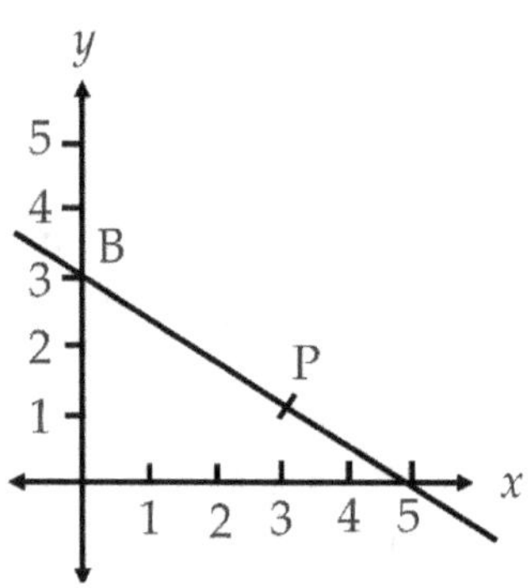

(a) Write down the coordinates of A and B.

(b) If P divides AB in the ratio 2: 3, find the coordinates of point P

(c) Find the equation of a line parallel to line AB and passing through the origin.

Solution:

(a) Co - ordinates of $A(5,0)$

o-ordinates of $B(0,3)$

(b) Let $P(x, y)$

$A(5,0) \rightarrow (x_1, y_1)$

$B(0,3) \rightarrow (x_2, y_2)$

$m_1 : m_2 = 2 : 3$

Section formula

$$\text{A}(5, 0) \quad\underline{\quad 2 \quad\; \overset{\textstyle P}{\bullet} \quad 3 \quad\quad}\; \text{B}(0, 3)$$

$$(x, y)$$

$$(x_1 y) = \left\{\frac{m_1 x_2 + m_2 x_1}{m_1 + m_2}, \frac{m_1 y_2 + m_2 y_1}{m_1 + m_2}\right\}$$

$$= \left\{\frac{2 \times 0 + 3 \times 5}{2 + 3}, \frac{2 \times 3 + 3 \times 0}{2 + 3}\right\}$$

$$= \left\{\frac{15}{5}, \frac{6}{5}\right\}$$

$$= \left\{3, \frac{6}{5}\right\} \text{Ans.}$$

(c) $\because$ Line (required) is parallel to AB

$\therefore$solve Slope of required dine = slope of AB

$$= \frac{y_2 - y_1}{x_2 - x_1} = \frac{3 - 0}{0 - 5}$$

$$\text{let } m_1 = -\frac{3}{5}$$

and panning through Origin so $O(0,0)$ as (x_1, y_1)

$\therefore$ equation of line:$y - y_1 = m(x - x_1)$

$$\Rightarrow y - 0 = -\frac{3}{5}(x + 0)$$

$$5y = -3x + 0$$

$$3x + 5y = 0$$

(iii) Use a graph sheet for this question. Take $2cm - 1$ unit along the axes. **[5]**
Plot the $\triangle OAB$, where $O(0,0), A(3,-2), B(2,-3)$.
(a) Reflect the $\triangle OAB$ through the origin and name it as $\triangle OA'B'$.
(b) Reflect the $\triangle OA'B'$ on the $y - axis$ and name it as $\triangle OA''B''$.
(c) Reflect the $\triangle OA'B'$ on the x - axis and name it as $\triangle OA'''B'''$.
(d) Join the points $AA''B''B'A'A'''B'''B$ and give the geometrical name of the closed figure so
formed.
Solution:

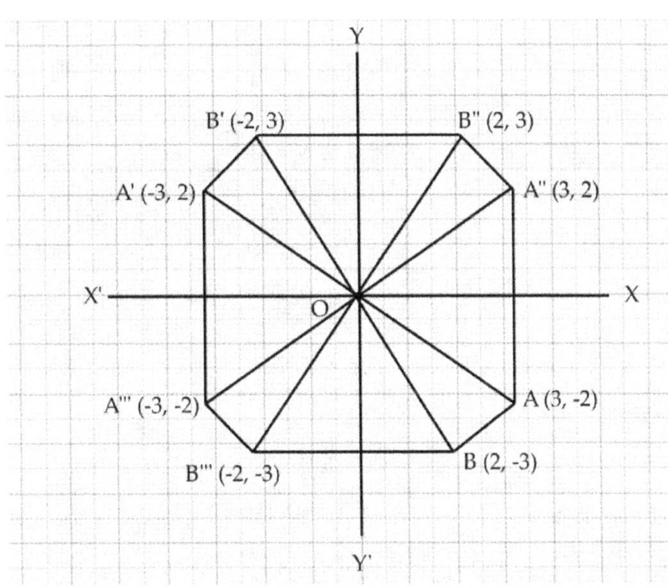

Question 4.

(i) The following bill shows the GST rates and the marked price of articles: [3]

BILL: COMPUTERS		
Articles	**Marked price**	**Rate of GST**
Graphic Card	Rs 15500.00	18%
Laptop adapter	Rs 1900.00	28%

Find the total amount to be paid for the above bill.

Solution:

M.P of Graphic Card $= $ Rs. 15500

$\therefore \quad GST = 18\%$

$\therefore \quad GST = \dfrac{18}{100} \times 15500$

$\qquad = $ Rs. 2790

MP of Adapted $= $ Rs. 1900

GST% $= 28\%$

GST $= \dfrac{28}{100} \times 1900$

$\qquad = $ Rs. 532

Total Amount to be paid $= 15500 + 2790 + 1900 + 532$

$$= \text{Rs. } 20722$$

(ii) Solve the following quadratic equation, [3]

$$7x^2 + 2x - 2 = 0$$

Give your answer correct to two places of decimal.

Solution:

$$7x^2 + 2x - 2 = 0$$
$$ax^2 + bx + c = 0; a \neq 0$$
$$a = 7, b = 2, c = -2$$

Quadratic formula:

$$x = \frac{-b \pm \sqrt{b^2 - 4ac}}{2a}$$

$$= \frac{-2 \pm \sqrt{(2)^2 - 4 \times 7 \times (-2)}}{2 \times 7}$$

$$= \frac{-2 \pm \sqrt{4 + 56}}{14}$$

$$= \frac{-2 \pm \sqrt{60}}{14}$$

$$= \frac{-2 \pm 2\sqrt{15}}{14} \Rightarrow \frac{-2 \pm 3.872 \times 2}{14}$$

$$= \frac{-2 \pm 7.74}{14}$$

$$= \frac{-2 + 7.744}{14}, \frac{-2 - 7.744}{14}$$

$$= 0.41, -0.70 \qquad \textbf{Ans.}$$

(iii) Use a graph sheet for this question. Draw a histogram for the daily earnings of 54 medical stores in the following table and hence estimate the mode for the following distribution. Take 2cm = ₹500 units along the x-axis and 2cm = 5 stores along the y-axis. **[4]**

Daily earnings (in Rs.)	4500 − 5000	5000 − 5500	5500 − 6000	6000 − 6500	6500 − 7000
No. of medical stores	20	14	12	5	3

Solution:

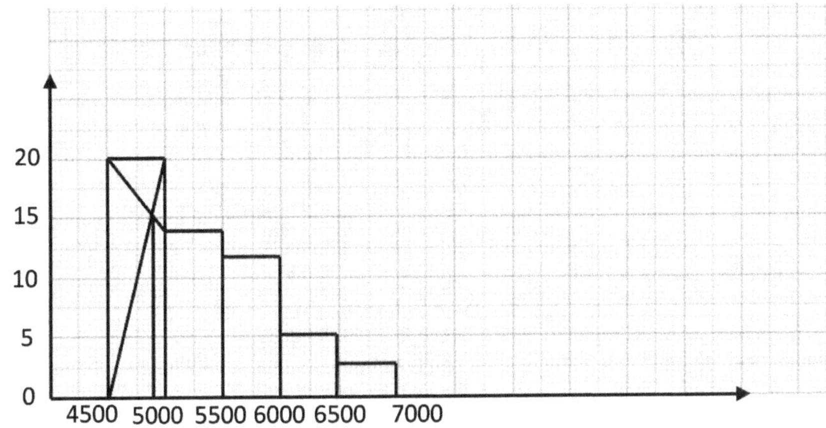

modal class = 4500 − 5000 so mode = Rs. 4900

Question 5.

(i) $A = \begin{bmatrix} 3 & -2 \\ -1 & 4 \end{bmatrix}, B = \begin{bmatrix} 6 \\ 1 \end{bmatrix}$ and $C = \begin{bmatrix} -4 \\ 5 \end{bmatrix}$, Evaluate AB − 5C **[3]**

Solution:

$$A = \begin{bmatrix} 3 & -2 \\ -1 & 4 \end{bmatrix}, B = \begin{bmatrix} 6 \\ 1 \end{bmatrix}, C = \begin{bmatrix} -4 \\ 5 \end{bmatrix}$$

$$\therefore \quad AB - 5C$$

$$= \begin{bmatrix} 3 & -2 \\ -1 & 4 \end{bmatrix}\begin{bmatrix} 6 \\ 1 \end{bmatrix} - 5\begin{bmatrix} -4 \\ 5 \end{bmatrix}$$

$$= \begin{bmatrix} 3 \times 6 + (-2) \times 1 \\ -1 \times 6 + 4 \times 1 \end{bmatrix} - \begin{bmatrix} -20 \\ 25 \end{bmatrix}$$

$$= \begin{bmatrix} 18 - 2 + 20 \\ -6 + 4 - 25 \end{bmatrix} = \begin{bmatrix} 36 \\ -27 \end{bmatrix} \; Ans.$$

(ii) In the given figure, O is the centre of the circle. The tangent PT meets the diameter RQ produced at P. **[3]**

(a) Prove $\triangle PQT \sim \triangle PTR$

(b) If $PT = 6cm, QR = 9cm$. Find the length of PQ

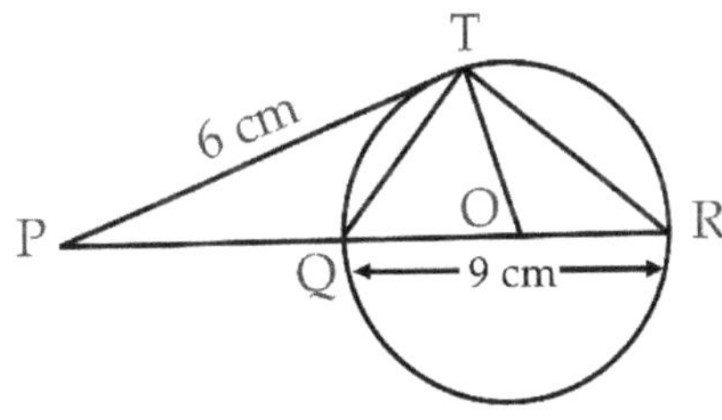

Solution:

(a) In $\triangle PQT$ and $\triangle PTR$

$\angle PTQ = \angle PRT$ (Angle in the alternate segment)

$\angle TPQ = \angle RPT$ (common)

$\therefore \triangle PQT \sim \triangle PTR$ (AA)

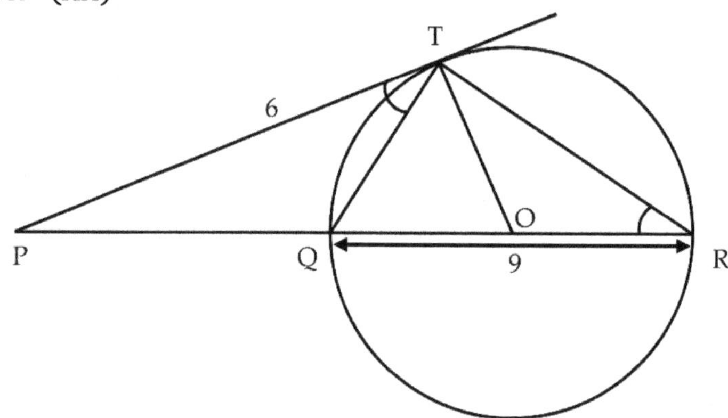

(b) $\therefore \dfrac{PQ}{PT} = \dfrac{QT}{TR} = \dfrac{PT}{PR}$ [corresponding sides of similar $\triangle'$ and proportional]

$$\frac{PQ}{6} = \frac{PT}{PR}$$
$$\frac{PQ}{P6} = \frac{6}{PQ + 9}$$
$$PQ^2 + 9PQ = 36$$
$$PQ^2 + 9PQ - 36 = 0$$
$$PQ^2 + 12PQ - 3PQ - 36 = 0$$
$$PQ(PQ + 12) - 3(PQ + 12) = 0$$
$$(PQ - 3)(PQ + 12) = 0$$
$$\therefore \quad PQ = 3, -12 \,(\text{ not Possible })$$
$$\therefore \quad PQ = 3\text{cm.} \qquad \textbf{Ans.}$$

(iii) Factorize the given polynomial completely, using Remainder Theorem: **[4]**
$$6x^3 + 25x^2 + 31x + 10$$

Solution:

$P(x) = 6x^3 + 25x^2 + 31x + 10$

$6 \times 10 = 60$

let $(x \pm 1), (x \pm 2), (x \pm 3)$ and $(x \pm 5)$ be factors

of $P(x)$

let $x + 1 = 0$

$$x = -1$$
$$P(-1) = 6(-1)^3 + 25(-1)^2 + 31(-1) + 10$$
$$= -6 + 25 - 31 + 10 \neq 0$$

let $x + 2 = 0$

$$x = -2$$
$$p(-2) = 6(-2)^3 + 25(-2)^2 + 31(-2) + 10$$
$$= -48 + 100 - 62 + 10$$
$$= -110 + 10 \Rightarrow 0$$

$\therefore x + 2$ is a factor of $P(x)$.

Now divide $p(x)$ by $x + 2$ to fedorite it

$$\therefore \quad 6x^3 + 25x^2 + 31x + 10$$

$$x + 2)\overline{6x^3 + 25x^2 + 31x + 10}$$
$$\underline{-6x^3 + 12x^2}$$
$$13x^2 + 31x + 10$$
$$13x^2 + 26x$$
$$\underline{(-)(-)}$$
$$5x + 10$$
$$5x + 10$$
$$\underline{(-)(-)}$$
$$0$$

$$= (x + 2)(6x^2 + 13x + 5)$$
$$= (x + 3)[6x^2 + 10x + 3x + 5]$$
$$= (x + 3)[2x(3x + 5) + 1(3x + 5)]$$
$$= (x + 3)(2x + 1)(3x + 5) \qquad \textbf{Ans.}$$

Question 6.

(i) ABCD is a square where B(1, 3), and D(3, 2) are the end points of the diagonal BD. Find: **[3]**

(a) The coordinates of a point of intersection of the diagonals AC and BD

(b) The equation of the diagonal AC

Solution:

Diagonals of a square bisects each other

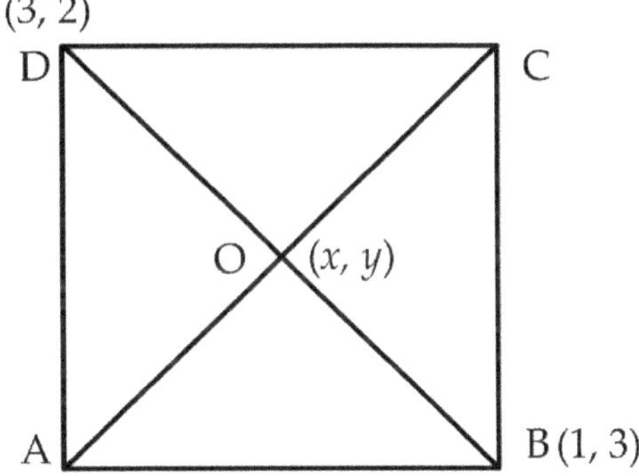

$\therefore$ O is the mid-pointof DB which is the point of intersection of both diagonals

mid-point formula $O(x, y) = \left\{ \dfrac{x_1 + x_2}{2}, \dfrac{y_1 + y_2}{2} \right\}$

$$= \left\{ \frac{3+1}{2}, \frac{2+3}{2} \right\}$$

$$= \left\{ 2, \frac{5}{2} \right\} \qquad \textbf{Ans.}$$

Slope of BD $(m_1) = \dfrac{y_2 - y_1}{x_2 - x_1}$

$$= \frac{3 - 2}{1 - 3} \Rightarrow -\frac{1}{2}$$

diagonal of a square of are perpendicular also.

Slope $_{(BD)} \times$ Slope $_{(BD)} = -1$

$$\frac{-1}{2} \times m_2 = -1$$

$$m_2 = 2$$

let $O\left(2, \frac{5}{2}\right)$ or (x_1, y_1), which lies on

$$\therefore \text{ equation} \Rightarrow y - y_1 = m(x + x_1)$$

$$y - \frac{5}{2} = 2(x - 2)$$

$$\frac{2y - 5}{2} = 2(x - 2)$$

$$2y - 5 = 2x - 4$$

$$0 = 2x - 2y - 4 + 5$$

$$\therefore \quad 2x - 2y + 1 = 0 \qquad \textbf{Ans.}$$

(ii) Prove that: $\sqrt{\sec^2 \theta + \operatorname{cosec}^2 \theta} = \sec \theta \cdot \operatorname{cosec} \theta$ **[3]**

Solution:

L.H.S

$$\sqrt{\frac{1}{\cos^2 \theta} + \frac{1}{\sin^2 \theta}} = \sqrt{\frac{\sin^2 \theta + \cos^2 \theta}{\sin^2 \theta \cos^2 \theta}}$$

$$= \sqrt{\frac{1}{\sin^2 \theta \cos^2 \theta}} = \frac{1}{\sin \theta \cos \theta} \ [\sin^2 \theta + \cos^2 \theta = 1]$$

$$= \operatorname{Sec} \theta \operatorname{cosec} \theta \qquad \text{R.H.S}$$

(iii) The first, the last term, and the common difference of an Arithmetic Progression are 98,1001 and 7 respectively. Find the following for the given Arithmetic Progression: **[4]**

(a) Number of terms 'n'.

(b) Sum of the 'n' terms.

Solution:

$$a = 98$$
$$l = 1001$$
$$d = 7$$
$$a + (n - 1)d = 1001$$
$$98 + (n - 1) \times 7 = 1001$$
$$(n - 1) \times 7 = 1001 - 98$$
$$n - 1 = \frac{903}{7}$$
$$n = 129 + 1 \Rightarrow 130 \text{ Ans.}$$

Sum of n terms:

$$S_n = \frac{n}{2}[2a + (n - 1)d]$$

$$S_{130} = \frac{65}{2}[2 \times 98 + (130 - 1) \times 7]$$

$$= 65[196 + 129 \times 7]$$

$$= 65 \times 1099 \Rightarrow 71435 \qquad \textbf{Ans.}$$

Question 7.

(i) A box contains some green, yellow and white tennis balls. The probability of selecting a green ball is $\frac{1}{4}$ and the yellow ball is $\frac{1}{3}$. If the box contains 10 white balls, then find: **[3]**

(a) Total number of balls in the box.

(b) Probability of selecting a white ball.

Solution:

Probability of green balls $= \frac{1}{4}$

Probability of yellow balls $= \frac{1}{3}$

No. of white belts $= 10$

det total No of bells $= x$

$\therefore$ probability of while belts $= \frac{10}{x}$

$\therefore \quad P(G) + P(V) + P(W) = 1$

$$\frac{1}{4} + \frac{1}{3} + \frac{10}{x} = 1$$

$$\frac{10}{x} = \frac{1}{1} - \frac{1}{4} - \frac{1}{3}$$

$$\frac{10}{x} = \frac{12 - 3 - 4}{12}$$

$$\frac{10}{x} = \frac{5}{12}$$

$$5x = 12 \times 10$$

$$x = \frac{12x + 02}{5} \Rightarrow 24 \text{ balls} \qquad \textbf{Ans.}$$

$$\therefore P(W) = \frac{\text{No. of fovorable outcome}}{\text{total number of outcome}}$$

$$= \frac{10}{24} \Rightarrow \frac{5}{12} \qquad \textbf{Ans.}$$

(ii) A cone and a sphere having the same radius are melted and recast into a cylinder. The radius and height of the cone are 3cm and 12cm respectively. If the radius of the cylinder so formed is 2cm, find the height of the cylinder. **[3]**

Solution:

Radius of cone $= 3$cm

height of cone $= 12$cm.

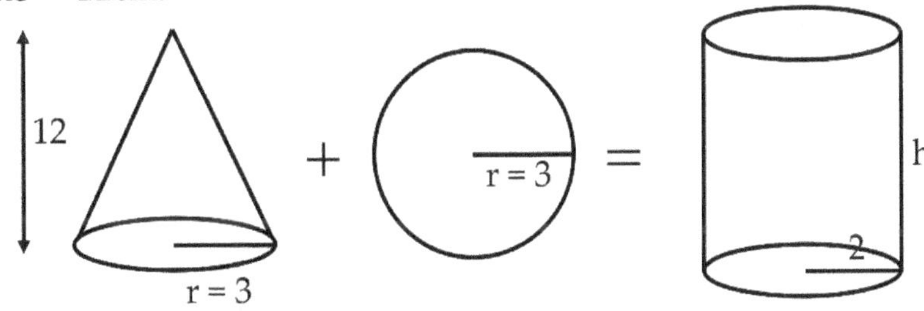

$$\text{Volume of cone} = \frac{1}{3}\pi r^2 h$$

$$= \frac{1}{3} \times \pi \times (3)^2 \times 12$$

$$= 36\pi\,\text{cm}^3 \qquad\qquad\qquad \ldots\ldots(i)$$

$$\text{radius of sphere} = 3cm$$

$$\text{volume of sphere} = \frac{4}{3}\pi r^3$$

$$= \frac{4}{3} \times \pi \times (3)^3 \Rightarrow 27\pi\,\text{cm}^3$$

Let height of cylinder $= h$ cm.

$A \cdot T \cdot Q.$

volume of Cone + vol. of sphese = vol of cylinder

$$3\pi + 27\pi = \pi \times 2^2 \times h$$

$$\frac{30\pi}{\pi \times 2^2} = h$$

$$h = \frac{30}{4} \Rightarrow 7.5\text{cm} \qquad\qquad \textbf{Ans.}$$

(iii) In the given diagram, ABCD is a cyclic quadrilateral and PQ is a tangent to the smaller circle at E. Given $\angle AEP = 70°, \angle BOC = 110°$. Find: **[4]**

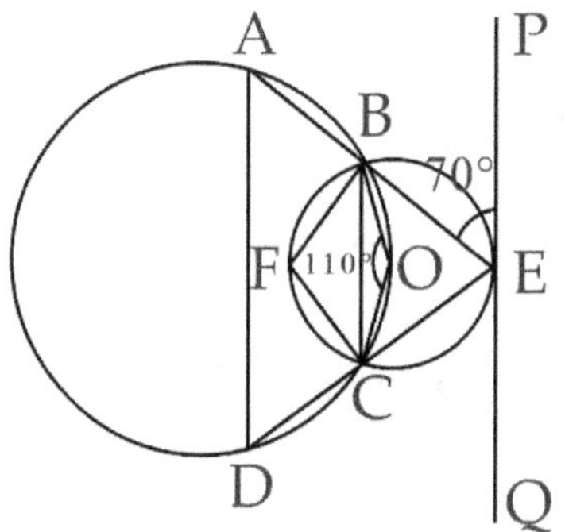

(a) $\angle ECB$,

(b) $\angle BEC$,

(c) $\angle BFC$,

(d) $\angle DAB$,

Solution:

(a) $\angle AEP = 70°$

$\quad \angle BOC = 110°$

$\quad \angle ECB = \angle BEP$ [angles in alternate segment]

$\quad \angle ECB = 70°$ \hfill **Ans.**

(b) $\angle BEC = \frac{1}{2}\angle BOC$[angle at the circumference $= \frac{1}{2}$ at the center]

$\quad \angle BEC = \frac{1}{2} \times 110$

$\quad\quad = 55°$ \hfill **Ans.**

(c) $\angle BFC + \angle BEC = 180$[opposite Angles of cyclic patrilateral]

$\quad \angle BFC = 180 - 55$

$\quad\quad\quad = 125$ \hfill **Ans.**

(d) $\angle DAB$

$\quad \angle DAB = \angle ECB$ [exterior angle of cyclic quadrilateral equals. opposite interior rectangle]

$$\angle DAB = 70° \qquad\qquad\qquad\qquad\qquad \textbf{Ans.}$$

Question 8.

(i) Solve the following inequation: **[3]**

$$-\frac{x}{3} - 4 \le \frac{x}{2} - \frac{7}{3} < -\frac{7}{6}, x \in R$$

Represent the solution set on a number line.

Solution:

$$-\frac{x}{3} - 4 \le \frac{x}{2} - \frac{7}{3} < -\frac{7}{6}, x \in R$$

$$-\frac{x}{3} - 4 \le \frac{3x - 14}{6} < -\frac{7}{6}$$

$$-\frac{x}{3} - 4 \le \frac{3x - 14}{6} \text{ and } \frac{3x - 14}{6} < -\frac{7}{6}$$

$$-x - 12 \le \frac{3x - 14}{2} \text{ and } 3x < -7 + 14$$

$$-2x - 24 \le 3x - 14 \text{ and } x < \frac{7}{3}$$

$$-2x - 3x \le -14 + 24 \text{ and } x < \frac{7}{3}$$

$$-5x \le 10$$

$$x \ge \frac{10}{-5}$$

$$x \ge -2 \text{ and } x < \frac{7}{3}$$

Solution Set: $\left\{ x : -2 \le x < \frac{7}{3}, x \in R \right\}$

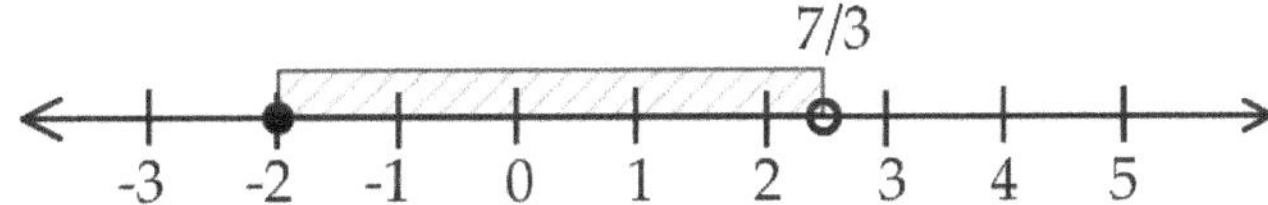

(ii) The following table gives the petrol prices per liter for a period of 50 days. **[3]**

Price (in Rs.)	85 − 90	90 − 95	95 − 100	100 − 105	105 − 110
No. of days	12	10	8	15	5

Find the mean price of petrol per litre to the nearest rupee using step-deviation method.

Solution:

CI	Landmarks(x)	f	$d = x - A$	$u = \dfrac{d}{h}$	fu
85 − 90	87.5	12	$87.5 - 97.5 = -10$	$-\frac{10}{5} = -2$	−24
90 − 95	92.5	10	−5	−1	−10
95 − 100	97.5	8	0	0	0
100 − 105	102.5	15	5	1	15
105 − 110	107.5	5	10	2	10

		$\sum f = 50$		$\Sigma fu = -9$

Let Assumed mean $(A) = 97.5$

Clam height $(h) = 90 - 85 \Rightarrow 5$

$$\text{mean}(n) = A + \left(\frac{\Sigma fu}{\Sigma f}\right) \times h$$

$$= 97.5 + \frac{-9}{5010} \times 5 \Rightarrow 97.5 - 0.9$$

$$\Rightarrow \text{Rs. } 96.6 \qquad \textbf{Ans.}$$

(iii) In the given diagram, ABC is a triangle and $BCFD$ is a parallelogram. $AD:DB = 4:5$ and $EF = 15$cm. **[4]**

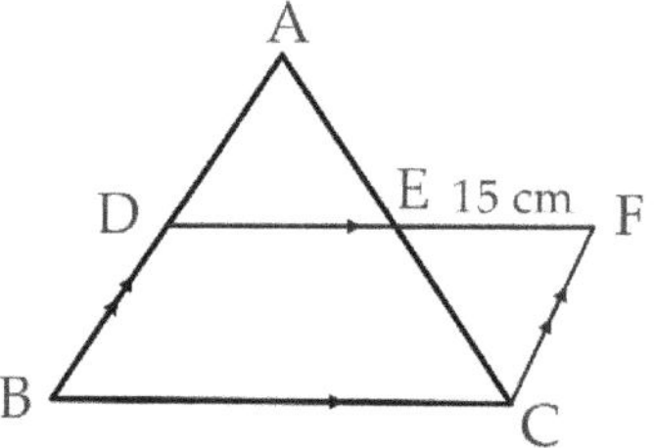

Find:

(a) $AE:EC$

(b) DE

(c) BC

Solution:

(a) BCFD is a ∥gm

∴ In $\triangle ABC$

$DE \parallel BC$ (opposite sides of ∥gm)

$$\frac{AD}{DB} = \frac{AE}{EC} \quad (BPT)$$

$$\frac{4}{5} = \frac{AE}{EC}$$

∴ $\frac{AE}{EC} = \frac{4}{5}$ or $AE!EC = 4:5$ $\qquad$ **Ans.**

(b) In $\triangle ADE$ and $\triangle CFF$

$\angle ADE = \angle CFE$ [Alternate angles]

$\angle DEA = \angle FEC$ [Vertically opposite]

∴$\triangle ADE \sim \triangle CFE \qquad (AA)$

$$\frac{DE}{FE} = \frac{AE}{CE} \text{ [Corresponding sides of similar are proposational]}$$

$$\frac{DE}{15} = \frac{4}{5}$$

$$DE = \frac{4 \times 15}{5}$$

$DE = 12$cm. $\qquad$ **Ans.**

$BC = DF$ (Opposite Sides of ∥ gm]

$\quad = OE + EF$

$$= 12 + 15$$
$$BC = 27 \text{ cm} \qquad \textbf{Ans.}$$

Question 9.

(i) Amit takes 12 days less than the days taken by Bijoy to complete a certain work. If both, working together, takes 8 days to complete the work, find the number of days taken by Bijoy to complete the work, working alone. **[4]**

Solution:

Let time taken by Bijoy to do work $= x$ days

$\therefore$ time is taken by a Amit $= (x - 12)$ days

Together they complete the work $= 8$ days

In I day Bijoy completes $= \dfrac{1}{x}$

In 1 day, Amit complete $= \dfrac{1}{x-12}$

Together in 1 day they do $= \dfrac{1}{8}$

$$\frac{x - 12 + x}{x(x - 12)} = \frac{1}{8}$$
$$x^2 - 12x = (2x - 12) \times 8$$
$$x^2 - 12x = 16x - 96$$
$$x^2 - 12x - 16x + 96 = 0$$
$$x^2 - 28x + 96 = 0$$
$$x^2 - 24x - 4x + 96 = 0$$
$$x(x - 24) - 4(x - 24) = 0$$
$$(x - 4)(x - 24) = 0$$
$$x = 4, 24$$
$$x = 4 \text{ is not possille as } 4 - 12 = -ve$$
$$\therefore x = 24 \text{ days}$$

Bijoy to complete the work $= 24$ day $\qquad$ **Ans.**

(ii) Use a graph sheet for this question. The daily wages of 120 workers working at a site is given below: **[6]**

Wages (₹)	250 − 300	300 − 350	350 − 400	400 − 450	450 − 500	500 − 550	550 − 600
No. of Workers	8	15	20	30	25	15	7

Use 2cm = ₹50 and 2cm − 20 workers along x - axis and y - axis respectively to draw an ogive and hence estimate:

(a) The median wages

(b) The inter-quartile range of wages

(c) Percentage of workers whose daily wage is above ₹ 475.

Solution:

Wages (f)	No. of wages (f)	$C.f$
$250 - 300$	8	8
$300 - 350$	15	23
$350 - 400$	20	43
$400 - 450$	30	73
$450 - 500$	25	98
$500 - 550$	15	113
$550 - 600$	7	120
	$f = 120$	

N= 120(even)

$$\text{Median wages} = \left(\frac{N}{2}\right)^{th} \text{ term}$$
$$= \left(\frac{120}{2}\right) th \text{ term}$$
$$= 60 \text{ th term}$$
$$= \text{Rs. } 435 \text{ (approx.)}$$

$$\text{Upper Quartile}(Q_3) \quad = \left(\frac{3}{4}N\right) \text{ th term}$$
$$= \left(\frac{3}{4} \times 120\right) \text{ th term}$$
$$= 90 \text{ th term}$$
$$= \text{Rs. } 475 \text{ (approx)}$$

$$\text{Lower Quartile} \quad (Q1) = \left(\frac{N}{4}\right) \text{ th term}$$
$$= \left(\frac{120}{4}\right) \text{ th term } = 30 \text{ th}$$
$$= \text{Rs. } 375 \text{ (approx)}.$$

$$\therefore \text{ ittinter quartice range} = Q_3 - Q_1$$
$$= 475 - 375$$
$$= Rs.\, 100$$

No of the worker's whose daily
wager above $475 = 120 - 90$
$$= 30$$
$$\% = \frac{30}{120} \times 100$$
$$= 25\% \qquad\qquad \textbf{Ans.}$$

Question 10.

(i) Solve for x, using the properties of proportion. **[3]**

$$\frac{\sqrt{2 + x} + \sqrt{3 - x}}{\sqrt{2 + x} - \sqrt{3 - x}} = 3$$

Solution:

$$\frac{\sqrt{2 + x} + \sqrt{3 + x}}{\sqrt{2 + x} - \sqrt{3 + x}} = 3$$

Apply components and dividends

$$\frac{\sqrt{2+x}+\sqrt{3-x}+\sqrt{2+x}-\sqrt{3-x}}{\sqrt{2+x}+\sqrt{3-x}+\sqrt{2+x}+\sqrt{3-x}}=\frac{3+1}{3-1}$$

$$\frac{2\sqrt{2+x}}{2\sqrt{3-x}}=\frac{4}{2}$$

$$\frac{\sqrt{2+x}}{\sqrt{3-x}}=2$$

Squaring both sides

$$\frac{2+x}{3-x}=\frac{4}{1}$$
$$2+x=12-4x$$
$$x+4x=12-2$$
$$5x=10$$
$$x=\frac{10}{5}$$
$$x=2 \qquad\qquad \textbf{Ans.}$$

(ii) Using ruler and compasses, construct a regular hexagon of side 4.5cm. Hence construct a circle circumscribing the hexagon. Measure and write down the length of the circum-radius.

[3]

Solution:

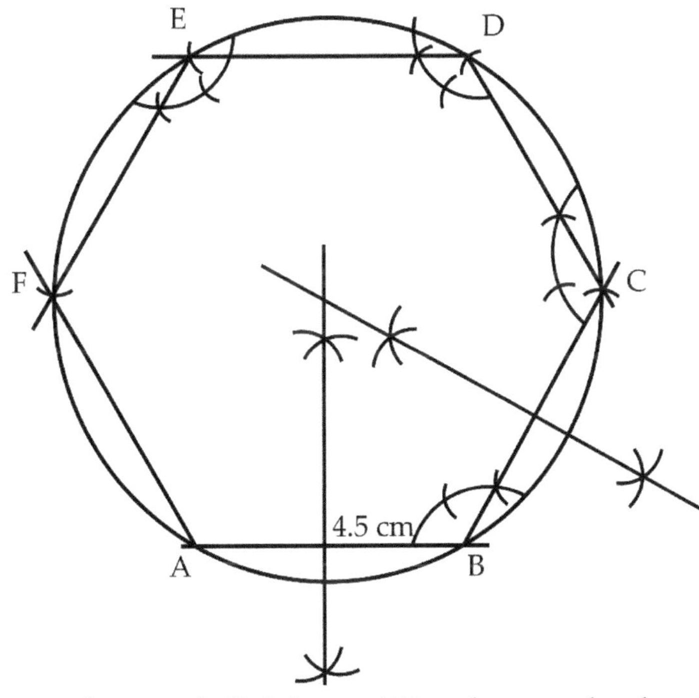

(iii) An observer standing on the top of a lighthouse 150m above sea level watches a ship sailing away. As he observes, the angle of depression of the ship changes from 50° to 30°. Determine the distance traveled by ship during the period of observation. Give your answer correct to the nearest meter. (Use Mathematical Table for this question.)

[4]

Solution:

let $AB = 150$m.

L $ADB = DAE$ and $\angle ACB = \angle CAE$ (angle of elevation= depression)

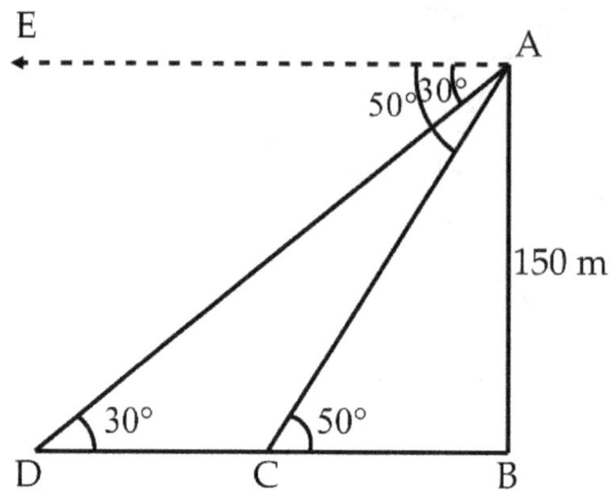

In $\triangle ACB$ $\text{ten}50 = \dfrac{AB}{CB}\left(\dfrac{perpendicuter}{Bare}\right)$

$$1.917 = \dfrac{150}{CB}$$

$$CB = \dfrac{150}{1-1917} \Rightarrow 125.87\text{m}.$$

In $\triangle ADB$

$$\tan 30 = \dfrac{AB}{BD}$$

$$\dfrac{1}{\sqrt{3}} = \dfrac{150}{BD}$$

$$BD = 150 \times \sqrt{3}$$
$$= 150 \times 1.732 = 259.80\text{m}$$

$\therefore$ Distance traveled by ship $= BO = CB$

$$= 259.80 - 125.87 \Rightarrow 13393$$
$$= 134\text{m} \qquad\qquad \textbf{Ans.}$$

$$\overline{}$$

ICSE EXAMINATION

SAMPLE PAPER-1

MATHEMATICS

Maximum Marks: 80

Time allowed: Two and a half hours

Answers to this Paper must be written on the paper provided separately.

You will not be allowed to write during first 15 minutes.

This time is to be spent in reading the question paper.

The time given at the head of this Paper is the time allowed for writing the answers.

Attempt all questions from Section *A* and any three questions from Section *B*.

The intended marks for questions or parts of questions are given in brackets [].

SECTION – A (40 Marks)

(Attempt all questions from this section)

Question 1.

Chose the correct answers to the questions from the given options: **[15]**

(i) Mr. Pankaj took a health insurance policy for his family and paid Rs. 900 as SGST. Find the total annual premium (Excluding GST) paid by him for this policy, the rate of GST being 18%.

(a) $Rs.\,9000$

(b) $Rs.\,10000$

(c) $Rs.\,10900$

(d) $Rs.\,5000$

Solution: Option (b)

Let the annual premium be Rs. X

$$\text{SGST} = Rs.\,900$$

So total GST $= Rs.\,1800$

$$18\ \%\ \text{of} = 1800$$

$$\frac{18}{100} \times x = 1800$$

$$x = \frac{1800 \times 100}{18}$$

$$= \text{Rs. } 10000$$

(ii) If discriminant (d) for a quadratic equation is given by $b^2 - 4ac = 0$, then roots are:

(a) Real and distinct

(b) Real and equal

(c) Imaginary

(d) None of the above

Solution: Option (b)

(iii) The value of 'm' for which (x – 1) is a factor of the polynomial $4x^3 + 3x^2 - 4x + m$ is:

    (a) 0

    (b) 3

    (c) –3

    (d) 1

    Solution: Option (c)

    Since $x - 1$ is a factor so $x = 1$

$$4(1)^3 + 3(1)^2 - 4 \times 1 + m = 0$$
$$4 + 3 - 4 + m = 0$$
$$m = -3$$

(iv) The order of Matrix M in $\begin{bmatrix} 3 & x \\ 9 & y \end{bmatrix} \times M = \begin{bmatrix} -2 \\ 8 \end{bmatrix}$ is:

    (a) 1×2

    (b) 2×2

    (c) 2×1

    (d) Multiplication not possible

    Solution: Option (c)

    Let order of $M = r \times c$

$$2 \times [2 = r] \times c = 2 \times 1$$

    So $r = 2$ and $c = 1$ i.e., order is 2×1

(v) The common difference of the AP $\frac{1}{2q}, \frac{1-2q}{2q}, \frac{1-4q}{2q}, ...$ is:

    (a) -1

    (b) 1

    (c) q

    (d) $2q$

    Solution: Option (a)

$$\frac{1-2q}{2q} - \frac{1}{2q} = \frac{1-2q-1}{2q} = \frac{-2q}{2q} = -1$$

(vi) A point P is reflected in the x-axis. Co-ordinate of its image are $(-4, 5)$. Co-ordinates of P?

    (a) $(4, 5)$

    (b) $(4, -5)$

    (c) $(-4, -5)$

    (d) $(-4, 5)$

    Solution: Option (c)

    When a point reflects in x axis sign of y coordinate changes

    So, P$(-4, -5)$

(vii) If ABC and DEF are similar triangles such that $\angle A = 47°$ and $\angle E = 83°$, then $\angle C =$

    (a) 50°

    (b) 80°

    (c) 70°

(d) Not possible to find

Solution: Option (a)

As triangle ABC and DEF are similar so their corresponding angles will be equal. So angle B = angle E= 83°. So, angle C = 180 – (47 + 83) = 50 degree (angle sum property)

(viii) The radius of the base and the height of a right circular cone are 7cm and 24cm respectively. The slant height of the cone is:

(a) 26cm

(b) 25cm

(c) 23cm

(d) 24cm

Solution: Option (b)

Slant height of the cone $= \sqrt{7^2 + 24^2} = \sqrt{49 + 576} = \sqrt{625} = 25\ cm$

(ix) The solution set for the given inequation is: $-\frac{5}{2} < x \le \frac{35}{6}, x \in N$

(a) $\{-2, -1, 0, 1, 2, 3, 4, 5\}$

(b) $\{1, 2, 3, 4, 5\}$

(c) $\{0, 1, 2, 3, 4, 5\}$

(d) None of these

Solution: Option (b)

$-2.5 < x \le 5\frac{5}{6}; x \in N$

So $(1, 2, 3, 4, 5)$

(x) Which of the following cannot be the probability of occurrence of an event?

(a) 0.2

(b) 0.4

(c) 0.8

(d) 1.7

Solution: Option (d)

1.7 as $0 \le P(E) \le 1$

(xi) The coordinates of the point where the line $x - y = 5$ cuts y- axis are:

(a) $(5, 0)$

(b) $(0, -5)$

(c) $(0, 5)$

(d) $(-5, 0)$

Solution: Option (b)

Since point of intersection is on y – axis so point will be $(0, y)$

$0 - y = 5 \Rightarrow y = -5$ so, coordinate $= (0, -5)$

(xii) Using the following figure, the value of x is:

(a) 120°

(b) 60°

(c) 240°

(d) 110°

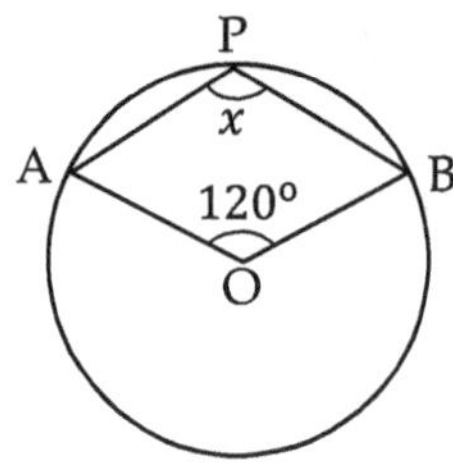

Solution: Option (a)

Take a point Q on the circumference and join AQ and BQ.

Angle AQB $=$ ½ of angle AOB $= 60°$ (angle at the center is double of the angle at the circumference)

So $x = 180° - 60° = 120°$

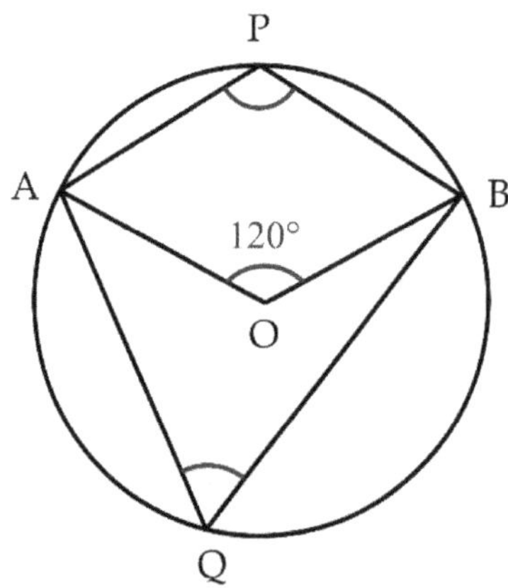

(xiii) The value of $\sin^2 45 + \cos^2 45$ is:

    (a) −1

    (b) 1

    (c) 0.5

    (d) $\frac{2}{\sqrt{2}}$

Solution: Option (b)

As $\sin^2 \theta + \cos^2 \theta$

(xiv) If $\Sigma f_i = 12$, $\Sigma f_i x_i = 2p + 52f$, and the mean of a distribution is 7, then the value of p

    (a) 14

    (b) 15

    (c) 12

    (d) 16

Solution: Option (d)

$$\text{mean} = \frac{\Sigma f_i x_i}{\Sigma f_i}$$

$$7 = \frac{2p + 52}{12}$$

$$2p + 52 = 84$$

$$2p = 84 - 52 = 32$$

$$p = \frac{32}{2} = 16$$

(xv) The sequence of numbers $-10, -6, -2, 2, \ldots$ is:

    (a) An AP with d $= -16$

    (b) An AP with d $= 4$

    (c) An AP with d $= -4$

    (d) Not an AP

    Solution: Option (b)

$$-6 - (-10) = -2 - (-6) = 2 - (-2)$$
$$-6 + 10 = -2 + 6 = 2 + 2$$
$$4 = 4 = 4 \ (\text{Common difference})$$

Question 2.

(i) Arvind deposits Rs 1600 per month in a cumulative account for 3 years at the rate of 9% p.a. simple interest. Find the amount Arvind will get at the time of maturity. **[4]**

Solution:

Per month installment (p) $= Rs.\,1600$

Time (n) $= 3$ years $= 36$ months

Rate $= 9\,\%$ p.a.

$$\text{M.A.} = p \times n + \frac{p \times n(n+1) \times r}{2400}$$
$$= 1600 \times 36 + \frac{1600 \times 36 \times 37 \times 9}{2400}$$
$$= 57600 + 7992$$
$$= Rs.\ 65{,}592 \qquad\qquad \textbf{Ans.}$$

(ii) What number should be subtracted from each of the numbers 23, 30, 57, and 78 so that the remainders are in proportion? **[4]**

Solution:

Let x should be subtracted

$$\frac{23 - x}{30 - x} = \frac{57 - x}{78 - x}$$
$$1794 - 23x - 78x + x2 = 1710 - 30x - 57x + x2$$
$$1794 - 101x = 1710 - 87x$$
$$-101x + 87x = 1710 - 1794$$
$$-14x = -84$$
$$x = 6$$

(iii) $(\operatorname{cosec}^2 A - 1)(\sec A + 1)(\sec A - 1) = 1$ **[4]**

Solution:

LHS

$$= (\operatorname{cosec}^2 A - 1)(\sec A + 1)(\sec A - 1)$$
$$= (\operatorname{cosec}^2 A - 1)(\sec^2 A - 1)$$
$$= \cot^2 A \times \tan^2 A \ [\text{as } 1 + \tan^2 A = \sec^2 A \text{ and } 1 + \cot^2 A = \operatorname{cosec}^2 A]$$
$$= \frac{1}{\tan^2 A} \times \tan^2 A$$

$= 1$

$= RHS$

Question 3.

(i) The area of curved surface of a right circular cylinder is 4400 cm² and the circumference of its base is 110 cm. Find the height of the cylinder. **[4]**

Solution:

Let radius of the cone be r cm and height = h cm.

Curved surface area of cone (CSA): $2\pi r h = 4400$ cm²

Circumference $(2\pi r) = 110$ cm

$$\frac{2\pi h}{2\pi r} = \frac{4400}{110}$$
$$h = 40\,cm \qquad\qquad \textbf{Ans.}$$

(ii) Given a line segment AB joining the points A $(-4, 6)$ and B$(8, -3)$. Find: **[2]**

(a) The ratio in which AB is divided by the y-axis.

(b) Find the coordinates of the point of intersection.

Solution:

Let point P(0, y) on y – axis which divide the

Join of A and B in $m_1 : m_2$

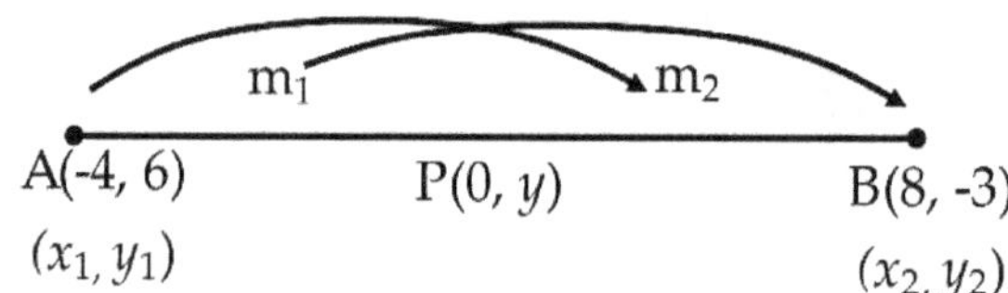

Using section formula:

$$x = \frac{m_1 x_2 + m_2 x_1}{m_1 + m_2}$$
$$0 = \frac{m_1 \times 8 + m_2 \times (-4)}{m_1 + m_2}$$
$$8\,m_1 - 4\,m_2 = 0$$
$$8\,m_1 = 4\,m_2$$
$$\frac{m1}{m2} = \frac{4}{8} \Rightarrow \frac{m1}{m2} = \frac{1}{2}$$

Now to find point of intersection

$$y = \frac{m_1 y_2 + m_2 y_1}{m_1 + m_2}$$
$$y = \frac{1 \times (-3) + 2 \times 6}{1 + 2}$$
$$y = \frac{-3 + 12}{3}$$
$$y = \frac{9}{3} \Rightarrow y = 3$$

So, co-ordinates of point of intersection $= (0,3)$

(iii) Use graph paper for this question (Take 2 cm = 1 unit along both x and y axis). ABCD is a quadrilateral whose vertices are $A(2, 2), B(2, -2), C(0, -1)$ and $D(0, 1)$. [5]

(a) Reflect quadrilateral ABCD on the y-axis and name it as A'B'CD.

(b) Write down the coordinates of A' and B'.

(c) Name two points which are invariant under the above reflection.

(d) Name the polygon A'B'CD.

Solution:

(b) Co – ordinates of A' (image of A under reflection

In y – axis) = $(-2, 2)$

Co – ordinates of B' (image of B under reflection

In y – axis) = $(-2, -2)$

(c) Point C and D are invariants.

(d) Name of polygon A'B'CD is isosceles trapezium.

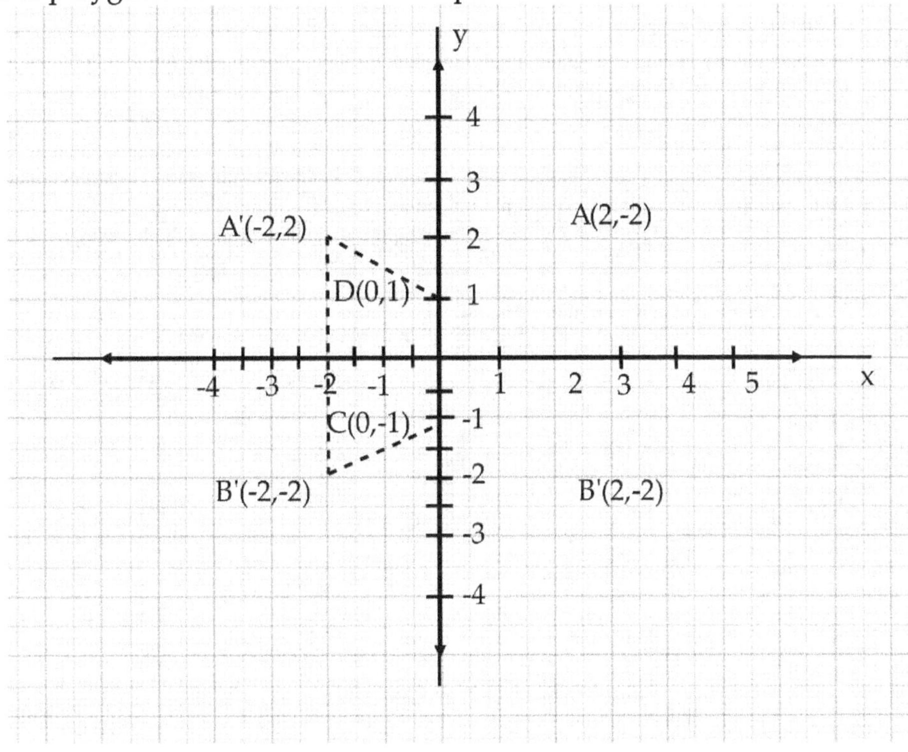

SECTION – B

(Attempt any four questions from this section)

Question 4.

(i) Find the amount of bill for the following intra-state transaction of goods/services. The GST rates and Marked price of each article are given: [3]

Article	A	B	C
Marked Price	$Rs. 3000$	$Rs. 6000$	$Rs. 4800$
GST%	12	12	18

Solution:

Total $GST = 12\%$ of $3000 + 12\%$ of $6000 + 18\%$ of 4800

$$= \frac{12}{100} \times 3000 + \frac{12}{100} \times 6000 + \frac{18}{100} \times 4800$$

$$= 360 + 720 + 864$$

$$= \text{Rs. } 1944$$

Total amount of Bill $= 3000 + 6000 + 4800 + 1944 = Rs.\,15{,}744$

(ii) Find the value of ' m ', if the following equation has equal roots:

$(4 + m)x^2 + (m + 1)x + 1 = 0$ [3]

Solution

Since roots are equal so $b^2 - 4a\,c = 0$

$$(m + 1)^2 - 4 \times (4 + m) \times 1 = 0$$
$$m^2 + 2\,m + 1 - 16 - 4\,m = 0$$
$$m^2 - 2\,m - 15 = 0$$
$$m^2 - 5\,m + 3\,m - 15 = 0$$
$$m(\,m - 5) + 3(\,m - 5) = 0$$
$$(\,m + 3)(m - 5) = 0$$
$$m = -3, 5$$

(iii) Find the mode of the following distribution by drawing a histogram: [3]

Height (in cm)	30 − 40	40 − 50	50 − 60	60 − 70	70 − 80	80 − 90
No of plants	4	3	8	11	6	2

Solution:

On x – axis heights of plants (in cm) plotted with the scale $2\,\text{cm} = 10\,\text{cm}$

On y – axis number of plants plotted with the scale $2\,\text{cm} = 2$ plants.

Since the highest column is 60 – 70 so it is modal class.

Mode $= 64$ cm. **Ans.**

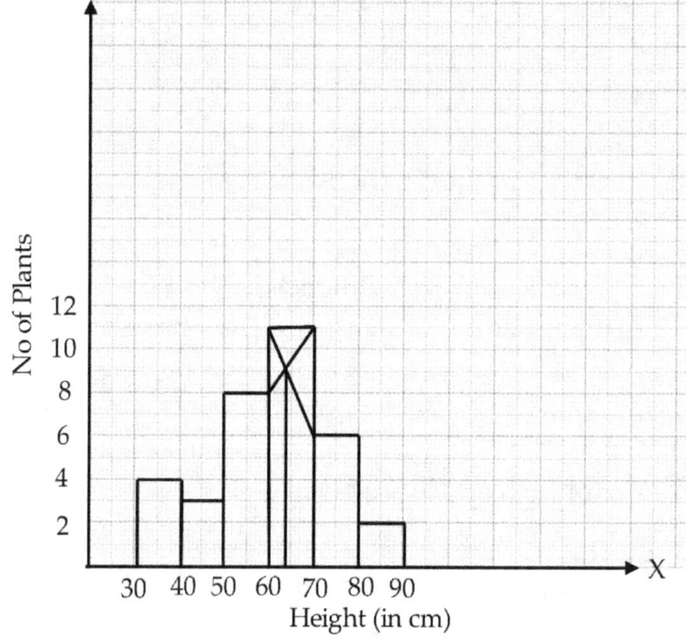

Question 5.

(i) Evaluate x, y if: $\begin{bmatrix} 3 & -2 \\ -1 & 4 \end{bmatrix}\begin{bmatrix} 2x \\ 1 \end{bmatrix} + 2\begin{bmatrix} -4 \\ 5 \end{bmatrix} = \begin{bmatrix} 8 \\ 4y \end{bmatrix}$ **[3]**

Solution:

$$\begin{bmatrix} 3 & -2 \\ -1 & 4 \end{bmatrix}\begin{bmatrix} 2x \\ 1 \end{bmatrix} + 2\begin{bmatrix} -4 \\ 5 \end{bmatrix} = \begin{bmatrix} 8 \\ 4y \end{bmatrix}$$

$$\begin{bmatrix} 3 \times 2x + (-2) \times 1 \\ -1 \times 2x + 4 \times 1 \end{bmatrix} + \begin{bmatrix} -8 \\ 10 \end{bmatrix} = \begin{bmatrix} 8 \\ 4y \end{bmatrix}$$

$$\begin{bmatrix} 6x - 2 \\ -2x + 4 \end{bmatrix} + \begin{bmatrix} -8 \\ 10 \end{bmatrix} = \begin{bmatrix} 8 \\ 4y \end{bmatrix}$$

$$\begin{bmatrix} 6x - 2 - 8 \\ -2x + 4 + 10 \end{bmatrix} = \begin{bmatrix} 8 \\ 4y \end{bmatrix}$$

$$\begin{bmatrix} 6x - 10 \\ -2x + 14 \end{bmatrix} = \begin{bmatrix} 8 \\ 4y \end{bmatrix}$$

So
$$6x = 8 + 10 = 18$$
$$x = 3$$
$$-2 \times 3 + 14 = 4y$$
$$8 = 4y$$
$$y = 2,$$

So, $\qquad x = 3$ and $y = 2$ **Ans.**

(ii) PQR is a triangle. S is a point on the side QR of triangle PQR such that $\angle PSR = \angle QPR$. Given QP $= 8$ cm, PR $= 6$ cm and SR $= 3$ cm. **[3]**

(a) Prove that: $\Delta PQR \sim \Delta SPR$

(b) Find the length of QR and PS.

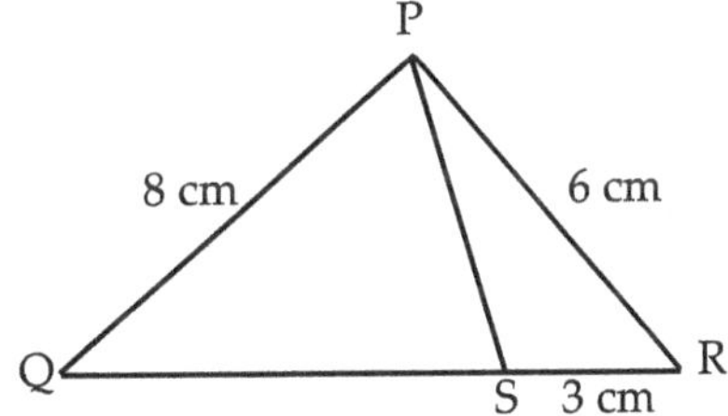

Solution:

In Δ PQR and Δ SPR

$\angle QPR = \angle PSR$ $\qquad$ (Given)

$\angle QRP = \angle PRS$ $\qquad$ (common)

So Δ PQR $\sim \Delta$ SPR $\qquad$ (AA similarity criterian)

$\dfrac{PQ}{SP} = \dfrac{QR}{PR} = \dfrac{PR}{SR}$ $\qquad$ (Corresponding sides of similar triangles are proportional)

$\dfrac{8}{SP} = \dfrac{QR}{6} = \dfrac{6}{3}$

$\dfrac{QR}{6} = \dfrac{6}{3} \Rightarrow QR = \dfrac{36}{3} = 12$ cm $\qquad$ **Ans.**

$\dfrac{8}{SP} = \dfrac{6}{3} \Rightarrow SP = \dfrac{24}{6} = 4$ cm $\qquad$ **Ans.**

(iii) Given that $(x + 2)$ and $(x + 3)$ are factors of $2x^3 + ax^2 + 7x - b$. Determine the values of a and b. **[4]**

Solution:

$$x + 2 = 0 \Rightarrow x = -2$$
$$\text{so, } 2(-2)^3 + a(-2)^2 + 7(-2) - b = 0$$
$$-16 + 4a - 14 - b = 0$$
$$4a - b - 30 = 0$$
$$4a - b = 30 \qquad \text{.......(i)}$$
$$x + 3 = 0 \Rightarrow x = -3$$
$$2(-3)^3 + a(-3)^2 + 7(-3) - b = 0$$
$$-54 + 9a - 21 - b = 0$$
$$9a - b - 75 = 0$$
$$9a - b = 75 \qquad \text{.......... (ii)}$$

Substitute $b = 4a - 30$ from (i) in equation (ii)
$$9a - (4a - 30) = 75$$
$$9a - 4a + 30 = 75$$
$$5a = 75 - 30 = 45$$
$$a = 9$$

Substitute a in equation (i) we get
$$36 - b = 30$$
$$b = 36 - 30 = 6$$

Ans. $\qquad a = 9, b = 6$

Question 6.

(i) The line through $P(5, 3)$ intersects y-axis at Q. **[3]**
 (a) Write the slope of the line.
 (b) Write the equation of the line.
 (c) Find the co-ordinates of Q.

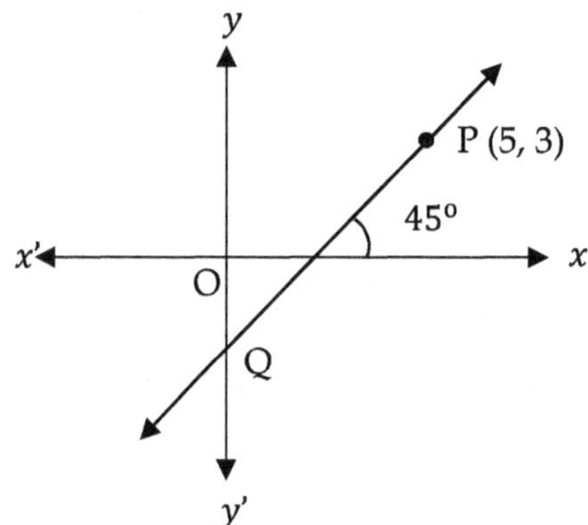

Solution:
(a) Slope of the line $m = \tan\theta$
$$= \tan 45° = 1 \qquad \textbf{Ans.}$$
(b) Required slope of the line $= 1$ and let $P(5, 3)$ as $x_1, y_1)$
Equation of the line: $\qquad y - y_1 = m(x - x_1)$

$$y - 3 = 1(x - 5)$$
$$x - y = -3 + 5$$
$$x - y = 2 \quad \text{Ans.}$$

(c) As Q lies on y axis so let Q $(0, y)$ and lies on the line $x - y = 2$

So $0 - y = 2 \Rightarrow y = -2$

So, Q $(0, -2)$ **Ans.**

(ii) Prove the identity: $1 + \dfrac{\cot^2 A}{1 + \csc A} = \csc A$ **[3]**

Solution:

$$= 1 + \frac{\cot^2 A}{1 + \csc A}$$
$$= 1 + \frac{\csc^2 A - 1}{(1 + \csc A)} \quad (\text{ as } 1 + \cot^2 A = \csc^2 A)$$
$$= 1 + \frac{(\csc A - 1)(\csc A + 1)}{(1 + \csc A)} \quad [a^2 - b^2 = (a + b)(a - b)]$$
$$= 1 + \csc A - 1$$
$$= \csc A$$
$$= \text{RHS}$$

(iii) Determine the value of a for which $2a + 1, a^2 + a + 1$ and $3a^2 - 3a + 3$ are in A.P. **[4]**

Solution:

Since these terms are in A.P. so their common difference will be equal.

$$a^2 + a + 1 - (2a + 1) = 3a^2 - 3a + 3 - (a^2 + a + 1)$$
$$a^2 + a + 1 - 2a - 1 = 3a^2 - 3a + 3 - a^2 - a - 1$$
$$a^2 - a = 2a^2 - 4a + 2$$
$$a^2 - 3a + 2 = 0$$
$$a^2 - 2a - a + 2 = 0$$
$$a(a - 2) - 1(a - 2) = 0$$
$$(a - 1)(a - 2) = 0$$
$$a = 1, 2 \quad \text{Ans.}$$

Question 7.

(i) Cards marked with numbers $1, 2, 3, 4, \ldots .20$ are well shuffled, and a card is drawn at random. What is the probability that the number on the card is: **[3]**

(a) A prime number?

(b) Divisible by 3?

(c) A perfect square?

Solution:

(a) Prime numbers among cards $= 2, 3, 5, 7, 11, 13, 17, 19$

No. of favorable outcomes $= 8$

Total number of outcomes

$$P(E) = \frac{\text{no.of favorable outcomes}}{\text{total number of outcomes}} = \frac{8}{20} = \frac{2}{5}$$

(b) Divisible by 3 $= 3, 6, 9, 12, 15, 18$

$$P(E) = \frac{6}{20} = \frac{3}{10}$$

(c) Perfect square $= 1, 4, 9, 16$

$$P(E) = \frac{4}{20} = \frac{1}{5}$$

(ii) A toy is in the shape of a right circular cylinder with a hemisphere on one end and a cone on the other. The radius and height of the cylindrical parts are 5cm and 13cm respectively. The radii of hemispherical and conical parts are the same as that of the cylindrical part. Find the surface area of the toy if the total height of the toy is 30cm and the cost of painting the toy at the rate of RS. 5.50 per cm^2. **[3]**

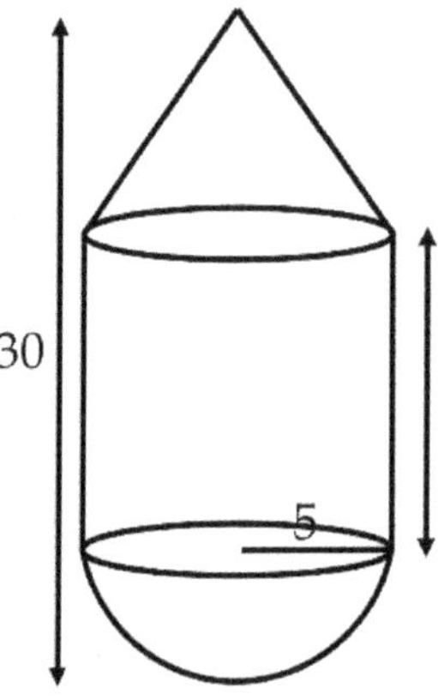

(iii) In the adjoining figure, AT is a tangent to a circle at A. If $\angle CAB = 60^o$ and $\angle TAB = 55^o$, Find $\angle ABC$. **[4]**

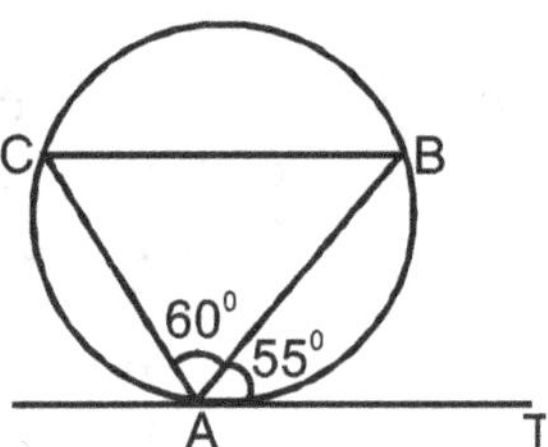

Solution:

$\angle ACB = \angle BAT$ (angles in alternate segment)

$\angle ACB = 55^o$,

In $\triangle ABC$: $\angle ABC + \angle ACB + \angle CAB = 180^o$ (angle sum property of triangle)

$$\angle ABC + 55^o + 60^o = 180^o$$
$$\angle ABC = 180^o - 115^o$$
$$\angle ABC = 65^o \qquad\qquad \textbf{Ans.}$$

Question 8.

(i) Solve the inequation and represent the solution on the number line: **[3]**

$$-\frac{2}{3} < -\frac{x}{3} + 1 \le \frac{2}{3}, x \in R.$$

Solution:

$$-\frac{2}{3} < -\frac{x}{3} + 1 \le \frac{2}{3}$$
$$-2 < -x + 3 \le 2 \text{[Multiply by 3]}$$

$$-2 < -x + 3 \text{ and } -x + 3 \leq 2$$
$$-2 - 3 < -x \text{ and } -x \leq 2 - 3$$
$$-5 < -x \text{ and } -x \leq -1$$
$$5 > x \text{ and } x \geq 1$$
$$\{x : 1 \leq x < 5, x \in R\}$$

Ans.

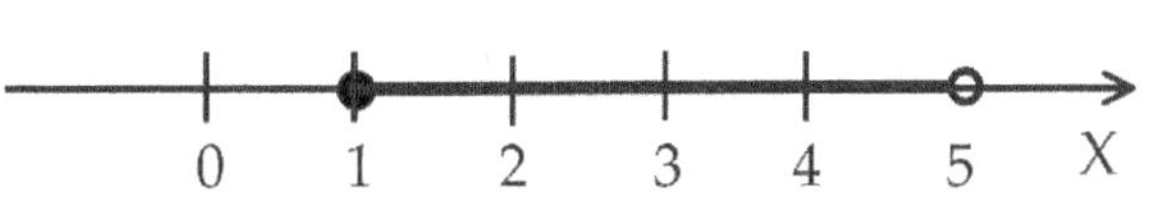

(ii) Find the mean of the following distribution. **[3]**

Class	0 – 10	10 – 20	20 – 30	30 – 40	40 – 50
Frequency	12	16	6	7	9

Solution:

Class	class mark (x)	frequency (f)	fx
0 – 10	5	12	60
10 – 20	15	16	240
20 – 30	25	6	150
30 – 40	35	7	245
40 – 50	45	9	405
		$\sum f = 50$	$\sum fx = 1100$

$$\text{Mean} = \frac{\sum fx}{\sum f}$$
$$= \frac{1100}{50}$$
$$= 22$$

(ii) In the adjoining figure; DE || BC and D divide AB in the ratio of 2:3. Find: **[4]**

(a) $\dfrac{AE}{EC}$

(b) $\dfrac{AE}{AC}$

(c) DE, if BC = 7.5 cm.

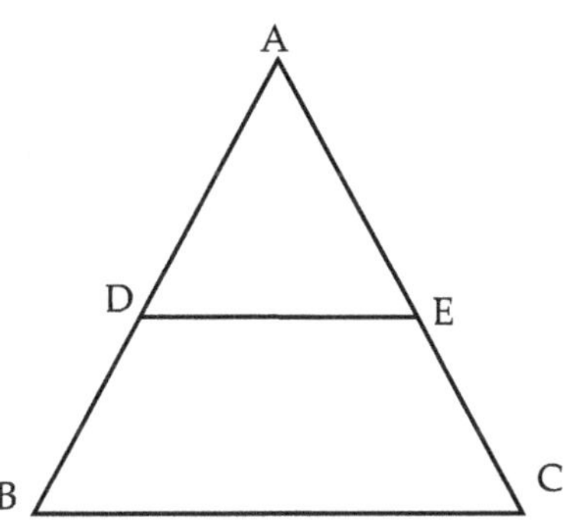

Solution:

(a) As $\quad$ DE || BC

$$\frac{AD}{AE} = \frac{AE}{EC} \text{[BPT]}$$

So $\quad \dfrac{AE}{EC} = \dfrac{2}{3}$ $\qquad$ **Ans.**

(b) now let AE = 2k and EC = 3k so AC = 2k + 3k = 5k

$$\frac{AE}{AC} = \frac{2k}{5k} = \frac{2}{5} \qquad \text{Ans.}$$

(c) In ΔADE and ΔABC

$\angle ADE = \angle ABC$	[corresponding angles]
$\angle AED = \angle ACB$	[corresponding angles]
$\Delta ADE \sim \Delta ABC$	[AA criterion]

So $\dfrac{AE}{AC} = \dfrac{DE}{BC}$ [corresponding sides of similar triangles are proportional]

$$\frac{2}{5} = \frac{DE}{7.5}$$

So, DE $= \dfrac{7.5 \times 2}{5} = 3$ cm. **Ans.**

Question 9.

(i) The sides of a right-angled triangle are $(x - 1)$cm, $3x$cm, and $(3x + 1)$cm. Find: **[4]**

(a) The value of x,

(b) The lengths of its sides

(c) Its area.

Solution:

Since 3x + 1 is largest so it will be hypotenuse

$$(3x + 1)^2 = (x - 1)^2 + (3x)^2$$
$$9^2 + 6x + 1 = x^2 - 2x + 1 + 9x^2$$
$$6x + 2x = x^2$$
$$x^2 - 8x = 0$$
$$x(x - 8) = 0$$
$$x = 0, 8$$

(ii) Use Graph paper for this question. **[3]**

A survey regarding height (in cm) of 60 boys belonging to Class 10 of a school was conducted. The following data was recorded:

Height in cm	135 – 140	140 – 145	145 – 150	150 – 155	155 – 160	160 – 165	165 – 170
No. of boys	4	8	20	14	7	6	1

Taking 2cm = height of 10 cm along one axis and 2 cm = 10 boys along the other axis draw an ogive of the above distribution. Use the graph to estimate the following:

(a) The median

(b) Lower Quartile

(c) If above 158 cm is considered as the tall boys of the class. Find the number of boys in the class who are tall.

Solution:

First construct a cumulative frequency table for the given distribution

Height in cm	Number of boys	Cumulative frequency
135 – 140	4	4
140 – 145	8	12

145 − 150	20	32
150 − 155	14	46
155 − 160	7	53
160 − 165	6	59
165 − 170	1	60
	$N = 60$	

Height (in cm) on x – axis with scale $2\,cm = 5\,cm$

Number of boys on y – axis with scale $2\,cm = 10$ boys

Plot the points $(140, 4), (145, 12), (150, 32), (155, 46), (160, 53), (165, 59)$ and $(170, 60)$ on the graph paper. Draw a free hand curve passing through the points marked, starting from the lower limit of first class to the upper limit of the last class.

Since the sum of all frequencies $N = 60$ (even)

(a) Median $= \left(\frac{N}{2}\right)^{th}$ observation $= \left(\frac{60}{2}\right)$ th

$\qquad$ = 30th observation $\qquad$ = 149 cm (approximately)

(b) Lower quartile (Q1) $= \left(\frac{N}{4}\right)^{th}$ observation $= \left(\frac{60}{4}\right)^{th}$

$\qquad$ =15th observation $\qquad$ = 146 cm (approximately)

(c) To find number of tall boys draw a vertical line through 158 cm (given), which meets the ogive at a point. Through this point draw a horizontal line which meets y – axis at the mark 51. This 51st student is also considered as tall boy. So number of tall boys = 60 – 50 = 10 boys.

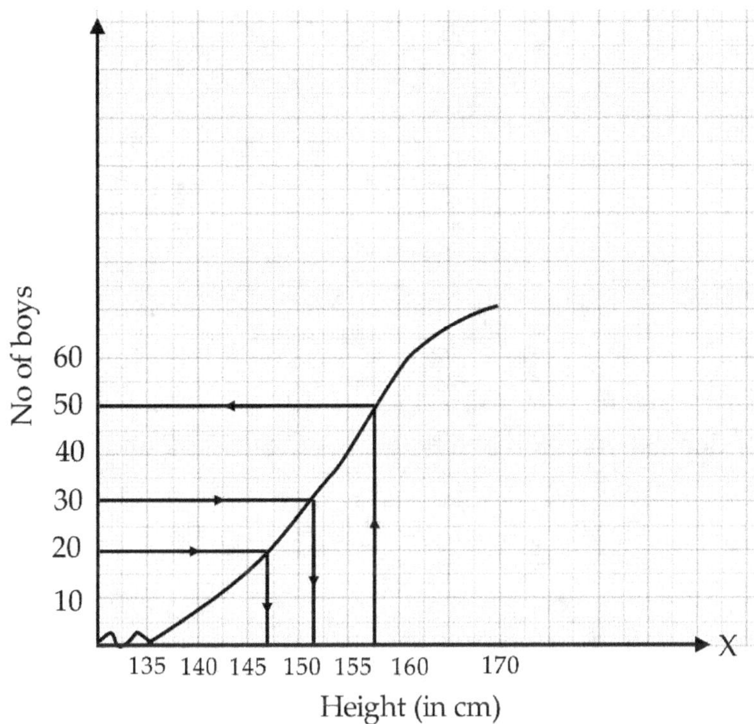

Question 10.

(i) Given, $\dfrac{a}{b} = \dfrac{c}{d}$, prove that: $\dfrac{3a-5b}{3a+5b} = \dfrac{3c-5d}{3c+5d}$ **[3]**

Solution:

Given $\dfrac{a}{b} = \dfrac{c}{d}$

Multiply by $\dfrac{3}{5}$ both side

$$\frac{3a}{5b} = \frac{3c}{5d}$$

Apply componendo and dividend

$$\frac{3a+5b}{3a-5b} = \frac{3c+5d}{3c-5d}$$

Apply invertendo

$$\frac{3a-5b}{3a+5b} = \frac{3c-5d}{3c+5d}$$

Hence proved

(ii) Using a ruler and compasses only, draw an equilateral triangle of side 5cm. Draw its inscribed circle. Measure the radius of the circle. **[3]**

(iii) From the top of a cliff 90 m high, the angles of depression of the top and bottom of a tower are observed to be 30 and 60 respectively. Find the height of tower. **[4]**

Solution:

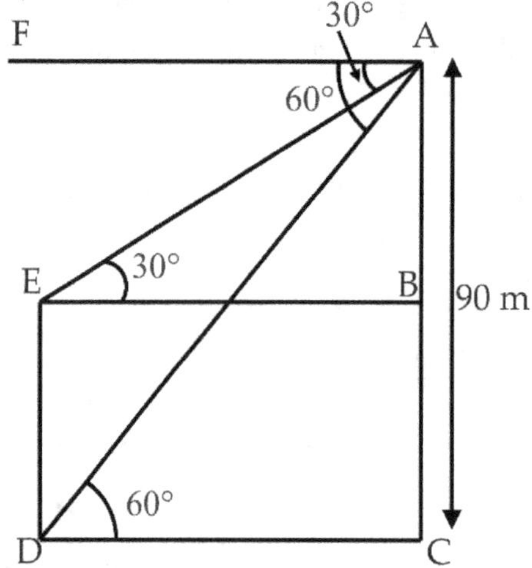

In the adjacent diagram from the top A of a cliff AC
the angle of depression of top and bottom of the tower E and D
are 30° and 60° respectively.

In $\triangle$ ACD: $\tan 60° = \dfrac{AC}{DC}$ $\left(\tan \theta = \dfrac{\text{perpendicular}}{\text{base}}\right)$

$$\sqrt{3} = \frac{90}{DC}$$

$$DC = \frac{90}{\sqrt{3}} = \frac{90\sqrt{3}}{\sqrt{3} \times \sqrt{3}} = \frac{90\sqrt{3}}{3} = 30\sqrt{3} \text{ m}$$

In $\triangle$ ABE $\tan 30° = \dfrac{AB}{BE}$

$$\frac{1}{\sqrt{3}} = \frac{AB}{DC} \quad (\underline{as}\ BE = DC)$$

$$\frac{1}{\sqrt{3}} = \frac{AB}{30\sqrt{3}}$$

$$AB\sqrt{3} = 30\sqrt{3} \Rightarrow AB = \frac{30\sqrt{3}}{\sqrt{3}}$$

$$AB = 30\ m$$

So BC $= AC - AB = 90 - 30 = 60$ m

So $DE = BC = 60\ m$

Height of the tower $= 60\ m$ **Ans.**

<table>
<tr><td align="center">Question 1.</td></tr>
</table>

(i) b, (ii) b, (iii) c, (iv) c, (v)a, (vi)c, (vii)a, (viii)b, (ix) b, (x) d, (xi)b,(xii)a, (xiii) b, (xiv) d, (xv)b

<table>
<tr><td align="center">Question 2.</td></tr>
</table>

(i) Rs. 65592, (ii) 6,

<table>
<tr><td align="center">Question 3.</td></tr>
</table>

(i) 40 cm, (ii) (a) 1:2 (b) (0, 3) (iii) (b) A'(-2, 2), B(-2, -2)   (c) Point C and D   (d) isosceles trapezium

<table>
<tr><td align="center">Question 4.</td></tr>
</table>

(i) Rs. 15744, (ii) m = 5, –3, (iii) 64 cm

<table>
<tr><td align="center">Question 5.</td></tr>
</table>

(i) $x = 3$, $y = 2$, (ii) (b) QR = 12 cm, PS = 4 cm, (iii) $a = 9, b = 6$

<table>
<tr><td align="center">Question 6.</td></tr>
</table>

(i) (a) 1(b) $y = x - 2$ (c) (0, –2) (iii) 1, 2

<table>
<tr><td align="center">Question 7.</td></tr>
</table>

(i) (a) $\frac{2}{5}$ (b) $\frac{3}{10}$ (c) $\frac{1}{5}$ (ii) 770cm^2, Rs. 4235 (iii) 65°

<table>
<tr><td align="center">Question 8.</td></tr>
</table>

(i) $\{x : x \in R, 1 \leq x < 5\}$

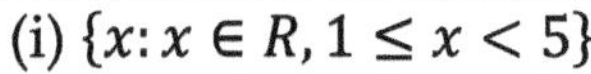
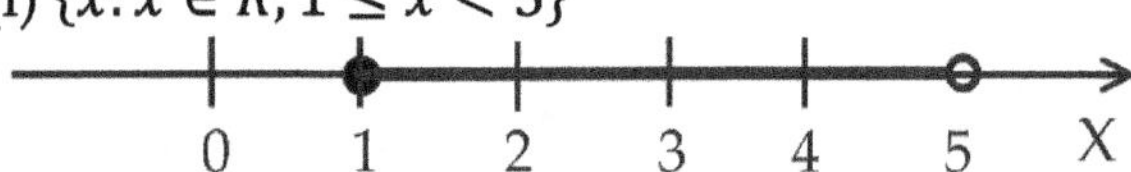

(ii) 22, (iii) (a) $\frac{2}{3}$ (b) $\frac{2}{5}$ (c) 3 cm

<table>
<tr><td align="center">Question 9.</td></tr>
</table>

(i) (a) 8 (b) 7 cm, 24 cm, 25 cm (c) 84 sq. cm (ii) (a) 149 cm (b) 146 cm (c) 10 boys

<table>
<tr><td align="center">Question 10.</td></tr>
</table>

(iii) 60 m

MATHEMATICS

Maximum Marks: 80
Time allowed: Two and a half hours
Answers to this Paper must be written on the paper provided separately.
You will not be allowed to write during first 15 minutes.
This time is to be spent in reading the question paper.
The time given at the head of this Paper is the time allowed for writing the answers.

Attempt all questions from Section *A* and any three questions from Section *B*.
The intended marks for questions or parts of questions are given in brackets [].

SECTION-A
(Attempt all questions from this section)

Question 1.

Chose the correct answers to the questions from the given options:

(i) The tax invoice of an article shows the cost of the article is Rs. 750. If the GST rate is 18%, find the amount of the bill.

(a) Rs. 885

(b) Rs. 750

(c) Rs. 785

(d) Rs. 800

Solution:(a)

Cost of the article $=$ Rs. 750

GST $= 18\%$

Bill $= 750 + \dfrac{18}{100} \times 750 =$ Rs. 885

(ii) If $x = -3$ is a solution of the quadratic equation $2x^2 + kx - 39 = 0$, the value of k is:

(a) -7

(b) 5

(c) 6

(d) 7

Solution:(a)

Since $x = -3$ is a solution of $2x^2 + kx - 39 = 0$ so replace x with -3 we get

$2(-3)^2 + k(-3) - 39 = 0$

$18 - 3k - 39 = 0$

$-3k - 21 = 0$

$K = -7$

(iii) $(x + 1)$ is a factor of the polynomial:

(a) $x^3 + x^2 - x + 1$

(b) $x^3 + x^2 + x + 1$

(c) $x^4 + x^3 + x^2 + 1$

(d) $2x^3 + x^2 - x + 1$

Solution:(b)

$$x + 1 = 0 \; so \; x = -1$$

In part (b) $(-1)^3 + (-1)^2 + (-1) + 1 = 0$

(iv) The order of Matrix M in $M \times [x \quad y] = \begin{bmatrix} a & b \\ d & c \end{bmatrix}$ is:

    (a) 2×1

    (b) 1×2

    (c) 2×2

    (d) Multiplication not possible

    Solution:(a)

        Let order of M is $r \times c$ then $(r \times c)\,(1 \times 2) = 2 \times 2$

        So $r = 2$ and c = 1; order of $M = 2 \times 1$

(v) Which of the following is not an A.P.?

    (a) $13, \; 8, \; 3, -2, -7, -12$

    (b) $10.8, 11.2, 11.6, 12, 12.4$

    (c) $8\frac{1}{7}, \; 18\frac{2}{7}, \; 28\frac{3}{7}, \; 48\frac{4}{7}, \; 58\frac{5}{7}$

    (d) $8\frac{3}{23}, \; 11\frac{6}{23}, \; 14\frac{9}{23}, \; 17\frac{12}{23}$

    Solution: (c) as difference between consecutive terms are different.

(vi) The point A$(-3, 2)$ is reflected in the x - axis to the point A'. Point A' is then reflected in the origin to point A "Co - ordinates of A"

    (a) $(3, 2)$

    (b) $(3, -2)$

    (c) $(-3, -2)$

    (d) $(2, -3)$

    Solution: (a)

Since A is first reflect in x – axis then A' reflect in y – axis. So the reflection in equivalent to y –axis.

(vii) If $\triangle ABC$ and $\triangle DEF$ are similar triangles such that $2AB = DE$ and $BC = 8\,cm$, then EF =

    (a) 16 cm

    (b) 12 cm

    (c) 8 cm

    (d) 4 cm

    Solution: (a)

As $\triangle ABC \sim \triangle DEF$, then $\frac{AB}{DE} = \frac{BC}{EF} = \frac{AC}{DF}$ [corresponding sides of similar triangles are proportional]

$\frac{AB}{2AB} = \frac{8}{EF} => EF = 16$ cm

(viii) The curved surface area of a right circular cone of height of 15cm and base diameter 16cm is:

(a) $60\pi\,cm^2$

(b) $68\pi\,cm^2$

(c) $120\pi\,cm^2$

(d) $136\pi\,cm^2$

Solution: (d)

Slant height $(l) = \sqrt{15^2 + 8^2} = \sqrt{225 + 64} = \sqrt{289} = 17$ cm

Curved surface area $= \pi rl = \pi \times 8 \times 17 = 136\,\pi\ cm^2$

(ix) The solution set for the given inequation is: $-\dfrac{5}{2} < -x \leq \dfrac{14}{5}, x \in I$

(a) $\{0, 1, 3\}$

(b) $\{x: -2.8 \leq x < 2.5, x \in I\}$

(c) $\{-2, -1, 0, 1, 2\}$

(d) None of these

Solution: (c)

$$-\frac{5}{2} < -x \text{ and } -x \leq \frac{14}{5}$$

$$\frac{5}{2} > x \text{ and } x \geq -\frac{14}{5}$$

$$2.5 > x \text{ and } x \geq -2.8$$

$$-2.8 \leq x < 2.5 \text{ and } x \in I \text{ so } \{-2, -1, 0, 1, 2\}$$

(x) If the probability of an event is 0.65, then the probability of not happening that event is:

(a) 0.35

(b) 0.035

(c) 1.25

(d) 3

Solution:(a)

As $\qquad P(E) + P'(E) = 1$

So $\quad P'(E) = 1 - 0.65 = 0.35$

(xi) The abscissa of a point is zero, then it lies on:

(a) $x - $ axis

(b) I Quadrant

(c) II Quadrant

(d) y-axis

Solution:(d)

On $y - $ axis $x - $ coordinates (abscissa) are zero.

(xii) In the given figure the value of angle BCD is:

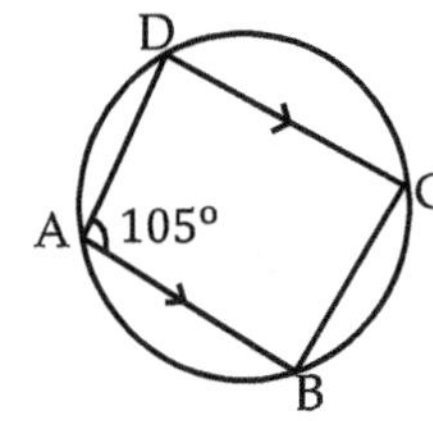

(a) 95°

(b) 75°

(c) 210°

(d) 52.5°

Solution:(b)

As ABCE is a cyclic quadrilateral so $\angle BCD + \angle BAD = 180°$

[Opposite angles of cyclic quadrilateral are supplementary]

$\angle BCD = 180° - 105° = 75°$

(xiii) if tan $A +$ cot $A = 2$, (A is acute) the value of $\tan^2 A + \cot^2 A$ is

(a) 0

(b) 1

(c) 2

(d) 4

Solution: (c)

$$(\tan A + \cot A)^2 = 2^2 \qquad \text{[squaring both sides]}$$
$$\tan^2 A + \cot^2 A + 2\tan A \cot A = 4$$
$$\tan^2 A + \cot^2 A + 2 = 4 \qquad \left[\text{as } \cot A = \frac{1}{\tan A}\right]$$
$$\tan^2 A + \cot^2 A = 4 - 2 = 2$$

(xiv) The median class of the following data:

Class intervals	10 − 20	20 − 30	30 − 40	40 − 50	50 − 60	60 − 70
Frequency	12	6	10	8	11	13

(a) 20 – 30

(b) 30 – 40

(c) 40 – 50

(d) 50 – 60

Solution:(c)

$12 + 6 + 10 + 8 + 11 + 13 = 60$; as $N = 60$ (even)

Class intervals	10 − 20	20 − 30	30 − 40	40 − 50	50 − 60	60 − 70
Frequency	12	6	10	8	11	13
	12	18	28	36	47	60

So median class $= \dfrac{N}{2} = 30$ th, which lies in 40 – 50.

(xv) If $p - 1, p + 3, 3p - 1$ are in A.P., then p is equal to:

    (a) 4

    (b) -4

    (c) 2

    (d) -2

    Solution: (a)

As these are in AP so their common difference will be same

$$p + 3 - (p - 1) = 3p - 1 - (p + 3)$$
$$p + 3 - p + 1 = 3p - 1 - p - 3$$
$$4 = 2p - 4$$
$$p = 4$$

Question 2.

(i) Mohan deposits Rs 80 per month in a cumulative deposit account for six years. Find the interest and amount payable to him on maturity, if the rate of interest is 6% per annum. **[4]**

Solution:

Per month installment (p) $=$ Rs. 80

Time (n) $=$ 6 years $=$ 72 months

$$\text{M.A.} = p \times n + \frac{p \times n(n + 1) \times r}{2400}$$
$$= 80 \times 72 + \frac{80 \times 72 \times 73 \times 6}{2400}$$
$$= 5760 + 1051.20$$
$$= \text{Rs. } 6811.20$$

Interest $=$ Rs. 1051.20   Ans.

(ii) Find two numbers whose mean proportional is 12 and the third proportional is 324.   **[4]**

Solution:

Let two numbers are x and y so that $x, 12, y$ and $x, y, 324$

$$\frac{x}{12} = \frac{12}{y} \qquad \text{[as 12 is the mean proportion]}$$
$$xy = 144 \qquad\qquad\qquad\qquad\qquad\qquad \text{.........(i)}$$
$$\frac{x}{y} = \frac{y}{324} \qquad \text{[as 324 is the third proportion]}$$
$$x = \frac{y^2}{324} \qquad\qquad\qquad\qquad\qquad \text{.............(ii)}$$

substitute x in equation (i) we get

$$\frac{y^2}{324}y = 144 => y^3 = 324 \times 144$$
$$y^3 = 27 \times 12 \times 144$$

so, $y = 3 \times 12 = 36$

Substitute $y = 36$ in equation (ii) we get $x = \dfrac{36^2}{324} = 4$ Ans.

(iii) Prove the identity: $\dfrac{\sin^3 A - \cos^3 A}{\sin A - \cos A} - \sin A . \cos A = 1$ **[4]**

Solution:

LHS

$$= \frac{\sin^3 A - \cos^3 A}{\sin A - \cos A} - \sin A . \cos A$$

$$= \frac{(\sin A - \cos A)(\sin^2 A + \cos^2 A + \sin A \cos A)}{\sin A - \cos A} - \sin A . \cos A$$

$$= 1 + \sin A \cos A - \sin A . \cos A \qquad\qquad [\sin^2 A + \cos^2 A = 1]$$

$$= 1 \qquad \text{RHS}$$

Question 3.

(i) In what ratio is the join of $(1, -5)$ and $(-4, 5)$ divided by the x-axis? Also, find the co-ordinates of the point of intersection. **[4]**

Solution:

Let the point $P(x, 0)$ on x - axis divides join of $(1, -5)$ and $(-4, 5)$ in the ratio $m_1 : m_2$

$(1, -5) = (x_1, y_1)$ and $(-4, 5) = (x_2, y_2)$

Using section formula $y = \dfrac{m_1 y_2 + m_2 y_1}{m_1 + m_2}$

$$0 = \frac{m_1 \times 5 + m_2(-5)}{m_1 + m_2}$$

$$5m_1 - 5m_2 = 0$$

$$5m_1 = 5m_2 \rightarrow m_1 : m_2 = 1 : 1$$

So point P is the mid-point

Now using the midpoint formula $x = \dfrac{x_1 + x_2}{2}$

$$x = \frac{1 + (-4)}{2} = \frac{-3}{2}$$

So, coordinates of point of intersection $P = (\frac{-3}{2}, 0)$ Ans.

(ii) 60 circular plates, each of radius 14cm and thickness of 0.5cm are placed one above the other to form a right circular cylinder. Find the total surface area and volume of the cylinder so formed. **[4]**

Solution:

Radius of circular plate $(r) = 14\ cm$

As thickness of one plate $= 0.5\ m$

So thickness of 60 plates $= 60 \times 0.5 = 30\ cm$ (height of cylinder)

Total surface area of cylinder $= 2\pi r(h + r)$

$$= 2 \times \frac{22}{7} \times 14(30 + 14)$$

$$= 88 \times 44 = 3872\ cm^2 \qquad\qquad \text{Ans.}$$

Volume of cylinder $= \pi r^2 h = \dfrac{22}{7} \times 14^2 \times 30 = 18480\ cm^3$ Ans.

(iii) Points $(-5, 0)$ and $(4, 0)$ are invariant points under reflection in the line $L1$; points $(0, -6)$ and $(0, 5)$ are invariant on reflection in the line $L2$. **[5]**

    (a) Name or write equations for the lines $L1$ and $L2$.

    (b) Write down the images of $P(2, 6)$ and $Q(-8, -3)$ on reflection in $L1$. Name the images as P' and Q' respectively.

    (c) Write down the images of P and Q on reflection in $L2$. Name the images as P" and Q" respectively.

    (d) State or describe a single transformation that maps Q' onto Q".

Solution:

    (a) Since $(-5, 0)$ and $(4, 0)$ lies on x – axis and a point on x – axis will be invariant if it reflects in x – axis. So L_1 will be x axis and its equation are $y = 0$.

    Since $(0, -6)$ and $(0, 5)$ lies on y – axis and a point on y – axis will be invariant if it reflects in y – axis. So L_2 will be y axis and its equation are $x = 0$.

    (b) image of $P(2, 6)$ in $L_1 = P'(2, -6)$ and $Q(-8, -3) = Q'(-8, 3)$.

    (c) image of $P(2, 6)$ in $L_2 = $ P"$(-2, 6)$ and $Q(-8, -3) = Q"(8, -3)$.

    (d) Single transformation that maps Q' onto Q" = Reflection in origin.

SECTION – B
(Attempt any four questions from this section)

Question 4.

(i) Find the amount of the bill for the following transaction. Marked price discount% and GST rates are given. All transactions are intra-state. **[3]**

Article	Washing Machine	Headphone	Smart Watch
Marked Price	Rs. 15000	Rs. 3000	Rs. 4500
Discount %	10	No discount	25
GST %	18	12	12

Solution:

Marked price of washing machine $=$ Rs. 15000

$$\text{Discount} = \frac{10}{100} \times 15000 = \text{Rs. } 1500$$

Sale price (after discount) $= 15000 - 1500 = $ Rs. 13500

$$\text{GST} = \frac{18}{100} \times 13500 = \text{Rs. } 2430$$

Marked price of headphone $=$ Rs. 3000

$$\text{GST} = \frac{12}{100} \times 3000 = \text{Rs. } 360$$

Marked price of smart watch $=$ Rs. 4500

$$\text{Discount} = \frac{25}{100} \times 4500 = \text{Rs. } 1125$$

Sale price (after discount) $= 4500 - 1125 = $ Rs. 3375

$$\text{GST} = \frac{12}{100} \times 3375 = \text{Rs. } 405$$

Total GST paid $= 2430 + 360 + 405 = $ Rs. 3195

Bill $= 13500 + 3000 + 3375 + 3195 = $ Rs. 23070 Ans.

(ii) Find the value of 'p', if the following quadratic equations have equal roots: $x^2 + (p - 3)x + p = 0$ [3]

Solution:

Given equation: $x^2 + (p - 3)x + p = 0$

$a = 1, b = p - 3, c = p$

Since roots are equal so $b^2 - 4a\,c = 0$

$(p - 3)^2 - 4 \times 1 \times p = 0$

$p^2 - 6p + 9 - 4p = 0$

$p^2 - 10p + 9 = 0$

$p^2 - 9p - p + 9 = 0$

$p(p - 9) - 1(p - 9) = 0$

$(p - 9)(p - 1) = 0$

$p = 1, 9$ Ans.

(iii) In a school, the weekly pocket money of 50 students is as follows: [4]

Weekly pocket money in Rs	$40 - 50$	$50 - 60$	$60 - 70$	$70 - 80$	$80 - 90$	$90 - 100$
No. of students	2	8	12	14	8	6

Draw a histogram on graph paper and find the mode from the graph.

Solution:

From the given information the following histogram is drawn

Mode from the graph = Rs. 72.50 (approx)

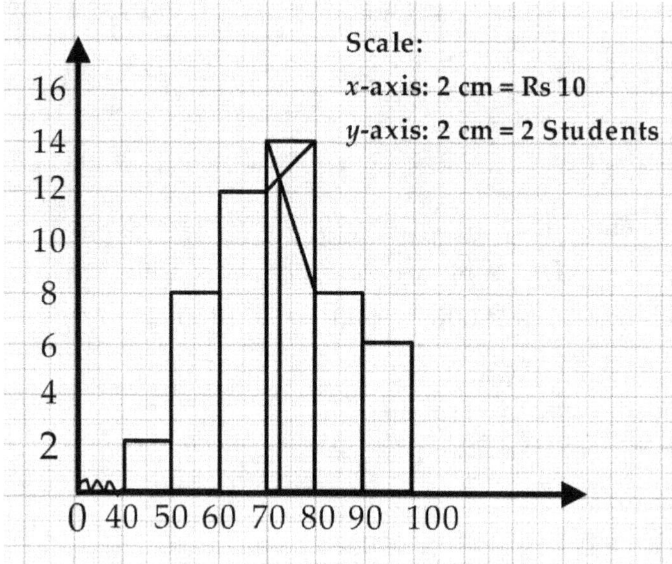

Question 5.

(i) Find the 2 × 2 matrix X which satisfies the equation:

$$\begin{bmatrix} 3 & 7 \\ 2 & 4 \end{bmatrix}\begin{bmatrix} 0 & 2 \\ 5 & 3 \end{bmatrix} + 2X = \begin{bmatrix} 1 & -5 \\ -4 & 6 \end{bmatrix}$$

[3]

Solution:

$$\begin{bmatrix} 3 & 7 \\ 2 & 4 \end{bmatrix}\begin{bmatrix} 0 & 2 \\ 5 & 3 \end{bmatrix} + 2X = \begin{bmatrix} 1 & -5 \\ -4 & 6 \end{bmatrix}$$

$$\begin{bmatrix} 0 + 7 \times 5 & 3 \times 2 + 7 \times 3 \\ 0 + 4 \times 5 & 2 \times 2 + 4 \times 3 \end{bmatrix} + 2X = \begin{bmatrix} 1 & -5 \\ -4 & 6 \end{bmatrix}$$

$$\begin{bmatrix} 35 & 27 \\ 20 & 16 \end{bmatrix} + 2X = \begin{bmatrix} 1 & -5 \\ -4 & 6 \end{bmatrix}$$

$$2X = \begin{bmatrix} 1 & -5 \\ -4 & 6 \end{bmatrix} - \begin{bmatrix} 35 & 27 \\ 20 & 16 \end{bmatrix} = \begin{bmatrix} 1 - 35 & -5 - 27 \\ -4 - 20 & 6 - 16 \end{bmatrix} = \begin{bmatrix} -34 & -32 \\ -24 & -10 \end{bmatrix}$$

$$X = \frac{1}{2}\begin{bmatrix} -34 & -32 \\ -24 & -10 \end{bmatrix} = \begin{bmatrix} -17 & -16 \\ -12 & -5 \end{bmatrix} \qquad \text{Ans.}$$

(ii) In the following figure, AB is the diameter of the larger circle with center O. Another circle is drawn with AO as the diameter to cut AD at C. [3]

(a) Prove $\triangle AOC \sim \triangle ABD$

(b) Also prove that: $BD = 2 \times OC$

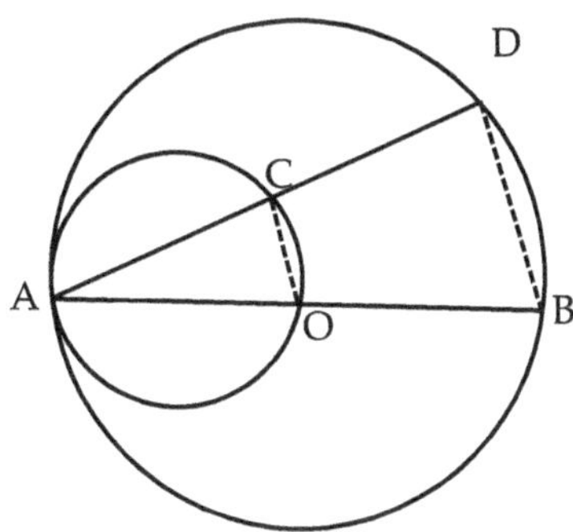

Solution:

(a) In $\triangle AOC$ and $\triangle ABD$

∠ACO = ∠ADB	(angle on diameter is 90°)
∠CAO = ∠DAB	(common)
So Δ AOC ~Δ ABD	(AA similarity criterian)

(b)

$$\frac{AO}{AB} = \frac{CO}{DB} \qquad \text{(Corresponding sides of similar triangles are proportional)}$$

$$\frac{AO}{2AO} = \frac{CO}{DB} \qquad \text{(O is the center and diameter} = 2 \times radius)$$

$$\frac{1}{2} = \frac{CO}{DB}$$

$$BD = 2\,OC \qquad \text{hence proved}$$

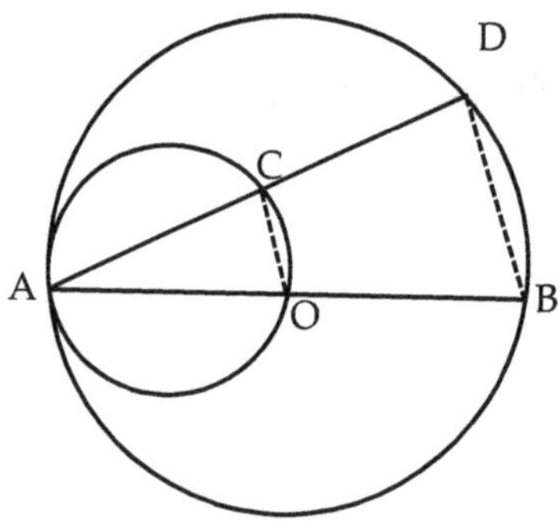

(iii) Find the values of m and n so that $x - 1$ and $x + 2$ both are factors of **[4]**
$$x^3 + (3m + 1)x^2 + nx - 18$$
Solution:
$$x - 1 = 0 \implies x = 1$$
$$\text{so, } (1)^3 + (3m + 1)(1)^2 + n(1) - 18 = 0$$
$$1 + 3m + 1 + n - 18 = 0$$
$$3m + n - 16 = 0$$
$$3m + n = 16 \qquad \qquad \text{.......(i)}$$
$$x + 2 = 0 \implies x = -2$$
$$(-2)^3 + (3m + 1)(-2)^2 + n(-2) - 18 = 0$$
$$-8 + 12m + 4 - 2n - 18 = 0$$
$$12m - 2n - 22 = 0$$
$$12m - 2n = 22 \qquad \qquad \text{....(ii)}$$
Substitute $n = 16 - 3m$ from (i) in equation (ii)
$$12m - 2(16 - 3m) = 22$$
$$12m - 32 + 6m = 22$$
$$18m - 32 = 22$$
$$18m = 22 + 32$$
$$m = \frac{54}{18} = 3$$
Substitute m in equation (i) we get
$$3m + n = 16$$
$$3 \times 3 + n = 16$$
$$n = 16 - 9 = 7$$
$$m = 3, n = 7$$

Question 6.

(i) A and B are two points on the x-axis and y-axis respectively. P(2, −3) is the midpoint of AB. Find the **[3]**

(a) Co-ordinates of A and B

(b) Slope of line AB

(c) Equation of line AB.

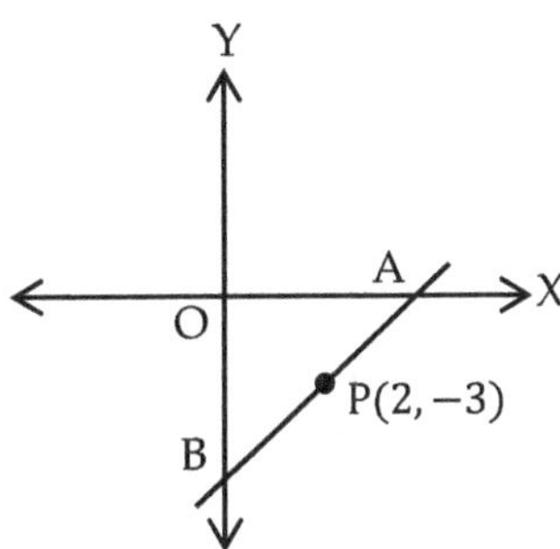

Solution:

(a) Coordinates of A (x, 0) and B (0, y)

Since P (2, -3) is the mid-point of AB so using mid-point formula

$$(x, y) = \left\{ \frac{x_1 + x_2}{2}, \frac{y_1 + y_2}{2} \right\}$$

$$2 = \frac{x + 0}{2} \rightarrow x = 4 \; so \; A\,(4, 0)$$

$$-3 = \frac{0 + y}{2} \rightarrow y = -6 \; so \; B\,(0, -6) \text{ Ans.}$$

(b) slope of line AB $= \frac{y_1 - y_2}{x_1 - x_2} = \frac{-6 - 0}{0 - 4} = \frac{-6}{-4} = \frac{3}{2}$ Ans.

(c) Slope of the line AB (m) $= \frac{3}{2}$ and line passes through P(2, -3) as (x_1, y_1)

Equation of the line: $y - y_1 = m(x - x_1)$

$$y + 3 = \frac{3}{2}(x - 2)$$

$$3x - 6 = 2y + 6$$

$$3x - 2y = 12 \text{Ans.}$$

(ii) Prove the identity: $\dfrac{1 + \cos A}{1 - \cos A} = \dfrac{\tan^2 A}{(\sec A - 1)^2}$ [3]

Solution:

LHS

$$\frac{1 + \cos A}{1 - \cos A} = \frac{1 + \frac{1}{\sec A}}{1 - \frac{1}{\sec A}} \qquad [\cos A = \frac{1}{\sec A}]$$

$$= \frac{\frac{\sec A + 1}{\sec A}}{\frac{\sec A - 1}{\sec A}}$$

$$= \frac{\sec A + 1}{\sec A - 1} \times \frac{\sec A - 1}{\sec A - 1} \qquad \text{[multiply by sec A − 1 in numerator and denominator]}$$

$$= \frac{\sec^2 A - 1}{(\sec A - 1)^2}$$

$$= \frac{\tan^2 A}{(\sec A - 1)^2} \qquad \text{RHS.}$$

(iii) An A.P. consists of 50 terms of which 3ʳᵈ the term is 12 and the last term is 106. Find the 29ᵗʰ term of this A.P and sum of 29 terms also.   [4]

Solution:

Let a is the first term and d is the common difference of the AP

nth term of an AP: $T_n = a + (n - 1)d$

$$a + 2d = 12 \; \ldots\ldots\ldots\ldots\ldots \text{ (i)}$$

$$a + 49d = 106 \ldots\ldots\ldots\ldots\ldots \text{(ii)}$$

subtract (i) from (ii)

     a + 2d = 12

$$a + 49\,d = 106$$
$$49d - 2d = 106 - 12$$

$$47\,d = 94 \rightarrow d = 2$$

Substitute d in (i) we get $a = 12 - 2 \times 2 = 8$

So 29th term is $\qquad = a + 28\,d$

$$= 8 + 28 \times 2 = 64 \text{ Ans.}$$

Sum of n terms of an AP is given by: $S_n = \dfrac{n}{2}[2a + (n-1)d]$

$$= \dfrac{29}{2}[2 \times 8 + (29 - 1)2]$$
$$= \dfrac{29}{2}[16 + 56]$$

$$= \dfrac{29 \times 72}{2} = 29 \times 36 = 1044 \text{ Ans.}$$

Question 7.

(i) A bag contains 6 red balls, 8 white balls, 5 green balls, and 3 black balls. One ball is drawn at random from the bag. Find the probability that the ball: [3]

(a) White

(b) Red or black

(c) Not green

(d) Neither white nor black.

Solution:

No of red balls n(R)=6

No of white balls n(W)=8

No of green balls n(G)=5

No of black balls n(B)=3

Total no of balls $= 6 + 8 + 5 + 3 = 22$

Probability on an event $P(E) = \dfrac{\text{no.of favorable outcomes}}{\text{total number of outcomes}}$

(a) probability of white ball $P(W) = \dfrac{\text{no of white balls}}{\text{total number of balls}} = \dfrac{8}{22} = \dfrac{4}{11}$ **Ans.**

(b) Red + Black balls $= 6 + 3 = 9$

probability of red or black $P(\text{red or black}) = \dfrac{9}{22}$ **Ans.**

(c) Not green $= 22 - 5 = 17$

probability of not green $P(\text{not green}) \dfrac{17}{22}$ **Ans.**

(d) Neither white nor black $= 22 - (8 + 3) = 11$

probability of neither white nor black $P(E) = \dfrac{11}{22} = \dfrac{1}{2}$ **Ans.**

(ii) A cylindrical container is filled with ice cream, whose radius is 6m and height of 15m. The whole ice cream is distributed to 10 children in equal cones having hemispherical tops. If the height of the conical portion is 4 times the radius of its base, find the radius of the cone.

[3]

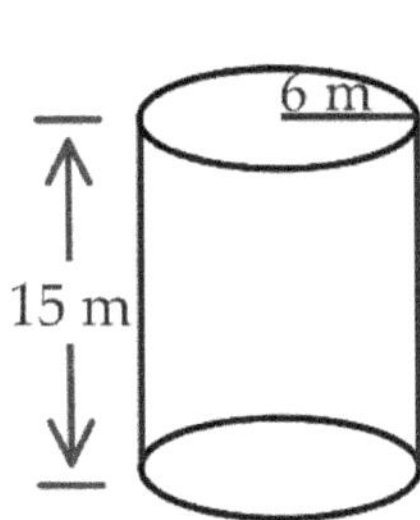

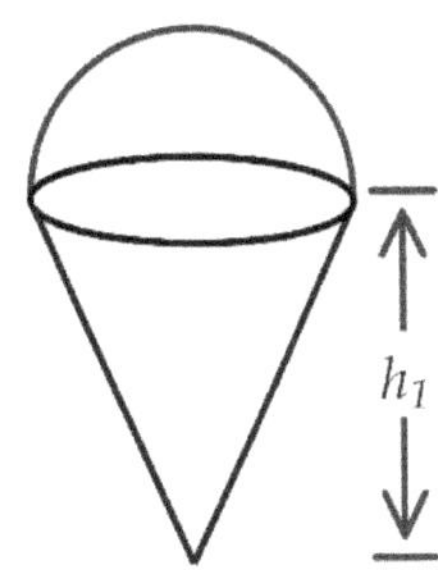

Solution:

Radius (R) of cylindrical container $= 6\ m$

Radius (H) of cylindrical container $= 15\ m$

Volume of ice cream in container $= \pi r^2 h$

$$= \pi \times 6^2 \times 15 = 540\ \pi cm^3$$

Let radius of the conical portion $= r$ cm

Height of the conical portion $= 4r$ cm

Volume of ice cream contained in 1 cone = volume f cone + volume of hemisphere

$$= \frac{1}{3}\pi r^2 h + \frac{2}{3}\pi r^3$$

$$= \frac{1}{3}\pi r^2 \times 4r + \frac{2}{3}\pi r^3$$

$$= \frac{1}{3}\pi r^3(4+2) = 2\pi r^3$$

Volume of ice cream contained in 10 cones $= 10 \times 2\pi r^3 = 20\pi r^3$

According to question $20\pi r^3 = 540\ \pi$

$$r^3 = 27 \rightarrow r = 3$$

Radius of the cone $= 3$ cm **Ans.**

(iii) In the figure given, 0 is the center of the circle. $\angle DAE = 70°$. Find giving suitable reasons, the measure of: **[4]**

(a) $\angle BCD$

(b) $\angle BOD$

(c) $\angle OBD$

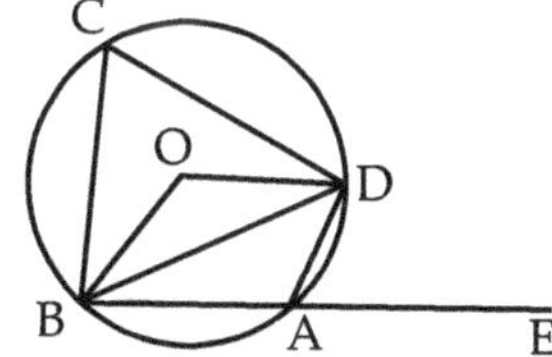

Solution:

Given $\angle DAE = 70°$

(a) $\angle BCD = \angle DAE$ [exterior angle of a cyclic quadrilateral equals to opposite interior angle]

$\angle BCD = 70°$ **Ans.**

(b) $\angle BOD = 2\angle BCD$ [(angle at the center is double of the angle at the circumference)]

$\angle BOD = 140°$ **Ans.**

(c) $\angle OBD = \angle ODB = x$ (let) [as OB = OD, radii]

So $\angle OBD + \angle ODB + \angle BOD = 180°$ [angle sum property of triangle]

$$x + x + 140° = 180°$$

$$2x = 180° - 140°$$
$$x = 40°/2 = 20°$$
$$\angle OBD = 20°$$

Ans.

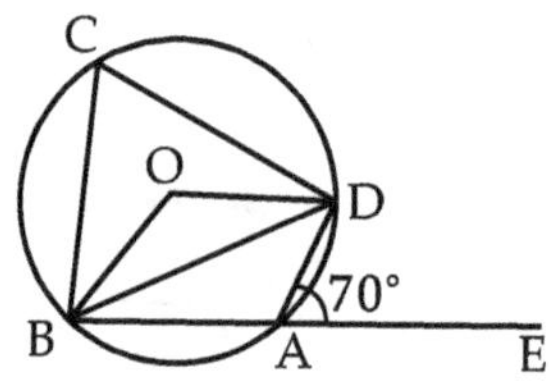

Question 8.

(i) Find the range of values of x, which satisfy $-\frac{1}{3} \leq \frac{x}{2} - 1\frac{1}{3} < \frac{1}{6}, x \in$ R. Graph these values of x on the real number line. **[3]**

Solution:

$$-\frac{1}{3} \leq \frac{x}{2} - \frac{4}{3} < \frac{1}{6}$$

$-2 \leq 3x - 8 < 1$

$-2 \leq 3x - 8$ and $3x - 8 < 1$

$-2 + 8 \leq 3x$ and $3x < 1 + 8$

$6 \leq 3x$ and $3x < 9$

$2 \leq x$ and $x < 3$

$x \geq 2$ and $x < 3$

$\{x : 2 \leq x < 3, x \in R\}$ **Ans.**

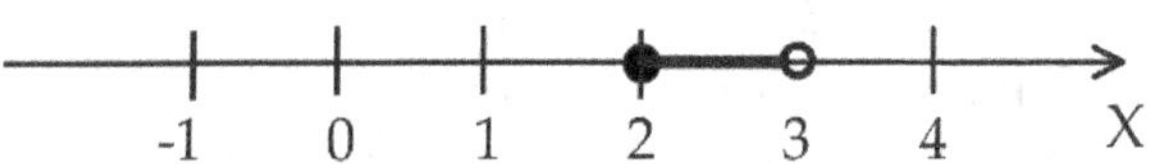

(ii) The mean of the frequency distribution is 18. The frequency f in the class interval $19 - 21$ is missing. Determine f.

Class Interval	$11-13$	$13-15$	$15-17$	$17-19$	$19-21$	$21-23$	$23-25$
Frequency	3	6	9	13	F	5	4

Solution:

Class Interval	Frequency (f)	Class marks(x)	fx
$11-13$	3	12	36
$13-15$	6	14	84
$15-17$	9	16	144
$17-19$	13	18	234
$19-21$	f	20	$20f$
$21-23$	5	22	110
$23-25$	4	24	96
Total	$\Sigma f_1 = 40 + f$		$\Sigma fx = 704 + 20f$

$$\text{Mean} = \frac{\Sigma f_i x_i}{\Sigma f_i}$$

$$\Rightarrow 18 = \frac{704 + 20f}{40 + f}$$
$$\Rightarrow 720 + 18f = 704 + 20f$$
$$\Rightarrow 16 = 2f$$
$$\Rightarrow f = 8 \qquad\qquad \textbf{Ans.}$$

(iii) In the following figure, DE || AC and DC || AP. Prove that: $\frac{BE}{EC} = \frac{BC}{CP}$ **[4]**

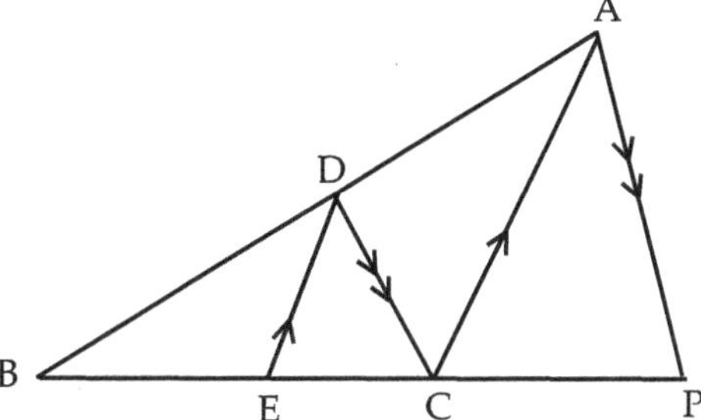

Solution:

In $\triangle BCA$

DE||AC   [given]

$\frac{BD}{DA} = \frac{BE}{EC}$ ....(i) [BPT]

In $\triangle BAP$

DC||AP   [given]

$\frac{BD}{DA} = \frac{BC}{CP}$ ....(ii) [BPT]

From (i) and (ii)

$\frac{BE}{EC} = \frac{BC}{CP}$ Proved.

Question 9.

(i) A can do a piece of work in 'x' days and B can do the same work in $(x + 16)$ days. If both working together can do it in 15 days; calculate 'x'. **[4]**

Solution:

A can do a piece of work = x days

A's one day word $= \frac{1}{x}$

B can do a piece of work = x+16 days

B's one day word $= \frac{1}{x+16}$

In 15 days together they finish work

Together their one day work $= \frac{1}{15}$

$$\frac{1}{x} + \frac{1}{x+16} = \frac{1}{15}$$
$$\frac{x+16+x}{x(x+16)} = \frac{1}{15}$$
$$x^2 + 16x = 30x + 240$$
$$x^2 - 14x - 240 = 0$$

$$x^2 - 24x + 10x - 240 = 0$$
$$x(x - 24) + 10(x - 24) = 0$$
$$(x - 24)(x + 10) = 0$$
$$x = 24, -10 \text{ (not possible)}$$

So value of $x = 24$ **Ans.**

(ii) The daily wages of 160 workers in a building project are given below:

[6]

Wages (in Rs)	$0 - 10$	$10 - 20$	$20 - 30$	$30 - 40$	$40 - 50$	$50 - 60$	$60 - 70$	$70 - 80$
No. of workers	12	20	30	38	24	16	12	8

Using graph paper, draw an ogive for the above distribution. Use your ogive to estimate :
(a) The median wage of the workers.
(b) The upper quartile wage of the workers.
(c) The lower quartile wage of the workers.
(d) The percentage of workers who earn more than Rs 45 a day.

Solution:

Wages (in Rs.)	Number of workers	Cumulative frequency
$0 - 10$	12	12
$10 - 20$	20	32
$20 - 30$	30	62
$30 - 40$	38	100
$40 - 50$	24	124
$50 - 60$	16	140
$60 - 70$	12	152
$70 - 80$	8	160
	$N = 160$	

(a) As sum of frequency N = 160 (even) so median class = 80 th i.e. $30 - 40$ (this class contains $N/2 = 80th$ term)

So median (from graph) = Rs. 34.50 (approx.)

(b) Upper quartile wages $(Q_3) = \frac{3}{4} \times 160 = 120^{th}$ term

So upper quartile wages from graph = Rs. 48 (approx.)

(c) Upper quartile wages $(Q_3) = \frac{1}{4} \times 160 = 40^{th}$ term

So upper quartile wages from graph = Rs. 23 (approx.)

(d) From graph no of workers who earn more that Rs. 45 $= 160 - 114 = 46$ workers

Percentage $= \frac{46}{160} \times 100 = 29\%$ (approx.)

Ans.

Question 10.

(i) If $\dfrac{8a-5b}{8c-5d} = \dfrac{8a+5b}{8c+5d}$; then prove that $a:b = c:d$ [3]

Solution:

Given that: $\dfrac{8a-5b}{8c-5d} = \dfrac{8a+5b}{8c+5d}$

$$\dfrac{8a-5b}{8a+5b} = \dfrac{8c-5d}{8c+5d} \qquad \text{[using alternendo]}$$

$$\dfrac{8a-5b+8a+5b}{8a-5b-8a-5b} = \dfrac{8c-5d+8c+5d}{8c-5d-8c-5d} \qquad \text{[using componendo and dividendo]}$$

$$\dfrac{16a}{-10b} = \dfrac{16c}{-10d}$$

$$\dfrac{a}{b} = \dfrac{c}{d} \;\to\; a:b = c:d \qquad \text{Proved}$$

(ii) Using ruler and compasses only: **[3]**

    (a) Construct a triangle ABC with the following data: Base

       $AB = 6\text{cm}, AC = 5.2\text{cm}$, and $\angle CAB = 60°$.

    (b) In the same diagram, draw a circle that passes through points A, B, and C, and mark its center O.

Solution:

Step 1. Draw a line segment AB = 6 cm.

Step 2. At point A make a ray, which make an angle = 60°

Step 3. From this ray cut an arc = 5.2 cm and name C.

Step 4. Join BC.

ABC is the required triangle.

Draw perpendicular bisector of AB and BC, which meet at O.

With O as center and OA = OB = OC as radius make a circle which passes through A, B and C.

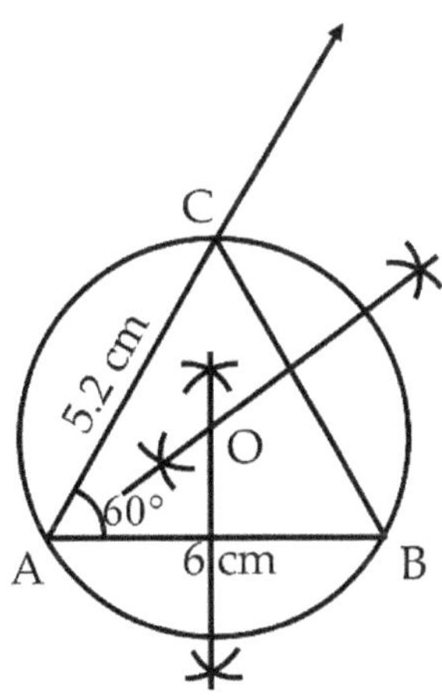

(iii) A man standing on the bank of a river observes that the angle of elevation of a tree on the opposite bank is 60°. When he moves 50m away from the bank. He finds the angle of elevation to be 30°. Calculate: **[4]**

    (a) The width of the river and

    (b) The height of the tree.

Solution:

In Δ DBC $\qquad\qquad \tan 60° = \dfrac{BC}{BD} =$

$$\sqrt{3} = \frac{BC}{BD}$$

$$\therefore BC = BD\sqrt{3} \qquad \ldots\ldots\ldots\ldots(i)$$

In ΔABC $\qquad \tan 30° = \dfrac{BC}{AB}$

$$\frac{1}{\sqrt{3}} = \frac{BD\sqrt{3}}{50 + BD}$$

$$3\,BD = 50 + BD$$

$$2BD = 50$$

$$BD = 25$$

(a) So, width of the river $= 25$ m $\qquad\qquad\qquad$ **Ans.**

(b) Height of the tree $\quad = BD\sqrt{3} = 25 \times 1.732 = 43.3$ m $\qquad$ **Ans.**

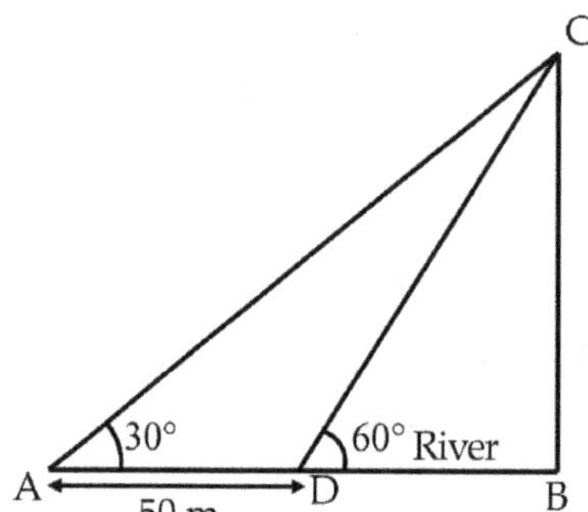

UNSOLVED SAMPLE PAPER

MATHEMATICS

Maximum Marks: 80
Time allowed: Two and a half hours
Answers to this Paper must be written on the paper provided separately.
You will not be allowed to write during first 15 minutes.
This time is to be spent in reading the question paper.
The time given at the head of this Paper is the time allowed for writing the answers.

Attempt all questions from Section *A* and any three questions from Section *B*.
The intended marks for questions or parts of questions are given in brackets [].

SECTION – A (40 Marks)
(Attempt all questions from this section)

Question 1.

Chose the correct answers to the questions from the given options: **[15]**

(i) A shopkeeper buys an article from a wholesaler for $Rs.\,20000$ and sells it to a consumer at a 10% profit. If the rate of GST is 12%, find the tax liability of the shopkeeper.

   (a) $Rs.\,2000$

   (b) $Rs.\,1100$

   (c) $Rs.\,2200$

   (d) None of the above

(ii) If $x = 3$ and $x = -2$ are the solution of the quadratic equation $x^2 + ax - b = 0$ and $a + 1 = 0$, find the value of 'b'

   (a) 6

   (b) 5

   (c) 6

   (d) -5

(iii) When $12x^3 - 13x^2 - 5x + 5$ is divided by $(3x + 2)$ the remainder is:

   (a) 1

   (b) -1

   (c) $\dfrac{70}{9}$

   (d) 8

(iv) The order of Matrix M in $M \times \begin{bmatrix} x & y \end{bmatrix} = \begin{bmatrix} p \\ q \end{bmatrix}$

   (a) 1×2

   (b) 2×1

   (c) 2×2

   (d) Multiplication not possible

(v) The first four terms of an A.P. whose first term is -2 and the common difference is -2 are:
   (a) $-2, 0, 2, 4$
   (b) $-2, 4, -8, 16$
   (c) $-2, -4, -6, -8$
   (d) $-2, -4, -8, -16$

(vi) Point $(3,0)$ is an invariant point under reflection in the line L. Name the line L.
   (a) $y - axis$
   (b) $x - $ axis
   (c) $y = 3$
   (d) $x = 3$

(vii) If in two triangles ABC and DEF, $\frac{AB}{DE} = \frac{BC}{FE} = \frac{CA}{FD}$, then
   (a) $\Delta FDE \sim \Delta CAB$
   (b) $\Delta FDE \sim \Delta ABC$
   (c) $\Delta CBA \sim \Delta FDE$
   (d) $\Delta BCA \sim \Delta FDE$

(viii) The height of the largest cone that can be carved out from a cylinder whose curved surface area is 4400cm^2 and the circumference of its base is 110cm.
   (a) 44cm
   (b) 40cm
   (c) 35cm
   (d) 17.5cm

(ix) The smallest value of $'x'$ of the inequation $27 - 4x \leq 13, x \in R$ is:
   (a) $\frac{3}{2}$
   (b) $-\frac{7}{2}$
   (c) $\frac{7}{2}$
   (d) None of these

(x) The probability of getting a bad egg from a lot of 600 eggs is 0.025. The number of bad eggs in the lot is:
   (a) 7
   (b) 15
   (c) 21
   (d) 28

(xi) The mid-point of line segment AB is the point $(0,4)$. If the coordinates of B are $(-2,3)$, then the coordinates of A are:
   (a) $(-2, -5)$
   (b) $(2, 9)$

(c) $(2, 5)$

(d) $(-2, 11)$

(xii) Find the length of the tangent drawn to a circle of radius of 3cm, from a point distant 5cm from the center.

(a) 3 cm

(b) 4 cm

(c) 6 cm

(d) 2.5 cm

(xiii) The value of $(\sin A + \cos A)^2 + (\sin A - \cos A)^2$ is:

(a) 2

(b) 1

(c) 4

(d) -2

(xiv) The modal class of the following data:

Class inter-vals	$10 - 20$	$20 - 30$	$30 - 40$	$40 - 50$	$50 - 60$	$60 - 70$
Frequency	12	6	13	8	11	10

(a) 20 – 30

(b) 30 – 40

(c) 40 – 50

(d) 50 – 60

(xv) 15th term of the A.P. $x - 7,\ x - 2,\ x + 3, \ldots$is:

(a) $x + 63$

(b) $x + 73$

(c) $x + 83$

(d) $x + 53$

Question 2.

(i) Prove the identity: $(\operatorname{cosec}^2 A - 1)(\sec A + 1)(\sec A - 1) = 1$ **[4]**

(ii) What number must be added to each of the numbers 6, 15, 20, and 43 to make them proportional? **[4]**

(iii) Richard has a recurring deposit account in a post office for 3 years at 8% p.a. simple interest. If he gets Rs 1998 as interest at the time of maturity, find **[4]**

(a) The monthly installment

(b) The amount of maturity

Question 3.

(i) How many cubic meters of the earth must be dug out to make a well 28m deep and 2.8m in diameter? Also, find the cost of plastering its inner surface at Rs. 4.50 per sq. meter. **[4]**

(ii) Calculate the ratio in which the line joining the points $(-3, -1)$ and $(5, 7)$ is divided by the line $x = 2$ Also, find the co-ordinates of the point of intersection. **[4]**

(iii) Use graph paper for this question. (Take two cm = 1 unit on both axes).
Plot the points P (3, 2) and Q (-3, - 2). From P and Q, draw perpendiculars PM and QN on the x-axis. **[5]**
   (a) Write the co-ordinates of points M and N.
   (b) Name the image of P on reflection in the origin.
   (c) Assign the special name to the geometrical figure PMQN and find its area.
   (d) Write the co-ordinates of the point to which M is mapped on reflection in:
       i. x-axis,
       ii. y-axis,
       iii.   Origin.

SECTION – B (40 Marks)

(Attempt any four questions from this section)

Question 4.

(i) Find the amount of bill for the following intra-state transaction of the following goods. The GST rate is 18%. **[3]**

Article	A	B	C
Quantity (No. of Articles)	40	47	20
Marked Price (in Rs.)	$Rs.\,420$	$Rs.\,600$	$Rs.\,350$
Discount %	10	10	20

(ii) Solve the following equation for x and give your answer correct to 2 decimal places:
$$x^2 - 3x - 9 = 0$$
[3]

(iii) IQ of 50 students were recorded as follows:

IQ score	$80 - 90$	$90 - 100$	$100 - 110$	$110 - 120$	$120 - 130$	$130 - 140$
No. of students	6	9	16	13	4	2

Draw a histogram for the above data and estimate the mode. **[4]**

Question 5.

(i) Find x and y if:
$$\begin{bmatrix} 3 & -2 \\ -1 & 4 \end{bmatrix}\begin{bmatrix} 2x \\ 2 \end{bmatrix} + 2\begin{bmatrix} -4 \\ 5 \end{bmatrix} = 4\begin{bmatrix} 2 \\ y \end{bmatrix}$$
[3]

(ii) In the given figure, given below, straight lines AB and CD intersect at P; and AC || BD. Prove that: **[3]**

(a) $\triangle APC \sim \triangle BPD$

(b) If BD = 2.4 cm, AC = 3.6 cm, PD = 4.0 cm and PB = 3.2 cm; find the length of PA and PC.

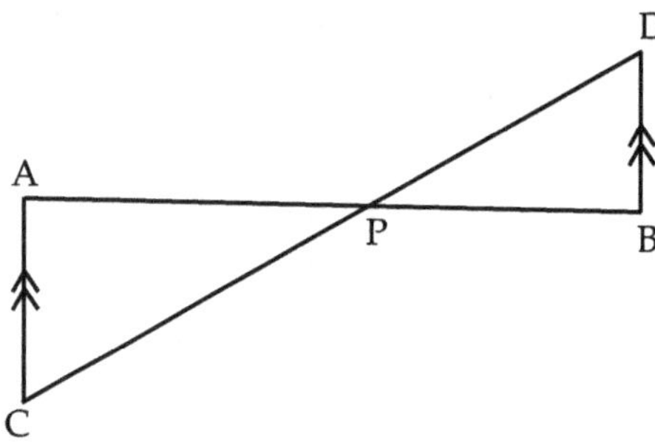

(iii) If $x^3 + ax^2 + bx + 6$ has $x - 2$ as a factor and leaves a remainder of 3 when divided by $x - 3$, find the values of a and b. **[4]**

Question 6.

(i) ABCD is a rhombus. The co-ordinates of A and C are (3,6) and (−1,2) respectively. Write down the equation of BD. **[3]**

(ii) Prove the identity: $\tan A + \cot A = \sec A \cdot \operatorname{cosec} A$ **[3]**

(iii) If the 8th term of an A.P. is 37 and the 15th term is 15 more than the 12th the term, find the A.P. Also, find the sum of the first 15 terms of this A.P. **[4]**

Question 7.

(i) A box contains some black balls and 30 white balls. If the probability of drawing a black ball is two-fifths of a white ball; find the number of black balls in the box. **[3]**

(ii) A hemispherical bowl on an internal radius of 15cm contains a liquid. The liquid is to be filled into cylindrical shaped bottles of diameter 5cm and a height of 6cm. How many bottles are necessary to empty the bowl? **[3]**

(iii) In the figure, $\angle DBC = 58°$. BD is the diameter of the circle. Calculate: **[4]**

(a) $\angle BDC$

(b) $\angle BEC$

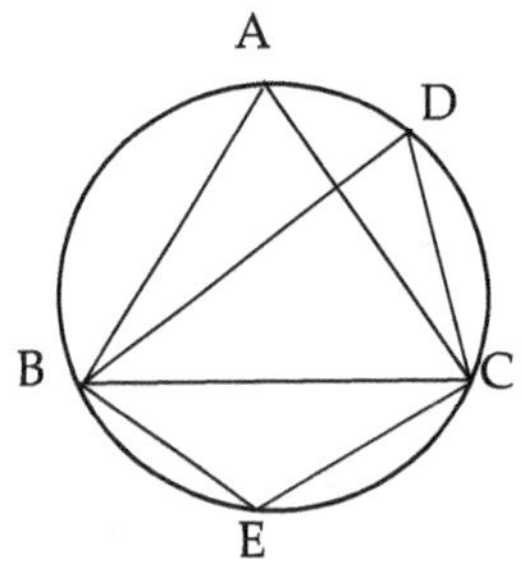

(c) ∠BAC

Question 8.

(i) Given: $P = \{x : 5 < 2x - 1 \le 11, x \in R\}$, $Q = \{x : -1 \le 3 + 4x < 23, x \in I\}$, where R = {real numbers}, I = {integers }. Represent P and Q on number lines. Write down the elements of $P \cap Q$.

[3]

(ii) Using the step-deviation method, calculate the mean marks of the following distribution. [3]

Class interval	$50 - 55$	$55 - 60$	$60 - 65$	$65 - 70$	$70 - 75$	$75 - 80$	$80 - 85$	$85 - 90$
Frequency	5	20	10	10	9	6	12	8

(iii) In the adjoining figure, ABC is a triangle. DE is parallel to BC and $\frac{AD}{DB} = \frac{3}{2}$. [4]

    (a) Determine the ratio of $\frac{AD}{AB}$ and $\frac{DE}{BC}$.

    (b) Prove that $\Delta DEF \sim \Delta CBF$. Hence find $\frac{EF}{FB}$.

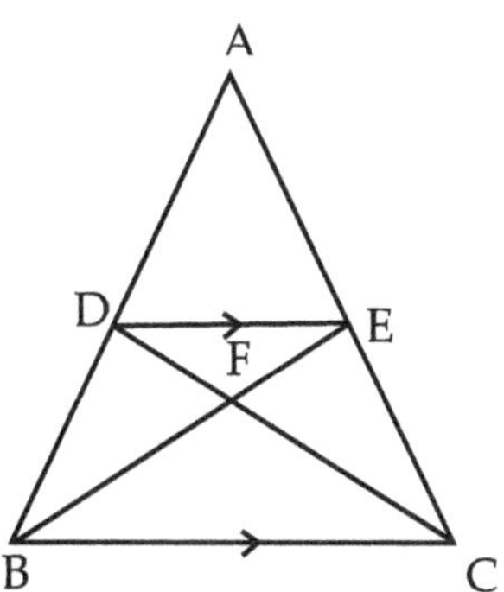

Question 9.

(i) A positive number is divided into two parts such that the sum of the squares of the two parts is 20. The square of the larger part is 8 times the smaller part. Taking x as the smaller part of the two parts, find the number. [4]

(ii) Marks scored by 400 students in an examination are as follows: [6]

Marks	$0 - 10$	$10 - 20$	$20 - 30$	$30 - 40$	$40 - 50$	$50 - 60$
No. of students	10	20	22	40	55	75

Continued			$60 - 70$	$70 - 80$	$80 - 90$	$90 - 100$
			80	58	28	12

Draw the ogive and from it determine:

(a) The median mark, and

(b) The pass marks if 80% of the students passes an examination.

Question 10.

(i) If $x = \dfrac{\sqrt{a+3b}+\sqrt{a-3b}}{\sqrt{a+3b}-\sqrt{a-3b}}$, prove that: $3bx^2 - 2ax + 3b = 0$ **[3]**

(ii) Draw a line AQ = 7cm. Mark a point P on AQ such that AP = 4cm. Using ruler and compasses only, construct: **[3]**

   (a) A circle with AP as a diameter

   (b) Two tangents to the above circle from point Q.

(iii) A vertical pole and a vertical tower are on the same level of ground. From the top of the pole, the angle of elevation of the top of the tower is 60° and the angle of depression of the foot of the tower is 30°. Find the height of the tower if the height of the pole is 20 m. **[4]**

Answers

Question 1.

(i) c, (ii) a, (iii) b, (iv) d, (v) c, (vi) b, (vii) a, (viii) b, (ix) c, (x) b, (xi) c, (xii) b, (xiii) a, (xiv) b, (xv) a

Question 2.

(ii)$x = 3$,   (iii) Rs. 450, Rs. 18198

Question 3.

(i) $172.48m^3$, Rs. 1108.80,   (ii) $5 : 3$, $(2, 4)$,   (iii) (a) M(3, 0), N(-3, 0)

(b) (-3, -2)

(c) Parallelogram, area = 12 sq. Units

(d) 1. (3, 0), 2. (-3, 0) 3. (-3, 0)

Question 4.

(i) Rs. 54398, (ii) 4.85, -1.85, (iii) 107

Question 5.

(i) $x = 3, y = 2$,   (ii) (b) PA = 4.8 cm, PC = 6 cm,   (iii) $a = 3, b = -1$

Question 6.

(i) $x + y = 5$,   (iii) AP is 2, 7, 12, 17, . . . sum = 555

Question 7.

(i) 12,   (ii) 60 ,   (iii) (a) 32°

(b) 148°

(c) 32°

Question 8.

(i) $P \cap Q = \{4\}$ (ii) 46.9,   (iii) (a) $\dfrac{3}{5}, \dfrac{3}{5}$

(b) $\dfrac{3}{5}$

Question 9.

(i) 6,   (ii) (a) 57.5

(b) 36

Question 10.

(iii) 80m

Maximum Marks: 80

Time allowed: Two and a half hours

Answers to this Paper must be written on the paper provided separately.

You will not be allowed to write during first 15 minutes.

This time is to be spent in reading the question paper.

The time given at the head of this Paper is the time allowed for writing the answers.

Attempt all questions from Section *A* and any three questions from Section *B*.

The intended marks for questions or parts of questions are given in brackets [].

SECTION -A (40 Marks)

(Attempt all questions from this section)

Question 1. [15]

Chose the correct answers to the questions from the given options:

(i) If the equation $x^2 + 4x + k = 0$ has real and distinct toots, then

   (a) $k < 4$

   (b) $k > 4$

   (c) $k \geq 4$

   (d) $k \leq 4$

(ii) Maya purchased an article for Rs. 5310, which includes a 10% rebate on the marked price and 18% tax (under GST) on the remaining price. Find the marked price of the article.

   (a) Rs. 4500

   (b) Rs. 5000

   (c) Rs. 5500

   (d) Rs. 6000

(iii) What is the order of the resultant Matrix of: $\begin{bmatrix} p \\ q \end{bmatrix} \times \begin{bmatrix} x & y \end{bmatrix}$

   (a) 2×2

   (b) 2×1

   (c) 1×2

   (d) Multiplication not allowed

(iv) When the polynomial $4x^3 - kx^2 + (4k - 3)x - 5$ is divided by $x - 2$, the remainder is 13. Find the value of 'k'

   (a) 2

   (b) $- 2$

   (c) 1

   (d) 3

(v) The common difference of an A.P. in which $a_{25} - a_{12} = -52$ is:

    (a) 4

    (b) -4

    (c) -3

    (d) 3

(vi) The point $P(4, 1)$ is reflected in the line $y = 3$ to become P'. Find the co - ordinates of P'.

    (a) $(-4, 5)$

    (b) $(4, -1)$

    (c) $(4, -5)$

    (d) $(4, 5)$

(vii) If the following figure, point D divides AB in the ratio $3:5$. Then the value of $\frac{AD}{AB}$ is

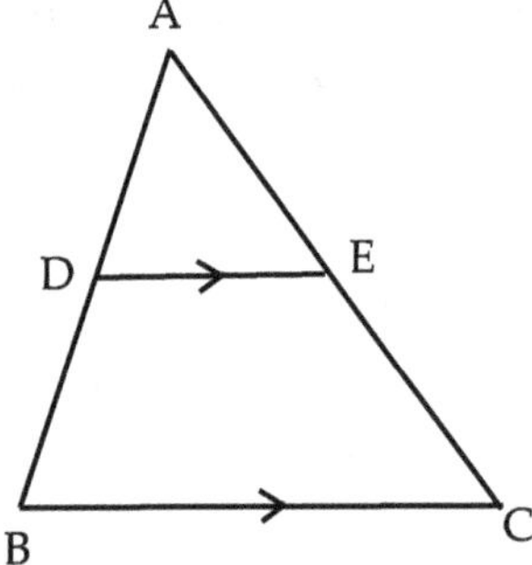

    (a) $\frac{5}{8}$

    (b) $\frac{3}{8}$

    (c) $\frac{3}{5}$

    (d) $\frac{5}{3}$

(viii) The radius of the largest cylinder is formed when a rectangular piece of paper 22 cm by 15 cm is rolled about its longer side:

    (a) 4.5cm

    (b) 7.5cm

    (c) 3.5cm

    (d) 7cm

(ix) The solution set for the following representation is:

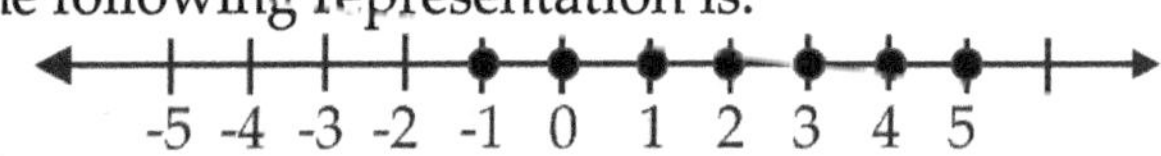

    (a) $\{-2 < x \leq 4, x \in R\}$

    (b) $\{-1, 0, 1, 2, 3, 4, 5\}$

    (c) $\{-1, 0, 1, 2, 3, 4\}$

    (d) $\{0, 1, 2, 3, 4,\}$

(x) In a throw of a pair of dice, the probability of getting a doublet (Same number on top of both dice) is:

(a) $\frac{1}{2}$

(b) $\frac{1}{3}$

(c) $\frac{1}{6}$

(d) $\frac{5}{6}$

(xi) If $P(\frac{a}{2}, 4)$ is the midpoint of the line segment joining the points A$(-6, 5)$ and B$(-2, 3)$, then the value of ' a ' is

(a) 3

(b) -8

(c) -4

(d) 4

(xii) In the figure given, O is the centre of the circle. AB is a diameter, TPT' is a tangent to the circle at P. If BPT' = 30°. The value of angle BAP is:

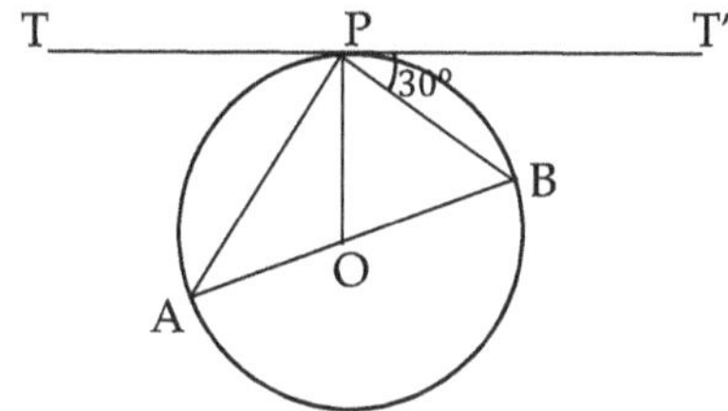

(a) 30°

(b) 60°

(c) 15°

(d) 45°

(xiii) The value of sec A$(1 - \sin A)(\sec A + \tan A)$ is:

(a) 2

(b) 1

(c) -1

(d) -2

(xiv) Most frequently occurring observation of data is called:

(a) Mean

(b) Median

(c) Mode

(d) Lower Quartile

(xv) If the common difference of an A.P. is 5, then the value of $a_{18} - a_{13}$ is:

(a) 5

(b) 20

(c) 25

(d) 30

Question 2.

(i) If $a, 15, 9$, and b are in continued proportion, fired a and b. [4]

(ii) Prove the identity: $\sqrt{\sec^2 A + \operatorname{cosec}^2 A} = \tan A + \cot A$ [4]

(iii) Mr. R.K. Nair gets Rs. 6,455 at the end of one year at the rate of 14% per annum in a recurring deposit account. Find the monthly installment. [4]

Question 3.

(i) Plot points A $(3, 5)$ and B$(-2, -4)$. Use 1 cm = 1 unit on both axes. [5]
    (a) A' is the image of A when reflected on the x-axis. Write down the co-ordinates of A' and plot them on graph paper.
    (b) B' is the image of B when reflected in the y-axis, followed by a reflection in the origin. Write down the co-ordinates of B' and plot them on graph paper.
    (c) Write down the geometrical name of the figure AA'BB'.
    (d) Name two invariant points under reflection on the x-axis.

(ii) Calculate the ratio in which the line joining A $(6,5)$ and B$(4,-3)$ is divided by the line $y = 2$. Also, find the co-ordinates of the point of division. [4]

(iii) The volume of a conical tent is $1232 m^3$ and the area of the base floor is $154 m^2$. Calculate the :
    (a) Radius of the floor,
    (b) Height of the tent,
    (c) Length of the canvas required to cover this conical tent if its width is 2m. [4]

SECTION – B (40 Marks)
(Attempt any four questions from this section)

Question 4.

(i) A shopkeeper bought an article with a market price of Rs. 12000 from the wholesaler at a discount of 10%. The shopkeeper sells this article to the customer at the market price printed on it. If the rate of GST is 18%, then find: [3]
    (a) GST paid by the wholesaler
    (b) Amount paid by the customer to buy the item.

(ii) Solve the following equation for x and give your answer correct to 2 decimal places:
$$5x(x + 2) = 3$$
[3]

(iii) A Mathematics aptitude test of 50 students was recorded as follows:

Marks	$50 - 60$	$60 - 70$	$70 - 80$	$80 - 90$	$90 - 100$
No. of Students	4	8	14	19	5

Draw a histogram for the above data using graph paper and locate the mode. **[4]**

Question 5.

(i) Find $A^2 - A + BC$.

$$A = \begin{bmatrix} 1 & 0 \\ 2 & 1 \end{bmatrix}, B = \begin{bmatrix} 2 & 3 \\ -1 & 0 \end{bmatrix}, C = \begin{bmatrix} 4 & 9 \\ 3 & 4 \end{bmatrix}$$ **[3]**

(ii) In the given figure, PM is a tangent to the circle, and PA = AM. Prove that: **[3]**
   (a) $\triangle$PMB ~ $\triangle$PAM
   (b) PA $\times$ PB = MB^2

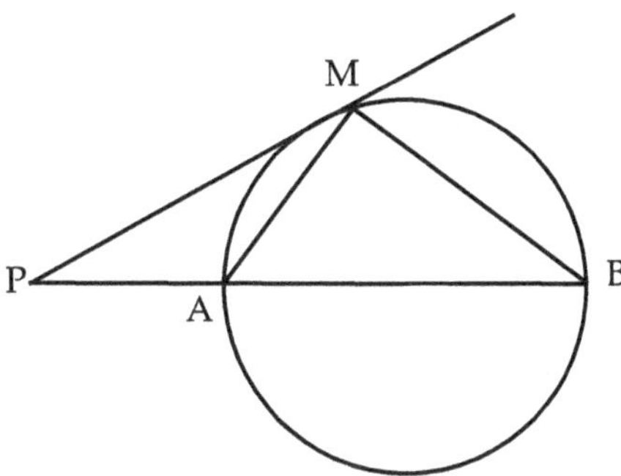

(iii) What number should be added to $3x^3 - 5x^2 + 6x$ so that when resulting polynomial is divided by $x - 3$, the remainder is 8? **[4]**

Question 6.

(i) Write down the equation of the line whose gradient is 3/2 and which passes through P, where P divides the line segment joining A (–2, 6) and B (3, –4) in the ratio 2: 3. Also find the coordinates of P. **[3]**

(ii) Prove the identity: $\dfrac{\sin A}{1+\cos A} = \text{cosec A} - \cot A$ **[3]**

(iii) The fourth term of an A.P. is 11 and the eighth term exceeds twice the fourth term by 5. Find the A.P. and the sum of the first 40 terms. **[4]**

Question 7.

(i) The queen, the jack, and 10 spades are removed from a pack of 52 cards. A card is drawn from the remaining well-shuffled pack. Find the probability of getting: **[3]**
   (a) Red card
   (b) King
   (c) Black card.

(ii) From a solid cylinder of height 36cm and radius 14cm, a conical cavity of radius 7cm and height 24cm is drilled out. Find the volume and the total surface area of the remaining solid.

[3]

(iii) In the given circle with center 0, $\angle ABC = 100°$, $\angle ACD = 40°$, and CT is a tangent to the circle at C. Find $\angle ADC$ and $\angle DCT$. [4]

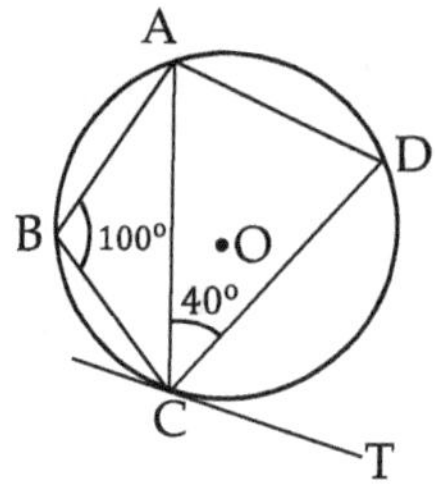

Question 8.

(i) Solve the inequation and represent the solution set on the number line:
$$-3 + x \leq \frac{8x}{3} + 2 \leq \frac{14}{3} + 2x, \text{ where } x \in I$$
[3]

(ii) Find the mean of the following distribution: [3]

Class-intervals	$20 - 30$	$30 - 40$	$40 - 50$	$50 - 60$	$60 - 70$	$70 - 80$
Frequency	10	6	8	12	5	9

(iii) In the given figure; AB||EF||CD. Given that $AB = 7.5\ cm$, EG = 2.5 cm, GC = 5 cm and DC = 9 cm. Calculate: [4]
(a) EF
(b) AC

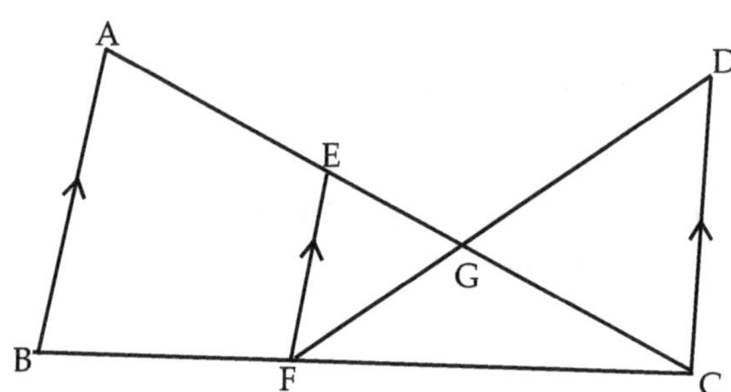

Question 9.

(i) An airplane traveled a distance of 400km at an average speed of x km/hr. On the return journey, the speed was increased by 40km/hr. Write down an expression for the time taken for:
(a) The onward journey:
(b) The return journey.
If the return journey took 30 minutes less than the onward journey, write down an equation in x and find its value. [4]

(ii) The marks obtained by 120 students in a Mathematics test are given below: **[6]**

Marks	0 − 10	10 − 20	20 − 30	30 − 40	40 − 50	50 − 60
No. of students	5	9	16	22	26	18

	60 − 70	70 − 80	80 − 90	90 − 100
Continued	11	6	4	3

Draw an ogive for the given distribution on a graph sheet. Use a suitable scale for your ogive.

Use your ogive to estimate:

(a) The median.

(b) The lower quartile.

(c) The number of students who obtained more than 75% marks on the test.

(d) The number of students who did not pass the test if the pass percentage was 40.

Question 10.

(i) Using properties of proportion, solve for : $\frac{\sqrt{x+2}+\sqrt{x-2}}{\sqrt{x+2}-\sqrt{x-2}} = 4,$ **[3]**

(ii) Using a ruler and compasses only: **[3]**

    (a) Construct a triangle ABC with the following data: AB = 3.5cm, BC = 6cm and ∠ABC = 120°

    (b) In the same diagram, draw a circle with BC as a diameter. Find a point P on the circumference of the circle which is equidistant from AB and BC.

    (c) Measure ∠BCP.

(iii) The figure drawn above is not to the scale. AB is a tower, and two objects C and D are located on the ground, on the same side of AB. When observed from the top A of the tower, their angles of depression are 45° and 60° . Find the distance between the two objects, if the height of the tower is 300 m, Give your answer to the nearest meter. **[4]**

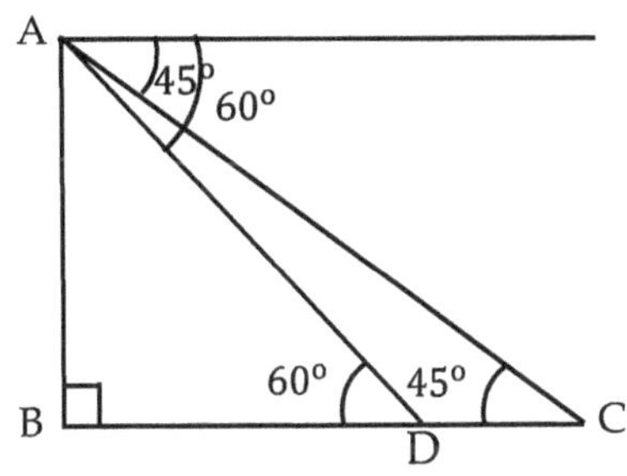

Answers.

Question 1.

(i) a , (ii) b, (iii) a , (iv) b , (v) b , (vii) d , (vii) b , (viii) c , (ix) c , (x) c , (xi) b , (xii) a , (xiii) b, (xiv) c , (xv) c

Question 2.

(i) 25, $\frac{27}{5}$, (iii) 4. Rs. 500

Question 3.

(i) (a) (3, -5) (b) (-2, 4) (c) Isosceles trapezium (d) (3, 0), (-2, 0) , (ii) 3:5, $\left(\frac{21}{4}, 2\right)$, (iii) (a) 7 m , (b) 24 m , (c) 275 m

Question 4.

(i) (a) Rs. 216 (b) Rs. 14160 , (ii) 0.26, -2.26],   (iii) 82 (appr.)

Question 5.

(i) $\begin{bmatrix} 4 & 9 \\ 5 & 4 \end{bmatrix}$,   (iii) -46

Question 6.

(i) $3x - 2y + 4 = 0$, (0, 2),   (iii) -1, 3, 7, 11, . . ., sum = 3080

Question 7.

(i) (a) $\frac{26}{49}$ (b) $\frac{4}{49}$ (c) $\frac{23}{49}$, (ii) 20944 cm^3, 4976 cm^2, (iii),60°

Question 8.

(i) {−3, −2, −1, 0, 1, 2, 3, 4}   (ii) 49.6 ,   (iii) (a) 4.5 cm (b) 12.5 cm

Question 9.

(i) (a) $\frac{400}{x}$ hrs, (b) $\frac{400}{x+40}$ hrs, $\frac{400}{x} - \frac{400}{x+40} = \frac{1}{2}$ and $x = 160$, (ii) (a) 43.5, (b) 30 , (c) 10 , (d) 52

Question 10.

(i) $\frac{17}{4}$,   (iii) 127m

Maximum Marks: 80

Time allowed: Two and a half hours

Answers to this Paper must be written on the paper provided separately.

You will not be allowed to write during first 15 minutes.

This time is to be spent in reading the question paper.

The time given at the head of this Paper is the time allowed for writing the answers.

Attempt all questions from Section *A* and any three questions from Section *B*.

The intended marks for questions or parts of questions are given in brackets [].

SECTION – A (40 Marks)

(Attempt all questions from this section)

Question 1. [15]

Chose the correct answers to the questions from the given options:

(i) Which term of the A.P.: $5, 2, -1, \ldots \ldots is -49$?

    (a) 19th

    (b) 15th

    (c) 16th

    (d) 20th

(ii) Find the values of x and y if $\begin{bmatrix} x-2 & y \\ 5 & 1 \end{bmatrix} = \begin{bmatrix} 3 & 1 \\ 5 & 1 \end{bmatrix}$:

    (a) $x = 5, y = 1$

    (b) $x = 1, y = 5$

    (c) $x = 5, y = 2$

    (d) $x = 1, y = 1$

(iii) If $(x - 2)$ is a factor of $2x^3 - x^2 - px - 2$, find the value of p:

    (a) -5

    (b) 5

    (c) 4

    (d) -4

(iv) If $ax^2 + bx + c = 0$ has equal roots, then c =

    (a) $\dfrac{-b}{2a}$

    (b) $\dfrac{b}{2a}$

    (c) $\dfrac{-b^2}{4a}$

    (d) $\dfrac{b^2}{4a}$

(v) If the cost of an article is Rs. 25000 and CGST paid by the owner is Rs. 2250, the rate of GST is:

(a) 15%

(b) 18%

(c) 10%

(d) 9%

(vi) The point $P(5,3)$ was reflected in the origin to get the image $P\,'$. Co-ordinates of $P\,'$.

(a) $(-5,3)$

(b) $(5,-3)$

(c) $-5,-3)$

(d) No change

(vii) In the given figure DE || AC, which of the following is true?

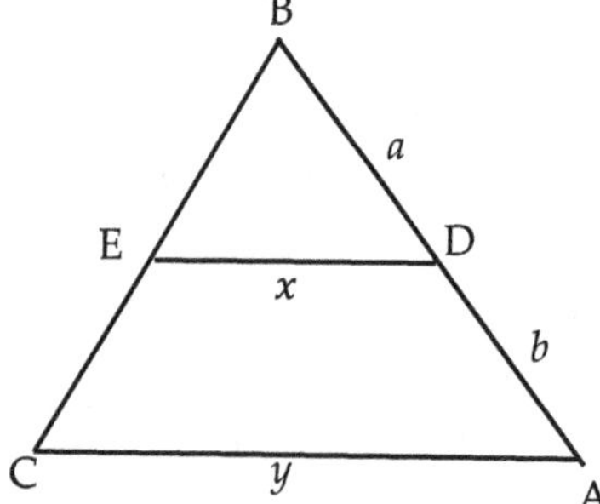

(a) $x = \dfrac{a+b}{xy}$

(b) $y = \dfrac{ax}{a+b}$

(c) $x = \dfrac{ay}{a+b}$

(d) $\dfrac{x}{y} = \dfrac{a}{b}$

(viii) The volume of a conical tent is 1232m^3 and the area of the base floor is 154m^2. The radius of the floor is:

(a) 7m

(b) 7.5m

(c) 3.5m

(d) 5m

(ix) The solution set of the following representation is:

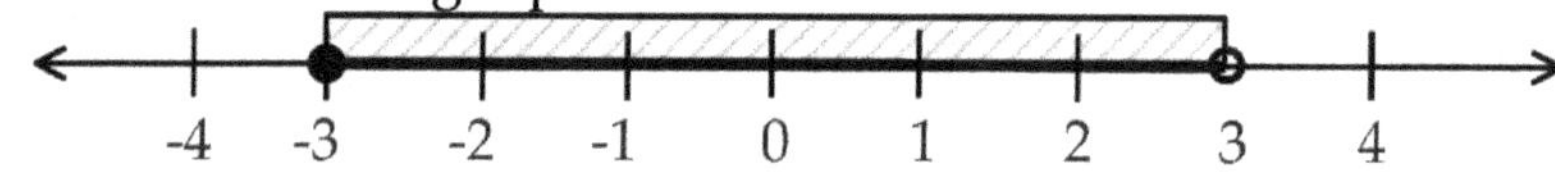

(a) $\{-3,-2,-1,0,1,2\}$

(b) $\{-3 \le x < 3, x \in R\}$

(c) $\{-3 \le x \le 3, x \in R\}$

(d) $\{-3 \le x < 3, x \in I\}$

(x) In a survey it is found that every sixth person possesses a car, what is the probability of a person not possessing the car?

(a) $\frac{1}{6}$

(b) 0

(c) $\frac{5}{6}$

(d) $\frac{6}{5}$

(xi) If the points $(7, -2), (5,1)$, and $(3, k)$ are collinear, then the value of ' k ' is:

(a) -4

(b) 0

(c) 4

(d) 11

(xii) Find the unknown length x in each of the following figures:

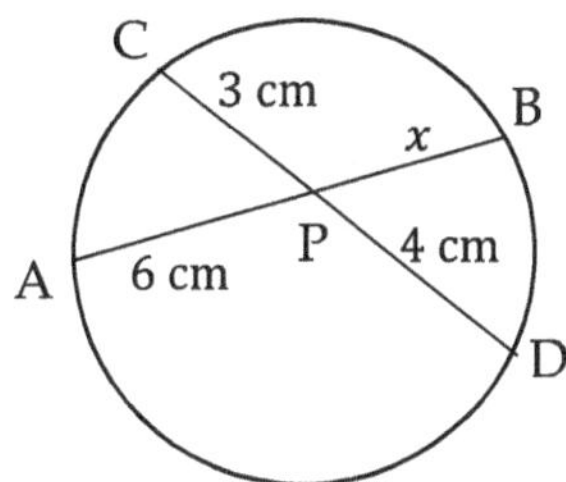

(a) 3cm

(b) 4cm

(c) 1.5cm

(d) 2cm

(xiii) Value of $\sec^2 A + \csc^2 A$ is equal to:

(a) $\cos^2 A$

(b) $\sin^2 A$

(c) $\sec^2 A \times \csc^2 A$

(d) $\tan A$

(xiv) The graphical representation of cumulative frequency distribution is called

(a) Median

(b) Ogive

(c) Histogram

(d) Frequency curve

(xv) 37th term of the A.P.:$\sqrt{x}, 3\sqrt{x}, 5\sqrt{x}, ...$ is :

(a) $37\sqrt{x}$

(b) $39\sqrt{x}$

(c) $73\sqrt{x}$

(d) $75\sqrt{x}$

Question 2.

(i) Prove the identity: $\dfrac{\sin A}{1+\cot A} - \dfrac{\cos A}{1+\tan A} = \sin A - \cos A$ **[4]**

(ii) Ahmed has a recurring deposit account in a bank. He deposits Rs. 2,500 per month for 2 years. If he gets Rs. 66,250 at the time of maturity, find: **[4]**
  (a) The interest paid by the bank
  (b) Rate of interest.

(iii) Find the third proportional to: $5\dfrac{1}{4}$ and 7. **[4]**

Question 3.

(i) In the figure given, alongside, line segment AB meets X-axis at A and Y-axis at B. The point P(−3, 4) on AB divides it in the ratio 2: 3. Find the coordinates of A and B. **[4]**

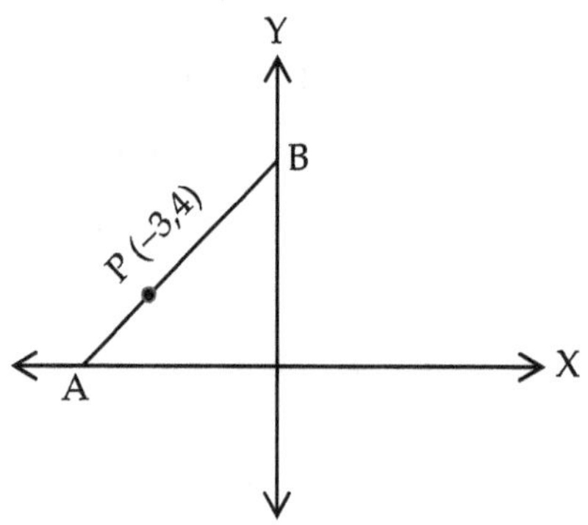

(ii) A conical tent is 10m high and radius of its base is 24m. Find: **[4]**
  (a) Slant height of the tent
  (b) Cost of canvas required to make the tent is the cost of $1m^2$ canvas is Rs. 70.

(iii) Use graph paper to answer this question. **[5]**
  (a) Plot points A (4, 6) and B (1, 2).
  (b) If A' is the image of A when reflected in the x-axis, write the co-ordinates of A'.
  (c) If B' is the image of B when reflected in the line AA', write the co-ordinates of B'.
  (d) Give the geometrical name for the figure ABA'B'.

SECTION – B (40 Marks)
(Attempt any four questions from this section)

Question 4.

(i) Find the amount of bill for the following intra-state transaction of goods/services. The GST rate is 5%. **[3]**

Quantity (No. of items)	MRP of each item(in Rs)	Discount %
18	150	Nil

24	240	20
30	100	30
12	120	20

(ii) Solve the following equation for x and give your answer corrects to 2 significant figures:
$(x-1)^2 - 3x + 4 = 0$ **[3]**

(iii) Calculate the mode of the following data: **[4]**

Classes	$10-20$	$20-30$	$30-40$	$40-50$	$50-60$	$60-70$
Frequency	30	16	12	18	5	10

Question 5.

(i) If $A = \begin{bmatrix} 2 & 3 \\ 0 & -2 \end{bmatrix}$ and $B = \begin{bmatrix} -8 \\ 8 \end{bmatrix}$, find matrix X such that $2AX = B$. **[3]**

(ii) In the given figure, chords AB and CD of a circle intersect at E. **[3]**
   (a) Prove that triangles ADE and CBE are similar.
   (b) Given DC = 12 cm, DE = 4 cm and AE = 16 cm, calculate the length of BE.

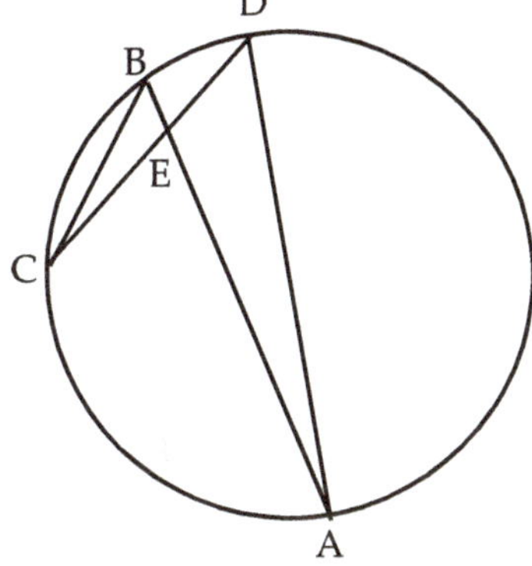

(iii) When divided by x–3 the polynomials $x^3 - px^2 + x + 6$ and $2x^3 - x^2 - (p+3)x - 6$ leave the same remainder. Find the value of 'p'. **[4]**

Question 6.

(i) The line $4x - 3y + 12 = 0$ meets the x-axis at A. Write down the coordinates of A. Determine the equation of the line passing through A and perpendicular to $4x - 3y + 12 = 0$. **[3]**

(ii) Prove the identity: $\sin^6 A + \cos^6 A = 1 - 3 \sin^2 A \cdot \cos^2 A$ **[3]**

(iii) Find the sum of first 22 terms of an A.P. in which 4th term is 15 and 8th term is one more than twice the 4th term. **[4]**

Question 7.

(i) Cards marked with numbers 5 to 50, are placed in a box and mixed thoroughly. A card is drawn from the box at random. Find the probability that the number on the card taken out is: **[3]**

    (a) A prime number less than 20

    (b) A perfect square numbers

    (c) A multiple of 5 or 6.

(ii) The adjoining figure represents a solid consisting of a cylinder surmounted by a cone at one end and a hemisphere at the other end. Given that the common radius = 3.5cm, the height of the cylinder = 6.5cm, and the total height = 12.8cm, calculate the volume of the solid, correct to the nearest cm^3. **[3]**

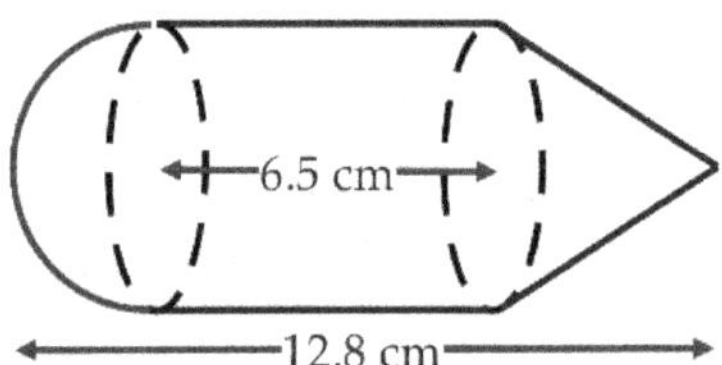

(iii) In the figure given below, AD is a diameter. O is the centre of the circle. AD is parallel to BC and ∠CBD = 32°. Find **[4]**

    (a) ∠OBD

    (b) ∠AOB

    (c) ∠BED.

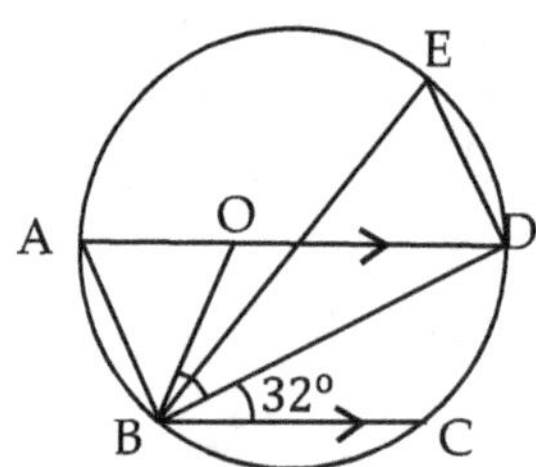

Question 8.

(i) Find the values of x, which satisfy the inequation $-2\frac{5}{6} < \frac{1}{2} - \frac{2x}{3} \leq 2, x \in W$. Graph the solution set on the number line. **[3]**

(ii) Given below are the weekly wages of 200 workers in a small factory. Find f, if the mean weekly wages is 145. **[3]**

Weekly wages	$80-100$	$100-120$	$120-140$	$140-160$	$160-180$
No. of workers	20	30	f	40	90

(iii) In the following figure, XY is parallel to BC, AX = 9 cm, XB = 4.5 cm and BC = 18 cm. Find: **[4]**

(a) $\dfrac{AY}{YC}$

(b) $\dfrac{YC}{AC}$

(c) XY

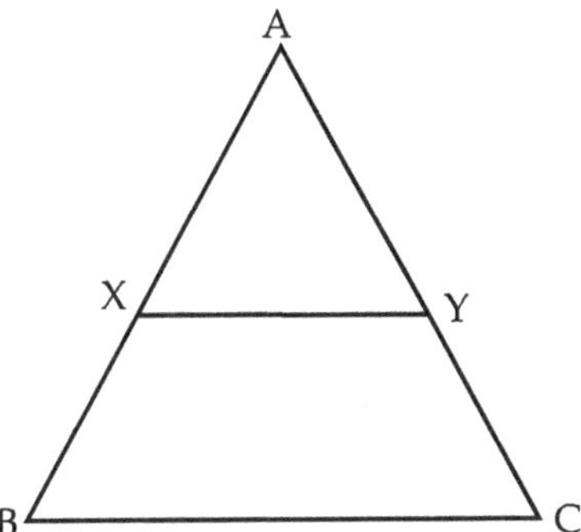

Question 9.

(i) Rs. 480 is divided equally among ' x ' children. If the number of children were 20 more than each would have got Rs. 12 less. Find ' x '. **[4]**

(ii) Attempt this question on graph paper: **[6]**

Marks obtained by 200 students in the examination are given below:

Marks	$0-10$	$10-20$	$20-30$	$30-40$	$40-50$	$50-60$
No. of students	5	10	14	21	25	34

Continued			$60-70$	$70-80$	$80-90$	$90-100$
			36	27	16	12

Draw an ogive for the given distribution. From the graph, find:

(a) The median

(b) The upper quartile

(c) The number of students scoring above 65 marks.

(d) If 10 students -qualify for a merit scholarship, find the minimum marks required to qualify.

Question 10.

(i) Using the properties of proportion, solve for x, given $\dfrac{x^4+1}{2x^2} = \dfrac{17}{8}$ **[3]**

(ii) Construct a regular hexagon of side 4cm. Construct a circle circumscribing the hexagon. **[3]**

(iii) Two lamp – posts of equal height stand on either side of a roadway which is 150 m wide. From a point on the roadway somewhere between the two lamp – posts, the elevation of the top of the lamp – posts are 60° and 30° respectively. Find the height of the lamp – posts and the position of the point. **[4]**

Answers

Question 1.
(i) a, (ii) a ,(iii) b ,(iv) d , (v) b ,(vi) c ,(vii) c ,(viii) a ,(ix) b ,(x) c , (xi) c , (xii) d ,(xiii) c ,(xiv) b , (xv) c
Question 2.
(ii) Rs. 6250, 10%, (iii) $9\frac{1}{3}$
Question 3.
(i) (−5,0) (0,10) , (ii) (a) 26 m, (b) Rs. 137280, (iii) (b) A′(4, -6) (c) B′(7, 2) (d) kite
Question 4.
(i) Rs. 11088, (ii) 3.6, 1.4,   (iii) 16.82
Question 5.
(i) $X = \begin{bmatrix} 1 \\ -2 \end{bmatrix}$, (ii) 2 cm, (iii) P=1
Question 6.
(i) (−3, 0), 3x + 4y + 9 = 0,   (iii) sum = 990
Question 7.
(i) (a) $\frac{3}{23}$ (b) $\frac{5}{46}$ (c) $\frac{17}{46}$,   (ii) 376 cm³,   (iii) (a) 60° (b) 64° (c) 58°
Question 8.
(i) {0, 1, 2, 3, 4}   (ii) 20,   (iii) (a) $\frac{2}{1}$ (b) $\frac{1}{3}$ (c) 12 cm
Question 9.
(i) $x = 20$,   (ii) (a) 58 marks (b) 72 marks (c) 72 (d) 92
Question 10.
(i)$x = \pm 2$,   (iii) 64.95 m, 37.50 m from one lamp - posts

MATHEMATICS

Maximum Marks: 80

Time allowed: Two and a half hours

Answers to this Paper must be written on the paper provided separately.

You will not be allowed to write during first 15 minutes.

This time is to be spent in reading the question paper.

The time given at the head of this Paper is the time allowed for writing the answers.

Attempt all questions from Section _A_ and any four questions from Section _B_.

The intended marks for questions or parts of questions are given in brackets [].

SECTION – A (40 Marks)

(Attempt all questions from this section)

Question 1. [15]

Chose the correct answers to the questions from the given options:

(i) The cost of some financial services is given below in the same city. Cost of services: Rs. 500, Rs. 700, Rs. 1200, and Rs. 600. If the rate of GST is 12%, then the amount of GST on the above services:

(a) Rs. 180

(b) Rs. 360

(c) Rs. 3360

(d) Rs. 540

(ii) If $x = 1$ is a common root of the equations $ax^2 + ax + 3 = 0$ and $x^2 + x + b = 0$, then $ab =$

(a) 3.5

(b) 3

(c) 6

(d) -3

(iii) When divided by $x-3$ the polynomials $x^3 - px^2 + x + 6$ and $2x^3 - x^2 - (p+3)x - 6$ leave the same remainder. Find the value of $'p'$.

(a) -1

(b) 2

(c) 1

(d) 3

(iv) If $2\begin{bmatrix} 3 & x \\ 0 & 1 \end{bmatrix} + 3\begin{bmatrix} 1 & 3 \\ y & 2 \end{bmatrix} = \begin{bmatrix} 9 & -7 \\ 15 & 8 \end{bmatrix}$, find x and y.

(a) $x = -8, y = 5$

(b) $x = 8, y = 5$

(c) $x = 4, y = 5$

(d) $x = 8, y = 7$

(v) The 21*st* term of the A.P. whose first two terms are -3 and 4 respectively, is

(a) 77

(b) 137

(c) 143

(d) -143

(vi) $P(0,5)$ is invariant when reflected in an axis. Name the axis.

(a) x-axis

(b) both a and b axis

(c) $y -$ axis

(d) None

(vii) In the given figure, if $\angle ADE = \angle ABC$, then CE is equal to:

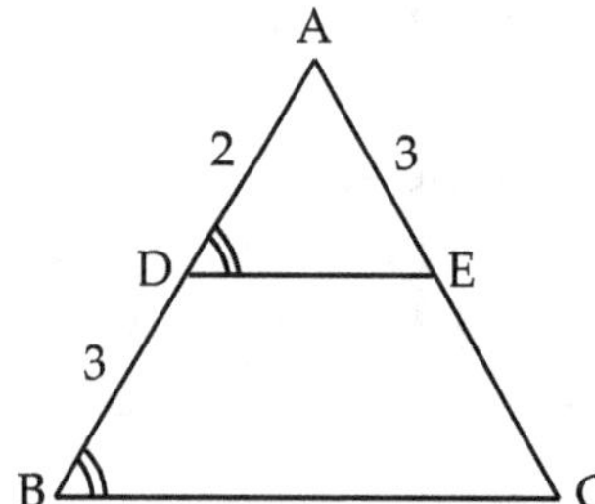

(a) 2

(b) 5

(c) 4.5

(d) 3

(viii) The total surface area of a right circular cone of radius 5cm is $90\pi\,cm^2$. Its slant height is:

(a) 13cm

(b) 14cm

(c) 12cm

(d) 11cm

(ix) Given $P = \{x: 5 < 2x - 1 < 11, x \in R\}$, $Q = \{x : -1 < 3 + 4x < 23, x \in I\}$. Where $R =$ real numbers, $I =$ integers. Write down the element. $P \cap Q$

(a) $\{-1, 0, 1, 2, 3, 4, 5, 6\}$

(b) $\{4\}$

(c) $\{3, 4, 5\}$

(d) $\{1, 2, 3, 4, 5\}$

(x) If $P(E)$ denotes the probability of an event K, then
    (a) $0 \leq P(E) \geq 1$
    (b) $0 \leq P(E) \leq 1$
    (c) $0 < P(E) \geq 1$
    (d) $-1 \leq P(E) \geq 1$

(xi) Find the value of k for which the lines $kx - 5y + 4 = 0$ and $4x - 2y + 5 = 0$ are perpendicular to each other.
    (a) $-\dfrac{2}{5}$
    (b) $\dfrac{5}{2}$
    (c) $-\dfrac{5}{2}$
    (d) 5

(xii) In the figure, chords AB and CD when extended meet at X. Given AB = 4cm, BX = 6cm, XD = 5cm, calculate the length of the CD.

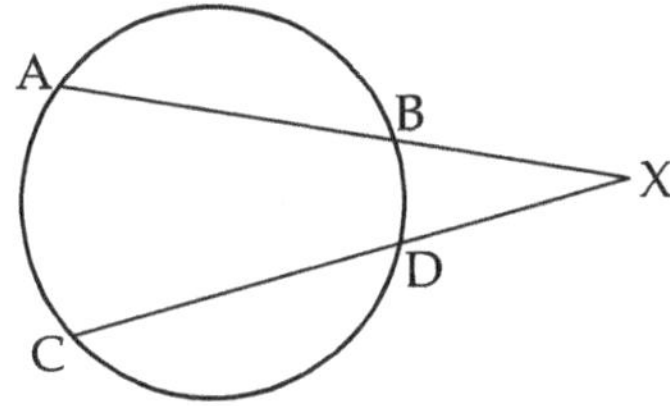

    (a) 5cm
    (b) 6cm
    (c) 7cm
    (d) 7.5cm

(xiii) If the height and length of the shadow of a man are the same, then the angle of elevation of the sun is:
    (a) 30°
    (b) 60°
    (c) 45°
    (d) 15°

(xiv) Mid value of class intervals is called:
    (a) Class mark
    (b) Assumed mean
    (c) Class height
    (d) Adjustment factor

(xv) If the first term of an A.P. is p and the common difference is q, its 10th term is :
    (a) $p + 9q$
    (b) $p + q$

(c) $p + 10q$

(d) $9p + q$

Question 2.

(i)   If x, y, z are continued proportion, prove that: $\dfrac{(x+y)^2}{(y+z)^2} = \dfrac{x}{z}$ [4]

(ii) Mr. Gupta opened a recurring deposit account in a bank for 2 years. At the time of maturity, he got Rs. 67,500 as maturity value and Rs. 7500 as interest. Find: [4]
(a) The monthly installment was deposited by Mr. Gupta.
(b) The rate of interest per annum.

(iii) Prove the identity:sin A(1 + tan A) + cos A(1 + cot A) = sec A + cosec A   [4]

Question 3.

(i)   A conical tent is to accommodate 77 persons. Each person must have $16m^3$ of air to breathe. Given the radius of the tent as $7m$ find the height of the tent and its curved surface area.
   [4]

(ii) The co-ordinates of the centroid of a triangle PQR are (4,3). If A = (1,3), B = (4, b) and C = $(a, 1)$; calculate the values of 'a' and 'b'.   [4]

(iii) Use graph paper for this question. (Take 10 small divisions = 1 unit on both axes).
P and Q have co-ordinates $(0, 5)$ and $(-2, 4)$.   [5]
(a) P is invariant when reflected in an axis. Name the axis.
(b) Find the image of Q on reflection in the axis found in (i).
(c) $(0, k)$ on reflection in the origin is invariant. Write the value of k.
(d) Write the co-ordinates of the image of Q, obtained by reflecting it in the origin followed by a reflection in the x-axis.

SECTION – B (40 Marks)
(Attempt any four questions from this section)

Question 4.

(i)   A shopkeeper bought a product at Rs. 12000 and then sold it to a customer at a profit of Rs. 4000. If the rate of GST is 18%, find: [3]
(a) SGST is paid by the shopkeeper.
(b) Tax received by central govt. on this whole transaction.
(c) Payment made by a customer (inclusive of tax) to buy this product.

(ii) Solve the following quadratic equation using the factorization method:
$$x^2 - 10x - 24 = 0$$
   [3]

(iii) Find the mode of the following data: **[4]**

Marks	$50 - 60$	$60 - 70$	$70 - 80$	$80 - 90$	$90 - 100$
No. of students	3	12	32	20	6

Question 5.

(i) Let $M \times \begin{bmatrix} 1 & 1 \\ 0 & 2 \end{bmatrix} = [1 \quad 2]$ where M is a matrix? **[3]**

(a) State the order of the matrix M.

(b) Find the matrix M.

(ii) In the adjoining figure, CBA is secant and CD is tangent to the circle. If AB = 7 cm and BC = 9 cm, then **[3]**

(a) Prove that $\Delta ACD \sim \Delta DCB$

(b) Find the length of CD.

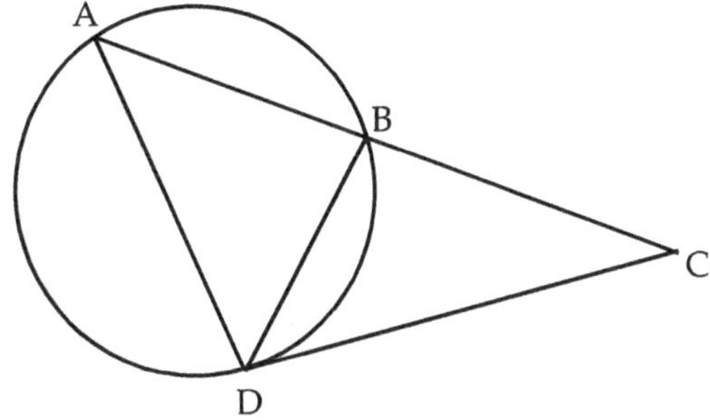

(iii) Using the Factor Theorem, show that:

$(x - 3)$ is a factor of $x^3 - 7x^2 + 15x - 9$. Hence, factorize the expression $x^3 - 7x^2 + 15x - 9$ completely. **[4]**

Question 6.

(i) $P\,(3, 4), Q\,(7, -2)$, and $R\,(-2, -1)$ are the vertices of triangle PQR. Write down the equation of the median of the triangle, through R. Also find the co-ordinates of the centroid of triangle PQR. **[3]**

(ii) Show that: $\dfrac{\sqrt{1-\cos A}}{\sqrt{1+\cos A}} = \dfrac{\sin A}{1+\cos A}$ **[3]**

(iii) If the sum of three numbers in A.P. is 21 and their product is 231, find the numbers. **[4]**

Question 7.

(i) A card is drawn at random from a well-shuffled deck of playing cards. Find the probability that the card drawn is: **[3]**

(a) A card of spades or an ace,

(b) A red king,

(c) Either a king or a queen,

(d) Neither a king nor a queen.

(ii) An iron sphere of diameter 12cm is dropped into a cylindrical can of diameter 24 cm containing water. Find the rise in the level of water when the sphere is completely immersed.

[3]

(iii) In the given figure PQ is a tangent to the circle at A. AB and AD are bisectors of $\angle CAQ$ and $\angle PAC$. If $\angle BAQ = 30°$, prove that: **[4]**

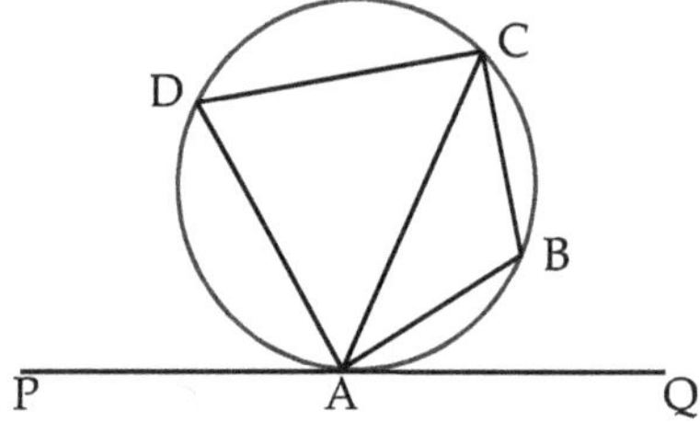

(a) BD is the diameter of the circle.

(b) ABC is an isosceles triangle.

Question 8.

(i) Solve the following inequation and represent the solution set on the number line.

$$-3 < -\frac{1}{2} - \frac{2x}{3} \leq \frac{5}{6}, x \in N.$$

[3]

(ii) In the following frequency distribution $\sum f = 50$ and mean $= 143$. Find the missing frequency $f1$ and $f2$

Class	$0 - 50$	$50 - 100$	$100 - 150$	$150 - 200$	$200 - 250$	$250 - 300$
Frequency	4	$f1$	$f2$	13	6	3

(iii) In the given figure, ABCD is a parallelogram, and AP: PB = 3: 5. Calculate: **[4]**
(a) BN: ND
(b) PN: BC

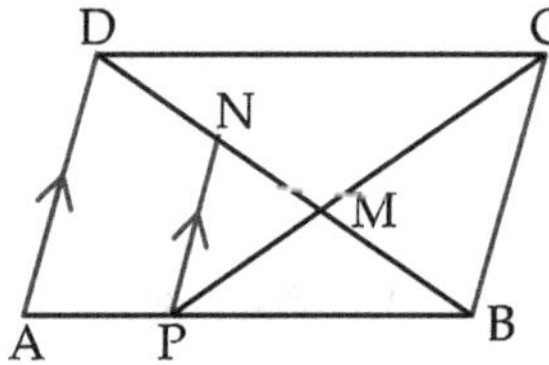

Question 9.

(i) The sum of the reciprocals of Rehman's ages (in years) 3 years ago and 5 years from now is 1/3. Find his present age. **[4]**

(ii) The mean of the following numbers is 68. Find the value of ' x '. $45, 2, 60, \ x, 69, 70, 26, 81$ and 94. Hence estimate the median. **[3]**

(iii) A toy is in the form of a cone mounted on a hemisphere of diameter 7cm. The total height of the toy is 15.5cm. Find the volume and the total surface area of the toy. **[3]**

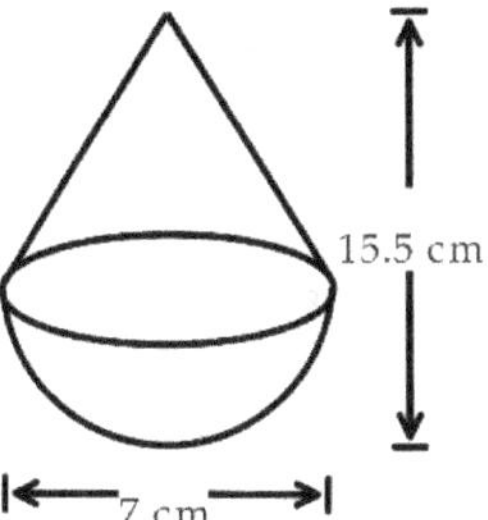

Question 10.

(i) If x, y, z are continued proportions, prove that: $\dfrac{(x+y)^2}{(y+z)^2} = \dfrac{x}{z}$ **[3]**

(ii) In triangle ABC, $\angle ABC = 90°$, side AB = 6cm, side BC = 7.2cm, and BD are perpendicular to side AC. Draw the circumcircle of triangle BDC and then state the length of the radius of this circumcircle drawn. **[3]**

(iii) A boy 2 m tall is standing at some distance from a 30 m tall building. The angle of elevation from his eyes to the top of the building increased from 30° to 60° as he walks toward the building. Find the distance he welded towards the building. **[4]**

Answers

Question 1.

(i)b ,(ii)b ,(iii)c,(iv)a ,(v)b ,(vi)c ,(vii)c,(viii) a, (ix)b, (x)b, (xi)c, (xii)c, (xiii)c, (xiv)a, (xv)a

Question 2.

(ii) Rs. 2500, 12%

Question 3.

(i) $h = 24m$, $550\ cm^2$, (ii) 7, 5 , (iii) (a) y-axis (b) (2, 4) (c) $k = 0$ (d) (-2, 4)
(b) 1232 cm^2

Question 4.

(i) (a) Rs. 360 (b) Rs. 1440 (c) Rs. 1880, (ii) 12, -2, (iii) 76.75

Question 5.

(a) 1×2 (b) $M = \begin{bmatrix} 1 & \frac{1}{2} \end{bmatrix}$, (ii) (b) 12 cm, (iii) $(x-3)^2(x-1)$

Question 6.

(i) $2x - 7y - 3 = 0$, $\left(\frac{8}{3}, \frac{1}{3}\right)$, (iii) 3, 7, 11 or 11, 7, 3

Question 7.

(i) (a) $\frac{4}{13}$ (b) $\frac{1}{26}$ (c) $\frac{2}{13}$ (d) $\frac{11}{13}$, (ii) 2 cm

Question 8.

(i) {1, 2, 3} (ii)$f1 = 8$, $f2 = 16$, (iii) (a) 5:3 (b) 5:8

Question 9.

(i) 7 years, (ii) 115, 69, (iii)$214.5\ cm^2$,$243.33\ cm^3$

Question 10.

(iii) $\frac{56\sqrt{3}}{3}$ m

Maximum Marks: 80

Time allowed: Two and a half hours

Answers to this Paper must be written on the paper provided separately.

You will not be allowed to write during first 15 minutes.

This time is to be spent in reading the question paper.

The time given at the head of this Paper is the time allowed for writing the answers.

Attempt all questions from Section *A* and any four questions from Section *B*.

The intended marks for questions or parts of questions are given in brackets [].

SECTION-A (40 Marks)

(Attempt all questions from this section)

Question 1. [15]

Chose the correct answers to the questions from the given options:

(i) A dealer bought goods from a Manufacturer at Rs. 20000 and sells them to a wholesaler at some profit. If the total GST paid by the dealer is Rs. 900. Calculate the profit avail by the dealer. The rate of GST is 18%.

   (a) Rs. 2500

   (b) Rs. 2000

   (c) Rs. 5000

   (d) Rs. None of these

(ii) Which of the following is not a quadratic equation?

   (a) $2(x - 2)^2 = 4x^2 - 2x + 1$

   (b) $(\sqrt{2}x + \sqrt{3})^2 + x^2 = 3x^2 - 5x$

   (c) $2x - x^2 = x^2 - 5$

   (d) $(x^2 + 1)^2 = x^4 + 3 + 4x^2$

(iii) Find the remainder when $2x^3 - 3x^2 + 7x - 8$ is divided by $x - 1$.

   (a) 3

   (b) 1

   (c) 2

   (d) – 2

(iv) If $\begin{bmatrix} 4 & -2 \\ 6 & -2 \end{bmatrix} + 3A = \begin{bmatrix} -2 & -2 \\ -3 & -1 \end{bmatrix}$, then matrix A is:

   (a) $\begin{bmatrix} 2 & 1 \\ -3 & -1 \end{bmatrix}$

   (b) $\begin{bmatrix} -2 & 0 \\ 3 & 0 \end{bmatrix}$

(c) $\begin{bmatrix} -2 & 3 \\ 3 & -1 \end{bmatrix}$

(d) $\begin{bmatrix} -2 & 0 \\ -3 & -1 \end{bmatrix}$

(v) The sum of all natural numbers from 1 to 100 is:
  (a) 4050
  (b) 5050
  (c) 6050
  (d) 7050

(vi) The point $P(5, -3)$ is reflected in the point $Q(2,2)$ to become a point R. Co-ordinates of R.
  (a) $(2,0)$
  (b) $(5,2)$
  (c) $(1,7)$
  (d) $(-1,7)$

(vii) In the following figure, if DE || BC, then x equals:

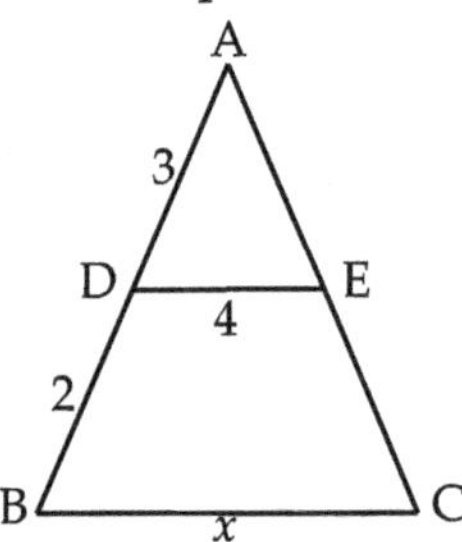

  (a) 3 cm
  (b) 2 cm
  (c) 4 cm
  (d) 6.7 cm

(viii) If a solid right circular cone of height 24cm and base radius 6cm is melted and recast in the shape of a sphere, then the radius of the sphere is:
  (a) 6 cm
  (b) 4 cm
  (c) 12cm
  (d) 8 cm

(ix) The solution set of the inequation $x - 3 \geq -5, x \in R$ is:
  (a) $\{x: x > -2, x \in R\}$
  (b) $\{x: x \leq -2, x \in R\}$
  (c) $\{x: x \geq -2, x \in R\}$
  (d) $\{-2, -1, 0, 1, 2\}$

(x) In a single throw of die, the probability of getting a multiple of 3 is

(a) $\frac{1}{2}$

(b) $\frac{1}{6}$

(c) $\frac{1}{3}$

(d) $\frac{2}{3}$

(xi) Given that the lines $\frac{y}{2} = x - p$ and $kx + 5 = 3y$ are parallel. Find the value of k

(a) 5

(b) $\frac{5}{2}$

(c) -6

(d) 6

(xii) In the given figure find TP if AT $= 16$cm and AB $= 12$cm.

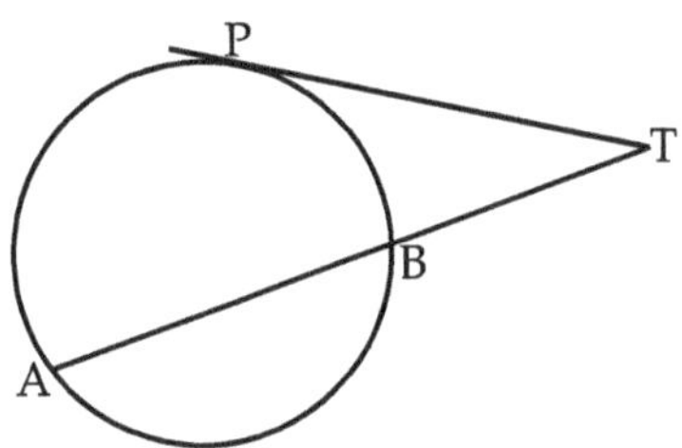

(a) 8 cm

(b) 7cm

(c) 6cm

(d) 12cm

(xiii) If a pole of the height of 6m casts a shadow of $2\sqrt{3}$m long on the ground, then the sun's elevation is:

(a) $30°$

(b) $60°$

(c) $45°$

(d) $90°$

(xiv) The following data have been arranged in ascending order. If their median is 66, find the value of x:

$35, 38, 52, 55, x, x + 2, 75, 83, 85, 100$

(a) 62

(b) 66

(c) 65

(d) 64

(xv) The sum of the first n terms of an A.P. is $2n^2 + 5n$. Then its nth term is:

(a) $4n + 3$

(b) $4n - 3$

(c) $3n - 4$

(d) $3n + 4$

Question 2.

(i) If a, b, and c are in continued proportion, prove that $(a + b + c)(a - b + c) = a^2 + b^2 + c^2$ [4]

(ii) Prove the identity: $\dfrac{1+\sec A - \tan A}{1+\sec A + \tan A} = \dfrac{1 - \sin A}{\cos A}$ [4]

(iii) Beena has a cumulative deposit account of Rs 500 per month at 10% per annum simple interest. If she gets Rs 28900 at the time of maturity, find the total time for which the account was held. [4]

Question 3.

(i) The midpoint of the line segment AB shown in the diagram is $(4, -3)$. Write down the coordinates of A, B. [4]

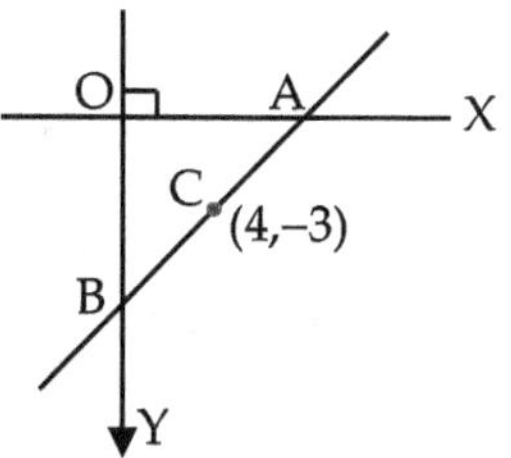

(ii) A hemispherical dome of a building needs to be painted. If the circumference of the base of the dome is 17.6m, find the cost of painting it. Given the cost of painting is Rs. 5 per 100cm². [4]

(iii) The triangle OAB is reflected in the origin O to triangle OA'B'. A' and B' have co-ordinates (-3, - 4) and (0, - 5) respectively. [5]
(a) Find the co-ordinates of A and B.
(b) Draw a diagram to represent the given information.
(c) What kind of figure is the quadrilateral ABA'B'?
(d) Find the co-ordinates of A", the reflection of A in the origin followed by a reflection in the y-axis.
(e) Find the co-ordinates of B", the reflection of B in the x-axis followed by a reflection in the origin.

SECTION – B (40 Marks)
(Attempt any four questions from this section)

Question 4.

(i) Mukherjee purchased a movie camera for Rs. 26550, which includes a 25% rebate on the list price and 18% tax (under GST) on the remaining price. Find the marked price of the camera. [3]

(ii) Solve the following equation and give your answer correct to 3 significant figures:

$$5x^2 - 3x - 4 = 0 \qquad [3]$$

(iii) A survey regarding the height (in cm) of 50 students of class X of a school was conducted and the following data was obtained.

Height (in cm)	$120 - 130$	$130 - 140$	$140 - 150$	$150 - 160$	$160 - 170$	Total
No. of students	2	8	12	20	8	50

Find the modal height. [4]

Question 5.

(i) Given $\begin{bmatrix} 2 & 1 \\ 1 & 2 \end{bmatrix} X = \begin{bmatrix} 4 \\ 5 \end{bmatrix}$. Write down [3]

(a) the order of the matrix X.

(b) the matrix X.

(ii) In the figure given below, chords AB and CD of a circle meet externally at O. Given that BO $= 4$ cm, CD $= 15$ cm, and DO $= 5$ cm. [3]

(a) Prove that triangles CAO and BDO are similar.

(b) Find AB.

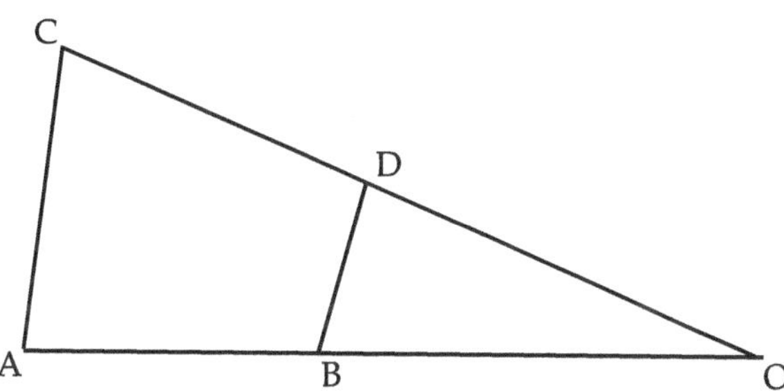

(iii) Using the Remainder Theorem, factorize each of the following completely:
$$3x^3 + 2x^2 - 19x + 6 \qquad [4]$$

Question 6.

(i) Find the equation of a line with x-intercept $= 5$ and passing through the point $(4, -7)$. [3]

(ii) Prove the identity: $(\cot A - \operatorname{cosec} A)^2 = \dfrac{1 - \cos A}{1 + \cos A}$ [3]

(iii) A manufacturer of TV sets produces 600 units in the third year and 700 units in the 7th year. Assuming that the production increases uniformly by a fixed number every year, find: [4]

(a) The production in the first year.

(b) The production in the 10th year.

(c) The total production in 7 years.

Question 7.

(i) A jar contains blue and green marble. The number of green marbles is 5 more than twice the number of blue. If the probability of drawing a blue one at random is 2/7, how many blue and green marbles are there in the jar? **[3]**

(ii) From a solid cylinder, whose height is 8cm and radius is 6cm, a conical cavity of the height of 8cm and with a base radius of 6cm is hollowed out. Find the volume of the remaining solid. Also, find the total surface area of the remaining solid. **[3]**

(iii) In the diagram given alongside, AC is the diameter of the circle, with center O. CD and BE are parallel. $\angle AOB = 80°$ and $\angle ACE = 10°$. **[4]**
Calculate:
(a) $\angle BEC$
(b) $\angle BCD$
(c) $\angle CED$

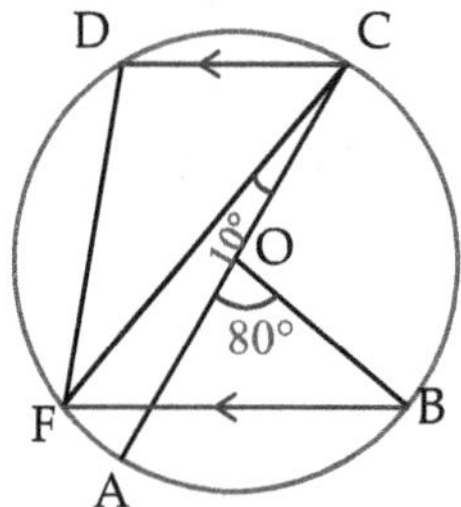

Question 8.

(i) Solve the following inequation and graph the solution on the number line:
$$-2\frac{2}{3} \le x + \frac{1}{3} < 3 + \frac{1}{3}, x \in \text{R}.$$
[3]

(ii) Calculate the mean for the following distribution: **[3]**

Pocket money (in Rs)	60	70	80	90	100	110	120
No. of students	2	6	13	22	24	10	3

(iii) In the following figure, DE ‖ OQ and DF ‖ OR and. **[4]**
(a) Show that EF ‖ QR.
(b) $\Delta PEF \sim \Delta PQR$
(c) If $\frac{PE}{EQ} = \frac{2}{3}$ and QR = 10 cm, find EF.

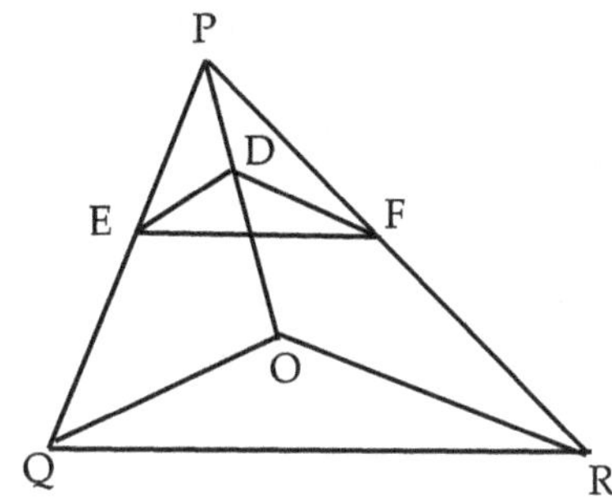

Question 9.

(i) A two-digit number is such that the product of the digits is 18. When 63 is subtracted from the number, the digits interchange their places. Find the number. **[4]**

(ii) Find the mode and median of the following frequency distribution. **[3]**

x	10	11	12	13	14	15
f	1	4	7	5	9	3

(iii) A wooden article was made by scooping out a hemisphere from each end of a solid cylinder, as shown in Fig. If the height of the cylinder is 10cm, and its base is of radius 3.5cm, find the total surface area of the article and volume (nearest integer) of the remaining solid.

[3]

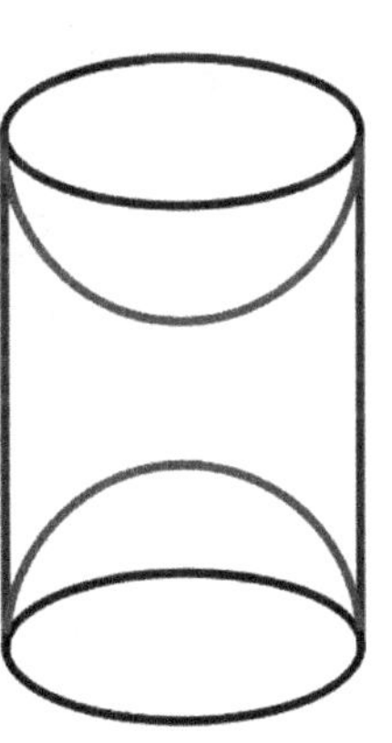

Question 10.

(i) Solve for x: $81\left(\dfrac{x-3}{x+3}\right)^3 = \dfrac{x+3}{x-3}$ **[3]**

(ii) Draw an inscribing circle of a regular hexagon of side 5.8cm. **[3]**

(iii) A man standing on the deck of the ship which is 10 m above sea level observes the angle of elevation of the top of the cloud as 30° and the angle of depression of its reflection in the sea was found to be 60° .Find the height of the cloud and also the distance of the cloud from the ship. **[4]**

Answers

Question 11.
(i)c ,(ii)b ,(iii)d ,(iv)d ,(v)b ,(vi)d ,(vii)d , (viii)a ,(ix)c , (x)c , (xi)d , (xii)a , (xiii)b , (xiv)c , (xv)a]

Question 12.
(iii)4 years

Question 13.
(i) (8,0), (0, –6), (ii) Rs. 24640, (iii) (a) A'(3, 4), B'(0, 5) (c) Rectangle (d) (3, -4) (e) (0, 5)

Question 14.
(i) Rs. 30000, (ii) 1.24, -0.643, (iii) 154 cm

Question 15.
(i) (a) 2×1 (b) $X = \begin{bmatrix} 1 \\ 2 \end{bmatrix}$, (ii) 21 cm, (iii) $(x-2)(x+3)(3x-1)$

Question 16.
(i) $7x - y - 35 = 0$, (iii) (a) 550 units (b) 775 units (c) 4375 units

Question 17.
(i) Blue = 10, Green = 25, (ii) $603\frac{3}{7}$ cm^3,$603\frac{3}{7}$ cm^2 , (iii) (i) 50°(ii) 100°(iii) 30°

Question 18.
(i) $\{x : x \in R, -3 \leq x < 3\}$ (ii) 92.75, (iii) (c) 4 cm

Question 19.
(i) 92, (ii) 14, 13, (iii) 374 cm^2,205 cm^3

Question 20.
(i) $x = 6, \frac{3}{2}$, (iii) height of the cloud = 20 m, distance = $10\sqrt{3}$

PREVIOUS YEAR PAPER

MATHEMATICS

Maximum Marks: 80
Time allowed: One and a half hours
Answers to this Paper must be written on the paper provided separately.
You will not be allowed to write during first 15 minutes.
This time is to be spent in reading the question paper.
The time given at the head of this Paper is the time allowed for writing the answers.

Attempt all questions from Section *A* and any four questions from Section *B*.
The intended marks for questions or parts of questions are given in brackets [].

SECTION A (40 Marks)
(Attempt all questions from this section)

Question 1.

(i) Solve the following in-equation and write down the solution set:
$11x - 4 < 15x + 4 \leq 13x + 14, x \in W$
Represent the solution set on the number line. [3]

(ii) A man invests Rs. 4500 in shares of a company that is paying a 7.5% dividend. If Rs. 100 shares are available at a discount of 10%. Find:
(a) A number of shares he purchases.
(b) His annual income.

[3]

(iii) In a class of 40 students, marks obtained by the students in a class test (out of 10) are given below: Calculate the following for the given distribution: [4]

Marks	1	2	3	4	5	6	7	8	9	10
Number of students	1	2	3	3	6	10	5	4	3	3

(a) Median
(b) Mode

Answer:

(i) Given $11x - 4 < 15x + 4 \leq 13x + 14, x \in W$
Case 1: $11x - 4 < 15x + 4$
$\Rightarrow -4x < 8 \Rightarrow -x < 2 \; or \; x > -2$
Case 2: $15x + 4 \leq 13x + 14$
$\Rightarrow 2x \leq 10 \Rightarrow x \leq 5$
$\therefore -2 < x \leq 5, x \in W$
$\therefore$ solution $x \in [0, 1, 2, 3, 4, 5]$

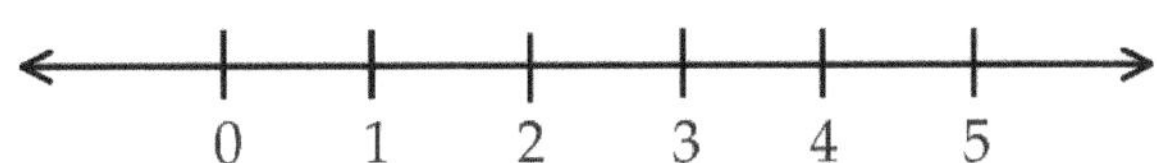

(ii) Out of syllabus

(iii) **(a)**

Marks	No. of students	Cumulative Frequency
1	1	1
2	2	3
3	3	6
4	3	9
5	6	15
6	10	25
7	5	30
8	4	34
9	3	37
10	3	40
Total	40	

Total number of students $= 40$ which is even

$$\text{Median} = \frac{1}{2}\left[\left(\frac{n}{2}\right)^{th} \text{term} + \left(\frac{n}{2} + 1\right)^{th} \text{term}\right]$$

$$= \frac{1}{2}\left[\left(\frac{40}{2}\right)^{th} \text{term} + \left(\frac{40}{2} + 1\right)^{th} \text{term}\right]$$

$$= \frac{1}{2}\left[20^{th} \text{term} + 21^{st} \text{term}\right]$$

$$= \frac{1}{2}[6 + 6]$$

$$= 6 \text{ marks}$$

Which is between 15 and 25. Therefore Median $= 6$

(a) The mode frequency of 6 is the highest. Therefore Mode $= 6$

Question 2.

(i) Using the factor theorem, show that $(x - 2)$ is a factor of $x^3 + x^2 - 4x - 4$. Hence factorize the polynomial completely. **[3]**

(ii) Prove that: $(\text{cosec } \theta - \sin \theta)(\sec \theta - \cos \theta)(\tan \theta + \cot \theta) = 1$ **[3]**

(iii) In an Arithmetic Progression (A.P.) the fourth and sixth terms are 8 and 14 respectively. Find the: **[4]**
(a) First term
(b) Common difference
(c) Sum of the first 20 terms.

Answer:

(i) $f(x) = x^3 + x^2 - 4x - 4$

Let

$$x - 2 = 0 \Rightarrow x = 2$$
$$\therefore\ f(2) = (2)^3 + (2)^2 - 4(2) - 4$$
$$\Rightarrow f(2) = 8 + 4 - 8 - 4 = 0$$
$$f(2) = 0$$

Therefore $(x - 2)$ is a factor of $f(x)$

$$
\begin{array}{r}
x^2 + 3x + 2 \\
x - 2 \overline{)\ x^3 + x^2 - 4x - 4} \\
x^3 - 2x^2 \\
\hline
3x^2 - 4x - 4 \\
3x^2 - 6x \\
\hline
2x - 4 \\
2x - 4 \\
\hline
\text{X}
\end{array}
$$

Hence $x^3 + x^2 - 4x - 4 = (x - 2)(x^2 + 3x + 2)$
$$\Rightarrow x^3 + x^2 - 4x - 4 = (x - 2)(x + 2)(x + 1)$$

(ii) To prove-($(\text{cosec } \theta - \sin \theta)(\sec \theta - \cos \theta)(\tan \theta + \cot \theta) = 1$

$$\text{LHS} = (\text{cosec } \theta - \sin \theta)(\sec \theta - \cos \theta)(\tan \theta + \cot \theta)$$
$$= \left(\frac{1}{\sin \theta} - \sin \theta\right)\left(\frac{1}{\cos \theta} - \cos \theta\right)\left(\frac{\sin \theta}{\cos \theta} + \frac{\cos \theta}{\sin \theta}\right)$$
$$= \left(\frac{1 - \sin^2 \theta}{\sin \theta}\right) \cdot \left(\frac{1 - \cos^2 \theta}{\cos \theta}\right) \cdot \left(\frac{\sin^2 \theta + \cos^2 \theta}{\sin \theta \cdot \cos \theta}\right)$$
$$= \left(\frac{\cos^2 \theta}{\sin \theta}\right) \cdot \left(\frac{\sin^2 \theta}{\cos \theta}\right) \cdot \left(\frac{1}{\sin \theta \cdot \cos \theta}\right)$$
$$= 1 = \text{RHS. Hence proved.}$$

(iii) Let the first term of the sequence is a and the common difference is d.

$$a_4 => a + 3d = 8 \qquad \dots\dots\dots\dots(i)$$
$$a_6 => a + 5d = 14 \qquad \dots\dots\dots\dots(ii)$$

Solving (i) and (ii) we get $d = 3$ and $a = -1$

Therefore

(a) First term $(a) = -1$

(b) Common difference $(d) = 3$

(c) Sum of the first 20 terms $= S_n = \frac{n}{2}[2a + (n - 1)d]$
$$= \frac{20}{2}[-2 + (20 - 1)d] = 10 \times 55 = 550$$

Question 3.

(i) Simplify: $\sin A \begin{bmatrix} \sin A & -\cos A \\ \cos A & \sin A \end{bmatrix} + \cos A \begin{bmatrix} \cos A & \sin A \\ -\sin A & \cos A \end{bmatrix}$ **[3]**

(ii) M and N are two points on the X-axis and Y-axis respectively. P(3,2) divides the line segment MN in the ratio of 2 : 3. Find: **[3]**

(a) The coordinates of M and N

(b) The slope of the line MN.

(iii) A solid metallic sphere of radius 6cm is melted and made into a solid cylinder of height 32cm. Find the: **[4]**

(a) Radius of the cylinder

(b) Curved surface area of the cylinder [take $\pi = 3.1$]

Answer:

(i) Given $\sin A \begin{bmatrix} \sin A & -\cos A \\ \cos A & \sin A \end{bmatrix} + \cos A \begin{bmatrix} \cos A & \sin A \\ -\sin A & \cos A \end{bmatrix}$

$$\Rightarrow \begin{bmatrix} \sin^2 A & -\sin A\cos A \\ \sin A\cos A & \sin^2 A \end{bmatrix} + \begin{bmatrix} \cos^2 A & \cos A\sin A \\ -\cos A\sin A & \cos^2 A \end{bmatrix}$$

$$\Rightarrow \begin{bmatrix} \sin^2 A + \cos^2 A & -\sin A\cos A + \cos A\sin A \\ \sin A\cos A - \cos A\sin A & \sin^2 A + \cos^2 A \end{bmatrix}$$

$$\Rightarrow \begin{bmatrix} 1 & 0 \\ 0 & 1 \end{bmatrix}$$

(ii) Let coordinates of M is $(x, 0)$ and N is $(0, y)$. Point P divides MN in a 2 : 3 ratio

$$\therefore 3 = \frac{3x_1 + 2 \times 0}{3 + 2} \Rightarrow 3x_1 = 15 \Rightarrow x = 5$$

And $\qquad 2 = \frac{3 \times 0 + 2 \times y_2}{3 + 2} \Rightarrow 3y_2 = 10 \Rightarrow y = 5$

Therefore

(a) The coordinates of M(5,0) and N(0,5)

(b) Slope of line MN $= \frac{(y_2 - y_1)}{(x_2 - x_1)} = \frac{0 - 5}{5 - 0} = -1$

(iii) Let the radius of the sphere is r_1 and the radius of a cylinder is r_2 and the height of the cylinder is h.

Therefore, Volume of sphere = Volume of cylinder

$$\Rightarrow \frac{4}{3}\pi r_1^3 = \pi r_2^2 h$$

$$\Rightarrow \frac{4}{3}(6^3) = r_2^2(32)$$

$$\Rightarrow r_2^2 = \frac{12 \times 6}{8} = 9$$

$$\Rightarrow r_2 = 3$$

Therefore, Radius of the cylinder is 3cm

Curved surface area $= 2\pi r h = 2 \times 3.14 \times 3 \times 32 = 595.20 \text{ cm}^2$

Question 4.

(i) The following numbers, $K + 3, K + 2, 3K - 7$, and $2K - 3$ are in proportion. Find K. **[3]**

(ii) Solve for x the quadratic equation x² − 4x − 8 = 0. Give your answer correct to three significant figures **[3]**

(iii) Use a ruler and compass only for answering this question. **[4]**
Draw a circle of radius 4cm. Mark the center as O. Mark a point P outside the circle at a distance of 7cm from the center. Construct two tangents to the circle from the external point P. Measure and write down the length of any one tangent.

Answer:

(i) Given $K + 3, K + 2, 3K − 7,$ and $2K − 3$ are in proportion.

$$\Rightarrow \frac{K + 3}{K + 2} = \frac{3K − 7}{2K − 3}$$

$$\Rightarrow (K + 3)(2K − 3) = (3K − 7)(K + 2)$$

$$\Rightarrow 2K^2 + 6K − 3K − 9 = 3K^2 − 7K + 6K − 14$$

$$\Rightarrow 2K^2 + 3K − 9 − 3K^2 − K − 14$$

$$\Rightarrow K^2 − 4K − 5 = 0$$

$$\Rightarrow K^2 − 5K + K − 5 = 0$$

$$\Rightarrow K(K − 5) + (K − 5) = 0$$

$$\Rightarrow (K − 5)(K + 1) = 0$$

$$\Rightarrow K = 5 \; or \; K = −1$$

(ii) Given $x^2 − 4x − 8 = 0$

Comparing the above equation by $ax^2 + bx + c = 0$

$a = 1, b = −4, c = −8$

$$x = \frac{−b \pm \sqrt{b^2 − 4ac}}{2a}$$

$$x = \frac{4 \pm \sqrt{(−4)^2 − 4(1)(−8)}}{2(1)}$$

$$x = \frac{4 \pm \sqrt{16 + 32}}{2}$$

$$x = \frac{4 \pm \sqrt{48}}{2}$$

$$x = \frac{4 \pm 6.928}{2}$$

$$x = 5.46 \; or \; x = −1.46$$

(iii) **(a)** Draw a line segment OP = 7cm

With center O and radius 4cm, draw a circle.

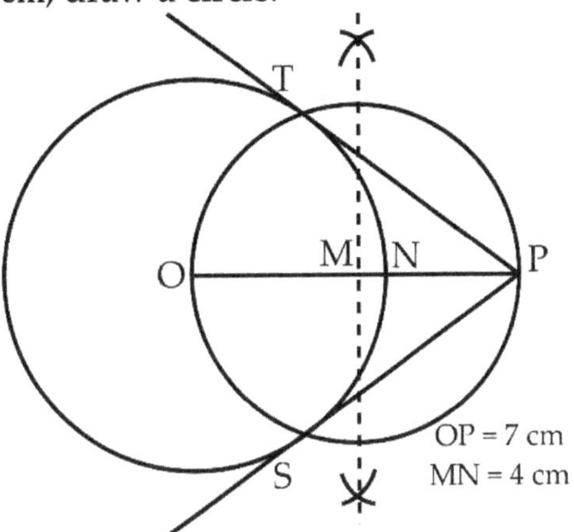

(b) Draw the midpoint of OP.

With center M and diameter OP, draw a circle that intersects the circle at T and S.

Joint PT and PS

PT and PS are the required tangents for measuring the length of PT = PS = 5.74cm (appr.)

SECTION B (40 Marks)

(Attempt any four questions from this Section)

Question 5.

(i) There are 25 discs numbered 1 to 25. They are put in a closed box and shaken thoroughly. A disc is drawn at random from the box. Find the probability that the number on the disc is:

(a) An odd number

(b) Divisible by 2 and 3 both.

(c) A number less than 16. [3]

(ii) Rekha opened a recurring deposit account for 20 months. The rate of interest is 9% per annum and Rekha receives Rs. 441 as interest at the time of maturity. Find the amount Rekha deposited each month. [3]

(iii) Use a graph sheet for this question. Take 1cm = 1 unit along both x and y-axis. [4]

(a) Plot the following points: $A(0, 5), B(3, 0), C(1, 0)$ and $D(1, -5)$

(b) Reflect the points B, C, and D on the y-axis and name them as B', C' and D' respectively.

(c) Write down the coordinates of B', C'' and D'.

(d) Join the points $A, B, C, D, D', C', B', A$ in order and give a name to the closed figure $ABCDD'C'B'$.

Answer:

(i) Total number of cases = 25

(a) An odd number $\{1, 3, 5, 7, 9, 11, 13, 15, 17, 19, 21, 23, 25\}$

Therefore, the probability of an odd number $= \dfrac{13}{25}$

(b) Divisible by 2 and 3 both $\{6, 12, 18, 24\}$

Probability of the number divisible by 2 and 3 both $= \dfrac{4}{25}$

(c) Probability of a number less than $16 = \dfrac{15}{25} = \dfrac{3}{5}$

(ii) Let the monthly installment i.e $P = Rs. \, x$

Since $n = 20$ months and $r = 9\%$

$$\text{Therefore Interest} \quad = P \times \frac{n(n+1)}{2\times 12} \times \frac{r}{100}$$

$$441 = \frac{x \times 20(20+1)}{2\times 12} \times \frac{9}{100}$$

$$441 = \frac{x \times 20 \times 21}{2 \times 12} \times \frac{9}{100}$$

$$441 = \frac{x \times 5 \times 7}{2} \times \frac{9}{100}$$

$$\Rightarrow 441 = 1.575x \Rightarrow x = Rs.\,280$$

(iii) Please refer to the graph below for answers. the shape of the figure is "Arrowhead".

    (a) $B'(-3, 0)$, $C'(-1, 0)$ and $D'(-1, -5)$

    (b) Arrowhead

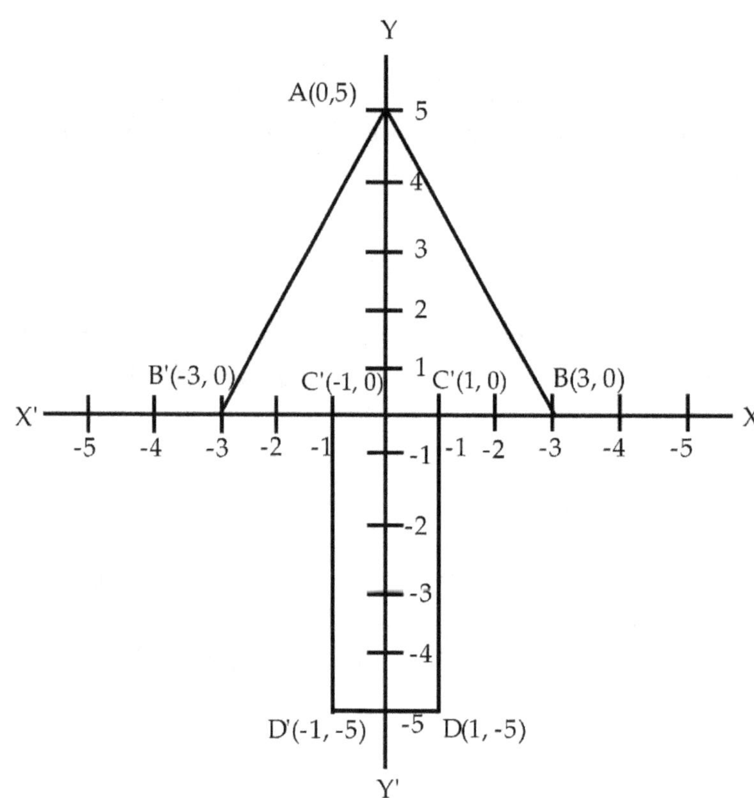

Question 6.

(i) In the given figure, $\angle PQR = \angle PST = 90°$, $PQ = 5$cm and $PS = 2$ cm . **[3]**

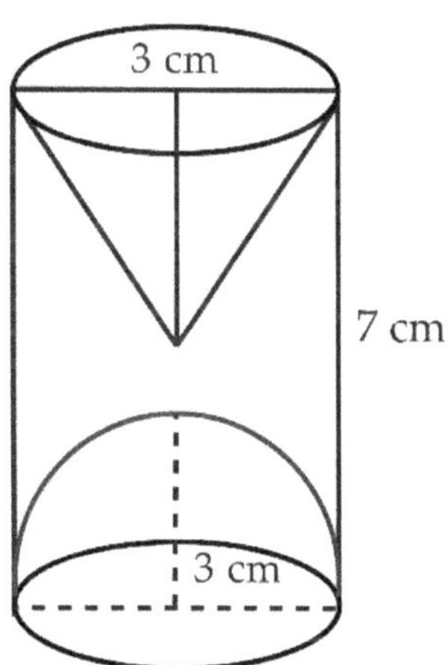

(a) Prove that $\triangle$ PQR $\sim \triangle$ PST.
(b) Find Area of $\triangle$ PQR : Area of quadrilateral SRQT.

(ii) The first and last terms of a Geometrical Progression (G.P) are 3 and 96 respectively. If the common ratio is 2, find: **[3]**
(a) ' n ' the number of terms of the G.P.
(b) Sum of the n terms.

(iii) A hemispherical and a conical hole is scooped out of a solid wooden cylinder. Find the volume of the remaining solid where the measurements are as follows: **[4]**
The height of the solid cylinder is 7cm, and the radius of each hemisphere, cone, and cylinder is 3cm. The height of a cone is 3cm Give your answer correct to the nearest whole number. Take $\pi = \dfrac{22}{7}$

Answer:

 (i)

  (a) To prove $\triangle$ POR $\sim \triangle$ PST
   Consider $\triangle$ PQR and $\triangle$ PST
   $\angle POR = \angle PST = 90°$ (Given)
   $\angle P$ is common
   $\therefore \triangle$ PQR $\sim \triangle$ PST (By AA criterian)
  (b) Out of syllabus

(ii) Out of syllabus

(iii) Required volume = Volume of a cylinder − (Volume of the hemisphere + Volume of cone)

Volume of cone $= \frac{1}{3}\pi r^2 h - \frac{1}{3} \times \pi \times \{3\}^2 \times 3 = 9\pi cm^3$

Volume of hemisphere $= \frac{2}{3}\pi r^3 = \frac{2}{3} \times \pi \times 3^3 - 18\pi cm^3$

Volume of cylinder $= \pi r^2 h = \pi \times 3^3 \times 7 = 63\pi cm^3$

Therefore, required volume $= 63\pi - 18\pi - 9\pi = 36\pi = 36 \times \frac{22}{7} = 113.14 cm^3 = 113\ cm^3$

Question 7.

(i) In the given figure AC s a tangent to the circle with center Q. If $\angle. ADB = 55^o$, find x and y. Give reasons for your answers. **[3]**

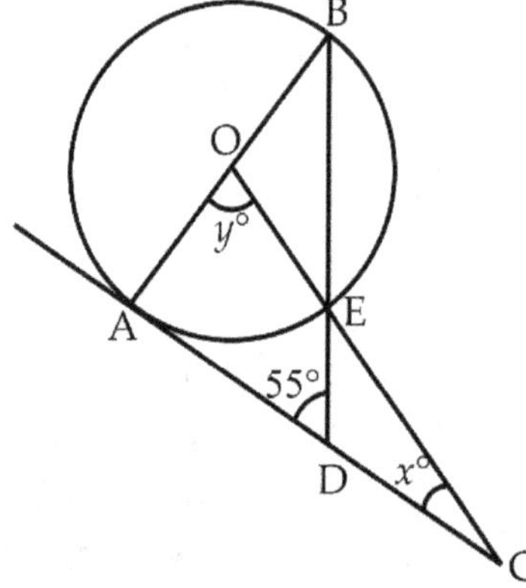

(ii) The model of a building is constructed with the scale factor of $1:30$
(a) If the height of the model is 80cm, find the 8ctual height of the building in meters.
(b) If the actual volume of a tank at the top of the building is $27m^3$, find the volume of the tank on the top of the model. **[3]**

(iii) Given $\begin{bmatrix} 4 & 2 \\ -1 & 1 \end{bmatrix} M = 6I$, where M a matrix and l is unit matrix of order 2x². **[4]**
(a) State the order of the Matrix M.
(b) Find the matrix M.

Answer:

(i)

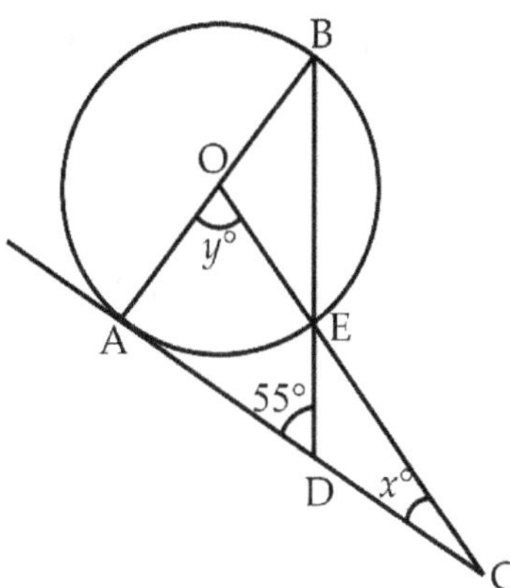

In $\triangle$ ABD, $\angle$BAD $= 90°$ [AB is diameter and angle on diameter is 90°]

$\therefore$ $\angle$ABD $+ \angle$BAD $+ \angle$ADB $= 180°$ [Angle sum property of a triangle]

$\therefore$ $\angle$ABD $+ 90° + 55° = 180°$

$\therefore$ $\angle$ABD $= 35°$

Also $\angle$AOE $= 2\angle$ABE $= 2\angle$ABD[angle at the center is double the angle in the remaining circconference]

$\Rightarrow y = 70°$

In $\triangle$ AOC.

$\angle$OAC $+ x + y = 180°$

$\therefore$ $90° + x + 70° = 180°$

$\therefore$ $90° + x + 70° = 180°$

$\Rightarrow x = 20°$

(ii) Out of syllabus

(iii) Given

(a) Let order of M is r×c

$$2 \times \boxed{2 = r} \times c = 2 \times 2$$

So order of   M $= 2 \times 2$

Let us assume M $= \begin{bmatrix} a & b \\ c & d \end{bmatrix}$

(b) $\therefore \begin{bmatrix} 4 & 2 \\ -1 & 1 \end{bmatrix}\begin{bmatrix} a & b \\ c & d \end{bmatrix} = \begin{bmatrix} 6 & 0 \\ 0 & 6 \end{bmatrix}$

$\Rightarrow \begin{bmatrix} 4a + 2c & 4b + 2d \\ -a + c & -b + d \end{bmatrix} = \begin{bmatrix} 6 & 0 \\ 0 & 6 \end{bmatrix}$

$\Rightarrow -a + c = 0 \Rightarrow a = c$

Similarly, $4b + 2d = 0 \Rightarrow d = -2b$

Now, $4a + 2c = 6 \Rightarrow 4a + 2a = 6 \Rightarrow 6a = 6 \Rightarrow a = 1$

also, $-b + d = 6 \Rightarrow -b + (-2b) = 6 \Rightarrow -3b = 6 \Rightarrow b = -2$

$\therefore$ $a = 1, b = -2, c = 1, d = 4$

$\therefore M = \begin{bmatrix} 1 & -2 \\ 1 & 4 \end{bmatrix}$

Question 8.

(i) The sum of the first three terms of an Arithmetic Progression (A.P.) is 42 and the product of the first and third terms is 52. Find the first term and the common difference. **[3]**

(ii) The vertices of an$\triangle$ ABC are A(3,8), B(−1,2), and C(6, −6) Find:
(a) Slope of BC.
(b) Equation of a line perpendicular to BC and passing through A. **[3]**

(iii) Using a ruler and a compass only construct a semi-circle with a diameter BC = 7cm. Locate a point A on the circumference of the semicircle such that A is equidistant from B and C. Complete the cyclic quadrilateral ABCD, such that D is equidistant from AB and BC. Measure $\angle$ADC and write it down. **[4]**

Answer:

(i) Let the three times terms of an A.P. be $(a - d), a, (a + d)$

Sum: $42 = (a - d) + a + (a + d) \Rightarrow 42 = 3a \Rightarrow a = 14$

Also
$$(a - d)(a + d) = 52$$
$$\Rightarrow a^2 - d^2 = 52$$
$$d^2 = a^2 - 52 = 196 - 52 = 144$$
$$\Rightarrow d = \pm 12$$

First term a = 14 and common difference $d = \pm 12$

(ii) Given A(3,8), B(−1,2), C(6, −6)

(a) Slope of BC Let us assume $= \dfrac{y_2 - y_1}{x_2 - x_1} = \dfrac{-6 - 2}{6 - (-1)} = -\dfrac{8}{7}$

(b) Slope of line perpendicular to Let us assume BC $= \dfrac{-1}{-\frac{1}{7}} = \dfrac{7}{8}$ $[m_1 \times m_2 = -1]$

So line passing through A(3, 8)

Required line is $y - y_1 = m(x - x_1)$

Let us assume $\Rightarrow y - 8 = \dfrac{7}{8}(x - 3)$
$$\Rightarrow 8y - 61 = 7x - 21$$
$$\Rightarrow 7x - 8y + 43 = 0$$

(iii) Draw a line segment BC = 7cm

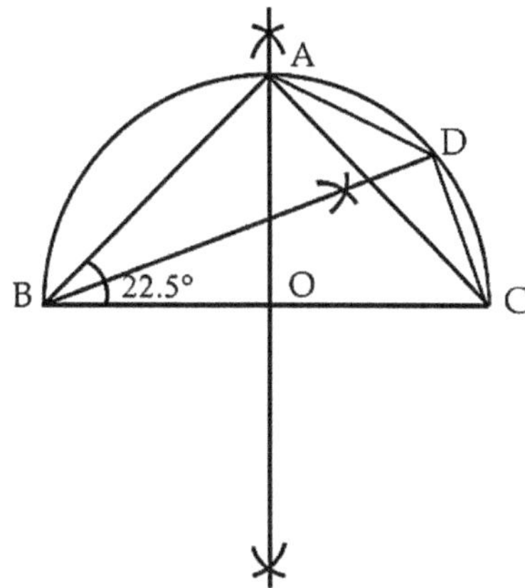

Taking the midpoint of BC as center O, draw a semi-circle with radius = of 3.5cm

Now, the semicircle circumscribes the △ ABC

Draw angle bisector of ∠ABC and make it intersect the semi-circle at D

Measure the angle ∠ADC which comes out to be 135°

Question 9.

(i) The data on the number of patients attending a hospital in a month is given below. Find the average (mean) number of patients attending the hospital in a month by using the shortcut method. Take the assumed mean as 45. Give your answer correct to 2 decimal places.   [3]

Number of Patients	$10-20$	$20-30$	$30-40$	$40-50$	$50-60$	$60-70$
Number of Days	5	2	7	9	2	5

(ii) Using properties of proportion solve for x, given $\dfrac{\sqrt{5x}+\sqrt{2x-6}}{\sqrt{5x}+\sqrt{2x-6}} = 4$ [3]

(iii) Sachin invests $Rs.\,8500$ in 10%, $Rs.\,100$ shares at $Rs.\,170$ He sells the shares when the price of each share rises by $Rs.\,30$. He invests the proceeds in 12% $Rs.\,100$ shares at $Rs.\,125$. Find: [4]

(a) The sale proceeds.

(b) The number of Rs. 125 shares he buys.

(c) The change in his annual income.

Answer:

(i)

Number of Patients	Number of Days (f_i)	Mid Value (x_i)	Assumed Mean $A = 45, d = x_i - A$	$f_i d_i$
$10-20$	5	15	-30	-150
$20-30$	2	25	-20	-40
$30-40$	7	35	-10	-70
$40-50$	9	45	0	0
$50-60$	2	55	10	20
$60-70$	5	65	20	100

Total	$\Sigma f_i = 30$			$\Sigma f_i d_i = -140$

$$\text{Mean} = A + \frac{\Sigma f_i d_i}{f_i} = 45 + \frac{-140}{30} = 45 - \frac{14}{3} = \frac{121}{3} = 40.33$$

(ii) Given $\dfrac{\sqrt{5x}+\sqrt{2x-6}}{\sqrt{5x}+\sqrt{2x-6}} = 4$

Using componendo and dividendo on both sides

$$\frac{(\sqrt{5x} + \sqrt{2x - 6}) + (\sqrt{5x} + \sqrt{2x - 6})}{\sqrt{5x} + \sqrt{2x - 6}) - (\sqrt{5x} + \sqrt{2x - 6})} = \frac{4 + 1}{4 - 1}$$

$$\frac{\sqrt{5x}}{\sqrt{2x - 6}} = \frac{5}{3}$$

On squaring both sides

$$\frac{5x}{2x - 6} = \frac{25}{9}$$

$$\Rightarrow 45x = 50x - 150$$

$$\Rightarrow 150 = 5x$$

$$\Rightarrow x = 30$$

(iii) Out of syllabus

Question 10.

(i) Use graph paper for this question. The marks obtained by 120 students in an English test are given below: **[6]**

Marks	0 − 10	10 − 20	20 − 30	30 − 40	40 − 50	50 − 60	60 − 70	70 − 80	80 − 90	90 − 100
No. of Students	5	6	16	22	26	18	11	6	4	3

Draw the ogive and hence, estimate:

(a) The median marks.

(b) The number of students who did not pass the test if the pass percentage was 50.

(c) The upper quartile marks.

(ii) A man observes the angle of elevation of the top of the tower to be 45°. He walks towards it in a horizontal line through its base. On covering 20m the angle of elevation changes to 60°. Find the height of the tower correct to 2 significant figures. **[4]**

Solution:

Class Interval	Frequency	Cumulative Frequency
0 − 10	5	5
10 − 20	9	14
20 − 30	16	30
30 − 40	22	52
40 − 50	26	78
50 − 60	18	96

$60 - 70$	11	107
$70 - 80$	6	113
$80 - 90$	4	117
$90 - 100$	3	120

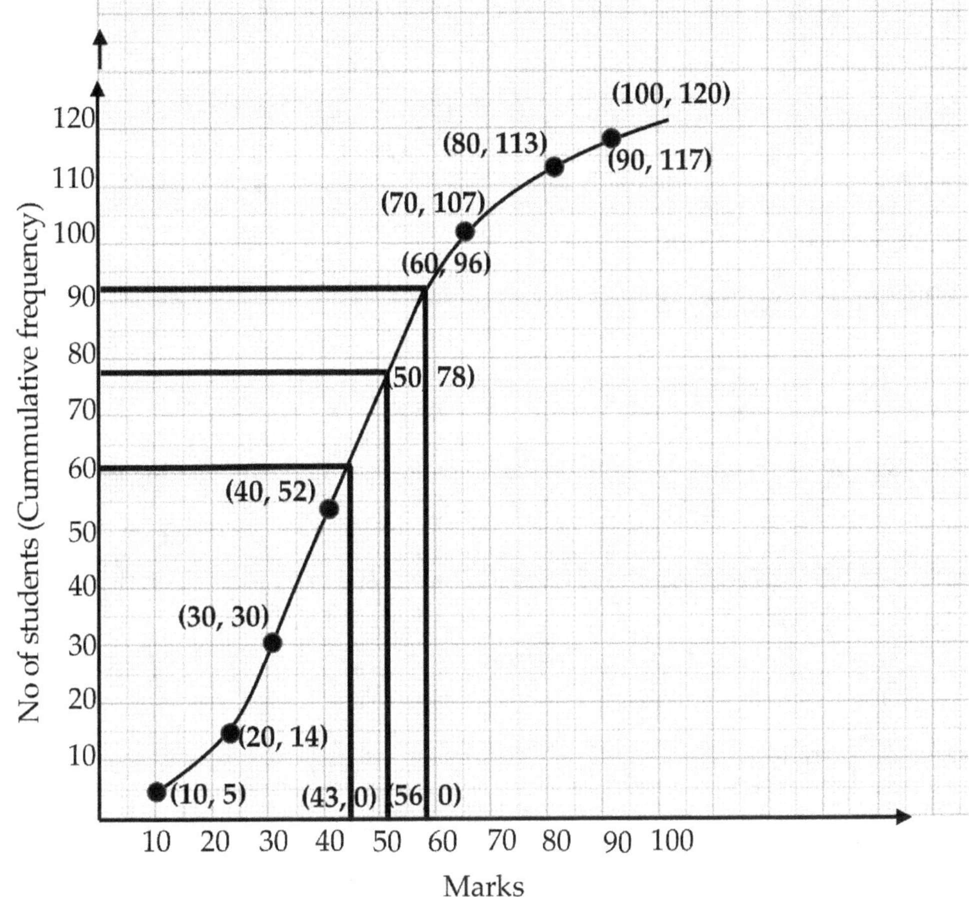

Here n = 120 (even), therefore $\frac{n}{2} = 60$

(a) Median = 43 marks

(b) Number of students who failed = 78

(c) The upper Quartile marks = $\frac{3}{4}n^{th}$ term = 90th term = 57 marks (appr.)

(ii)

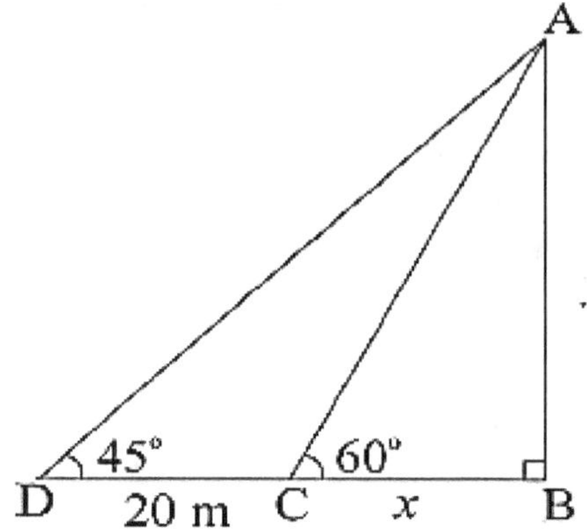

Let the height of the tower be h m.

In $\triangle ADB$, $\tan 45° = \dfrac{h}{20 + x}$

$$\Rightarrow 1 = \dfrac{h}{20 + x}$$

$$\Rightarrow h = 20 + x \qquad \qquad \text{.................(i)}$$

In $\triangle BDC$, $\tan 60° = \dfrac{h}{x}$

$$\sqrt{3} = \dfrac{h}{x}$$

$$\Rightarrow x = \dfrac{h}{\sqrt{3}} \qquad \qquad \text{.............(ii)}$$

Using (i) and (ii), we get

$$h - 20 + \dfrac{h}{\sqrt{3}}$$

$$\Rightarrow h - \dfrac{h}{\sqrt{3}} = 20$$

$$\Rightarrow h\left(\dfrac{\sqrt{3} - 1}{\sqrt{3}}\right) = 20$$

$$h = 20\left(\dfrac{\sqrt{3}}{\sqrt{3}-1} \times \dfrac{\sqrt{3}+1}{\sqrt{3}+1}\right)$$

$$h = 20\left(\dfrac{1.732 + 3}{3 - 1}\right)$$

$$h = 10 \times 4.732$$

Therefore, Height of the tower $=$ is 47.32m

Question 11.

(i) Using the Remainder Theorem find the remainders obtained when $x^3 + (kx + 8)x + k$ is divided by $x + 1$ and $x - 2$. Hence find k if the sum of the two remainders is 1. **[3]**

(ii) The product of two consecutive natural numbers which are multiples of 3 is equal to 8 Find the two numbers. **[3]**

(iii) In the given figure, ABCDE is a pentagon inscribed in a circle such that AC is the diameter and side BC ∥ AE, If ∠BAC = 50°, find giving reasons: **[4]**

[a图] 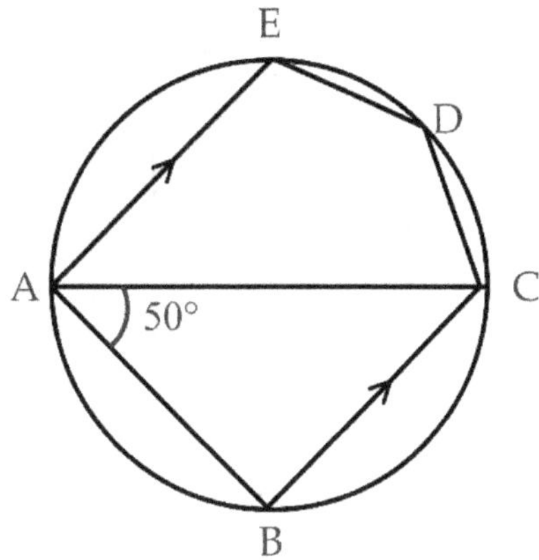

(a) ∠ACB

(b) ∠EDC

(c) ∠BEC

Hence prove that BE is also a diameter.

Answer:

(i) Remainder theorem:

Dividend = Divisors × Quotient + Remainder

∴ Let
$$f(x) = x^3 + (kx + 8)x + k = x^3 + kx^2 + 8x + k$$
Dividing $f(x)$ by x + 1 gives the remainder as R_1

∴ $f(-1) = R_1$

Also $f(2) = R_2$

∴ $f(-1) = (-1)^3 + k(-1)^2 + 8(-1) + k = -1 + k - 8 + k = 2k - 9 = R_1$

$f(2) = (2)^3 + k(2)^2 + 8 \times 2 + k = 8 + 4k + 16 + k = 5k + 24 = R_2$

Sum of remainder
$$= R_1 + R_2 = 1$$
∴ $2k - 9 + 5k + 24 = 1$

$\Rightarrow 7k + 15 = 1$

$\Rightarrow k = -2$

(ii) Let the numbers be $x, x + 3$

Therefore $x \times (x + 3) = 810$

$x^2 + 3x = 810$

$x^2 + 3x - 810 = 0$

$x^2 + 30x - 27c - 810 = 0$

$x(x + 30) - 27(x + 30) = 0$

$(x + 30)(x - 27) = 0$

$x = 27$ or $x = -30$(not a natural number)

Therefore $x = 27$

Therefore, the numbers are 27,30

(iii) Let $∠ACB = x, ∠EDC = y,$ and $∠BEC = z$

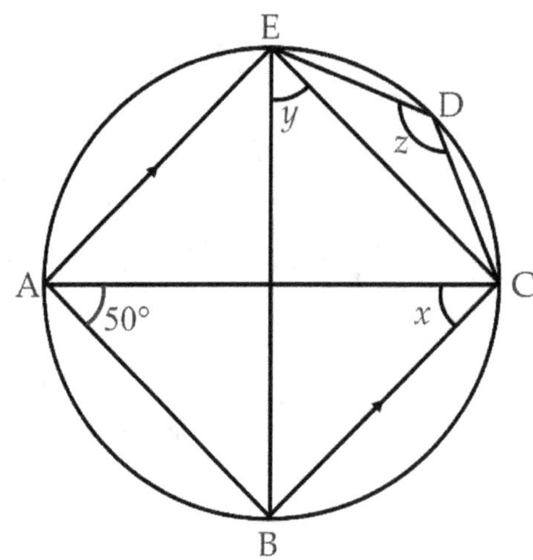

We know ∠ABC = 90° (Angle in a semi-circle)

(a) In △ ABC, ∠ABC + ∠BAC + ∠ACB = 180°[angle sum property of a triangle]

⇒ 90° + 50° + ∠ACB = 180°

⇒ ∠ACB = 40°

(b) We know ∠EAC = ∠ACB = 40°[as AE ∥ BC so alternate angles]

∠EAC + ∠EDC = 180°   [Opposite angles of a cyclic quadrilateral are supplementary

∠EDC = 180° − 40° = 140°

(c) ∠BEC = ∠BAC = 50°   [Angles in the same segment are equal]

Join BE

∠BAC + ∠CAE = 50° + 40°=90°

So   BAE = 90°

Since the angle on diameter is 90°, so BE is a diameter.

MATHEMATICS

Maximum Marks: 80
Time allowed: Two and a half hours
Answers to this Paper must be written on the paper provided separately.
You will not be allowed to write during first 15 minutes.
This time is to be spent in reading the question paper.
The time given at the head of this Paper is the time allowed for writing the answers.

Attempt all questions from Section *A* and any four questions from Section *B*.
The intended marks for questions or parts of questions are given in brackets [].
SECTION -A(40 Marks)
(Attempt all questions from this section)

Question 1.

(i) Solve the following quadratic equation: [3]
$x^2 - 7x + 3 = 0$
Give your answer correct to two decimal places.

(ii) Given $A = \begin{bmatrix} x & 3 \\ y & 3 \end{bmatrix}$ [3]
If $A^2 = 3I$, where I is the identity matrix of Order 2, find x and y.

(iii) Using ruler and compass construct a triangle ABC where $AB = 3cm, BC = 4cm$, and $\angle ABC \ 90°$.Hence construct a circle circumscribing the triangle ABC. Measure and write down the radius of the circle. [4]

Solution:

(i) Given $x^2 - 7x + 3 = 0$
Comparing it with $ax^2 + bx + c = 0$
we get, $a = 1, b = -7$, and $c = 3$
We know, $x = \dfrac{-b \pm \sqrt{b^2 - 4ac}}{2a}$
$= \dfrac{7 \pm \sqrt{49 - 12}}{2}$
$\Rightarrow x = \dfrac{7 \pm \sqrt{37}}{2}$
$\Rightarrow x = \dfrac{7 \pm 6.08}{2}$
Therefore $x = \dfrac{7 + 6.08}{2} = 6.54$ or
$x = \dfrac{7 - 6.08}{2} = 0.46$
Hence roots are 6.54 and 0.46

(ii) Given: $A = \begin{bmatrix} x & 3 \\ y & 3 \end{bmatrix}$ and $A^2 = 3I$

$$A^2 = \begin{bmatrix} x & 3 \\ y & 3 \end{bmatrix} \times \begin{bmatrix} x & 3 \\ y & 3 \end{bmatrix}$$

$$\Rightarrow A^2 = \begin{bmatrix} x^2 + 3y & 3x + 9 \\ xy + 3y & 3y + 9 \end{bmatrix}$$

$$3I = 3 \times \begin{bmatrix} 1 & 0 \\ 0 & 1 \end{bmatrix} = \begin{bmatrix} 3 & 0 \\ 0 & 3 \end{bmatrix}$$

Comparing we get

$$\begin{bmatrix} x^2 + 3y & 3x + 9 \\ xy + 3y & 3y + 9 \end{bmatrix} = \begin{bmatrix} 3 & 0 \\ 0 & 3 \end{bmatrix}$$

$$\Rightarrow 3x + 9 = 0 \Rightarrow \mathbf{x = -3}$$

Similarly, $3y + 9 = 3 \Rightarrow \mathbf{y = -2}$

(iii) Steps:

1. Draw BC = 4 cm.
2. Draw a line segment BA = 3 cm which makes 90 degrees with B.
3. Join AC. This is the required triangle ABC.
4. Draw perpendicular bisector of AB and BC, which intersect each other at point O on AC.
5. With O as center and OB (OA = OB = OC) as radius draw the required circumcircle.
   BC = 4cm and AB = 3cm
   Radius of the circle = 2.5cm

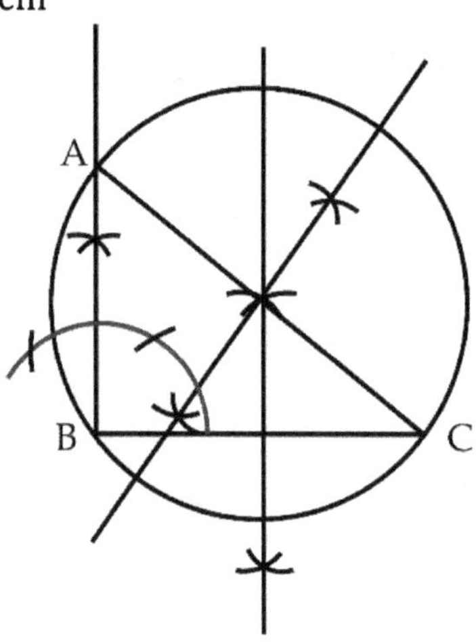

Question 2.

(i)   Use factor theorem to factorize $6x^3 + 17x^2 + 4x - 12$ completely. **[3]**

(ii) Solve the following in-equation and represent the solution set on the number line. **[3]**

$$\frac{3x}{5} < x + 4 \leq \frac{x}{5}, x \in R$$

(iii) Draw a histogram for the given data using graph paper. **[4]**

Weekly Wages (in Rs)	No. of People
3000 − 4000	4
4000 − 5000	9

$5000 - 6000$	18
$6000 - 7000$	6
$7000 - 8000$	7
$8000 - 9000$	2
$9000 - 10000$	4

Solution:

(i) Let $f(x) = 6x^3 + 17x^2 + 4x - 12$

By trial and error, let $x = -2$

Therefore $f(-2) = 6(-8) + 17(4) + 4(-2) - 12 = -48 + 68 - 8 - 12 = 0$

Hence we can say that $(x + 2)$ is a factor of $f(x)$

$$\begin{array}{r}
6x^2 + 5x - 6 \\
\hline
x + 2\overline{)6x^3 + 17x^2 + 4x - 12} \\
6x^3 + 12x^2 \\
-\quad - \\
\hline
5x^2 + 4x \quad - 12 \\
5x^2 + 10x \\
-\quad - \\
\hline
-6x \ - 12 \\
-6x \ - 12 \\
+\quad + \\
\hline
\times
\end{array}$$

So $6x^3 + 17x^2 + 4x - 12 = (x + 2)\,(6x^2 + 5x - 6)$

$$= (x + 2)(6x^2 + 9x - 4x - 6)$$
$$= (x + 2)[3x(2x + 3) - 2(2x + 3)]$$
$$= (x + 2)(3x - 2)(2x + 3)$$

Therefore, complete factorization is $f(x) = (x + 2)(3x - 2)(2x + 3)$

(ii) $\frac{3x}{5} + 2 < x + 4 \leq \frac{x}{2} + 5, x \in R$

First, solve: $\frac{3x}{5} + 2 < x + 4$

$\Rightarrow 3x + 10 < 5x + 20$ [Multiply by 5]

$\Rightarrow -2x < 10$

$\Rightarrow x > -5$

Also, solve $x + 4 \leq \frac{x}{2} + 5$

$\Rightarrow 2x + 8 \leq x + 10$

$\Rightarrow x \leq 2$ [Multiply by 2]

$\therefore -5 < x \leq 2, x \in R$

Hence the solution set $S = \{x : x \in R, -5 < x \leq 2\}$

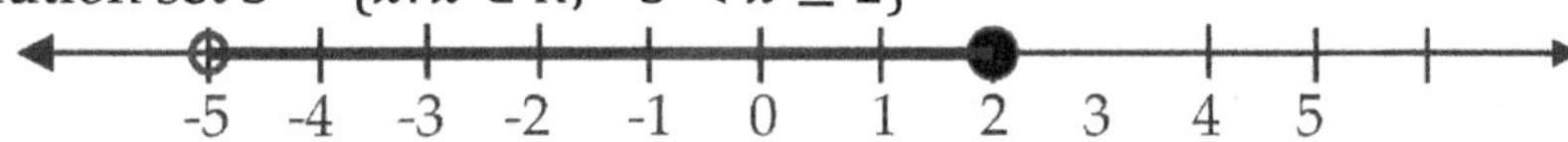

(iii) Histogram for the given data is given below:

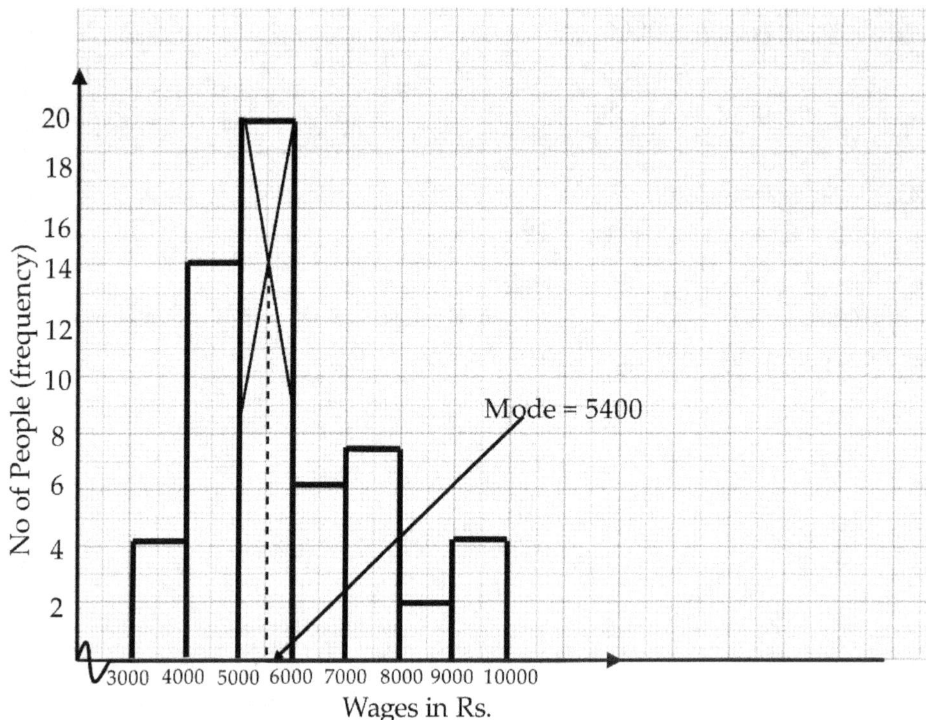

Question 3.

(i) In the figure given below, O is the center of the circle and AB is a diameter, if AC = BD and ∠ADC = 72°, find   **[3]**

  (a) ∠ABC

  (b) ∠BAD

  (c) ∠ABD

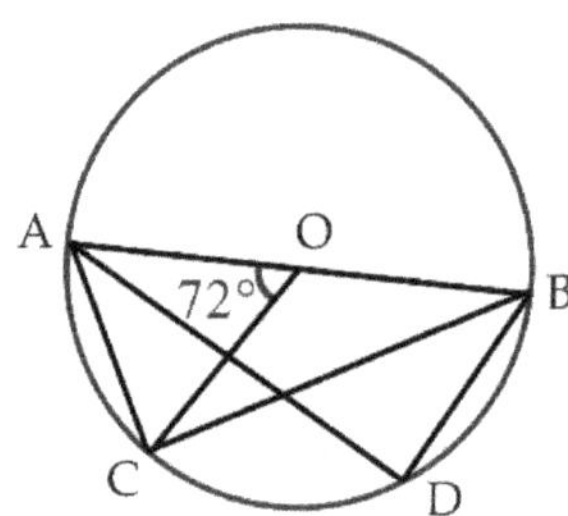

(ii) Prove that   **[3]**

$$\frac{\sin A}{1 + \cot A} - \frac{\cos A}{1 + \tan A} = \sin A - \cos A$$

(iii) In what ratio is the line joining P(5,3) and Q(−5,3) is divided by the y-axis? Also, find the coordinates of the point of intersection.   **[4]**

Solution:

(i)

(a) We know, the angle at which an arc of a circle subtends at the center is double that which it subtends on any point of the part of the circumference.

Therefore $\angle ABC = \frac{1}{2}\angle AOC = \frac{1}{2}(72) = 36°$

(b) Given $AC = BD$

The chord of the same length subtends the same angle

$\therefore \angle BAD = 36°$

(c) $\angle ABD = 90°$ (Angle on diameter is $90°$)

In $\triangle ABD, \angle ABD = 180° - 36° - 90° = 54°$

(ii) $LHS = \dfrac{\sin A}{1+\cot A} - \dfrac{\cos A}{1+\tan A}$

$$= \dfrac{\sin A}{1 + \dfrac{\cos A}{\sin A}} - \dfrac{\cos A}{1 + \dfrac{\cos A}{\sin A}}$$

$$= \dfrac{\sin A}{\dfrac{\sin A + \cos A}{\sin A}} - \dfrac{\cos A}{\dfrac{\sin A - \cos A}{\sin A}}$$

$$= \dfrac{\sin^2 A}{\sin A + \cos A} - \dfrac{\cos^2 A}{\cos A + \sin A}$$

$$= \dfrac{\sin^2 A - \cos^2 A}{\sin A + \cos A}$$

$$= \dfrac{(\sin A - \cos A)(\sin A + \cos A)}{\sin A + \cos A}$$

$= \sin A - \cos A = RHS$ Hence proved.

(iii) Let the point of intersection be $(0, b)$

Let the ratio of in which the line segment gets divided be $k: 1$

Using section formula

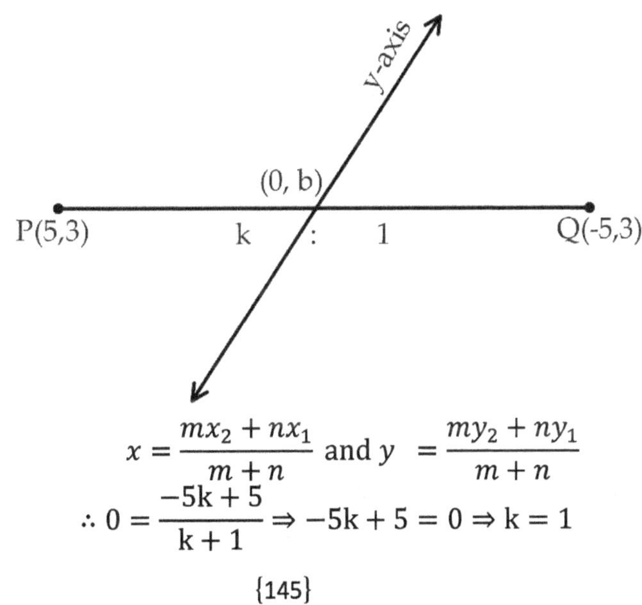

$$x = \dfrac{mx_2 + nx_1}{m + n} \text{ and } y = \dfrac{my_2 + ny_1}{m + n}$$

$$\therefore 0 = \dfrac{-5k + 5}{k + 1} \Rightarrow -5k + 5 = 0 \Rightarrow k = 1$$

Hence the ratio is $1:1$

Therefore $b = \dfrac{3+3}{1+1} = 3$

Therefore, the coordinates of the point of intersection is $(0,3)$

Question 4.

(i) A solid spherical ball of radius 6cm is melted and recast in 64 identical spherical marbles. Find the radius of each marble. [3]

(ii) Each of the letters of the word AUTHORIZES is written on identical circular discs and put in a bag. They are well shuffled. If a disc is drawn at random from the bag. what is the probability that the letter is

    (a) A vowel

    (b) One of the first 9 letters of the English alphabet which appears in a given word

    (c) One of the last 9 letters of the English alphabet which appears in a given word   [3]

(iii) Mr. Bedi visits the market and buys the following articles:

Medicines costing Rs. 950, GST @ 5%

A pair of shoes costing Rs.3000 GST @ 18%

A laptop bag costing Rs 1000 with a discount of 30%, GST @ 18%

    (a) Calculate the total amount of GST paid

    (b) The total bill amount including GST paid by Mr. Bedi   [4]

Solution:

(i) Let R be the radius of the spherical ball and r be the radius of the spherical marble

Volume of spherical ball $= \dfrac{4}{3}\pi R^3 = \dfrac{4}{3}\pi(6)^3$

Volume of spherical marble $= \dfrac{4}{3}\pi r^3$

$$\therefore \frac{4}{3}\pi(6)^3 = 64 \times \frac{4}{3}\pi r^3$$

$$r^3 = \frac{6^3}{64} = \frac{6^3}{4^3}$$

$$\Rightarrow r = \frac{6}{4} = \frac{3}{2} = 1\frac{1}{2}\,cm$$

(ii) Total outcomes $= 10$

    (a) No, of vowels $= 5$ (a, e, i, o, u)

        Therefore, probability P(Vowels) $= \dfrac{5}{10} = \dfrac{1}{2}$

    (b) First 9 letters: $A, B, C, D, E, F_1, G, H, I$

        Favorable A, E, H, I

        There are 4 favorable outcomes

        Therefore probability P(first 9 letters) $= \dfrac{4}{10} = \dfrac{2}{5}$

    (c) Last 9 letters: R, S, T, U, V, W, X, Y, Z

        Favorable U, T, R, Z and S

There are 5 favaorable outcomes

Therefore probability P(last 9 letters) $= \frac{5}{10} = \frac{1}{2}$

(iii)

Article	Cost (R$_5$)	Final Cost (Rs)	GST Rate	GST (Rs.)	Final Price (Rs.)
Medicines	950	950	5%	47.50	0997.50
Shoes	3000	3000	18%	540	3540
Laptop bag	1000@30% discount	700	18%	126	829
Total (Rs.)				713.50	5363.50

Therefore

(a) Calculate the total amount of GST paid = Rs. 713.50Rs.

(b) The total bill amount including GST paid by Mr. Bedi = Rs. 5363.50Rs.

SECTION B [40 Marks]
(Attempt any four questions from this Section.)

Question 5.

(i) A company with 500 shares of nominal value Rs. 120 declares and an annual dividend of 15%. Calculate:

(a) The total amount of dividend paid by the company

(b) Annual income of Mr. Sharma who holds 80 shares of the company.

If the return percent of Mr. Sharma for his shares is 10% find the market value of each share.

[3]

(ii) The mean of the following data is 16 Calculate the value of f.　　　　　　　　　　[3]

Marks	5	10	15	20	25
No, of Students	3	7	f	9	6

(iii) The 4th, 6th and the last term of a geometric progression is 10,40 and 640 respectively. If the common ratio is positive, find the first term, common ration and the number of terms of the series.　　　　[4]

Solution:

(i) Out of syllabus

(ii)

Marks (x)	No. of Students (f)	fx
5	3	15
10	7	70
15	f	$15f$
20	9	180
25	5	150

		$5f = 25 + f$	$\Sigma fr = 415 + 15f$

Given: Mean = 16

We know $\bar{x} = \dfrac{\Sigma fx}{\Sigma f}$

$$\Rightarrow 16 = \dfrac{415 + 15f}{25 + f}$$

$$\Rightarrow 400 + 16f = 415 + 15f$$

$$\Rightarrow f = 15$$

(iii) Out of syllabus

Question 6.

(i) If $A = \begin{bmatrix} 3 & 0 \\ 5 & 1 \end{bmatrix}$ and $B - \begin{bmatrix} -4 & 2 \\ 1 & 0 \end{bmatrix}$ Find: $A^2 - 2AB + B^2$ [3]

(ii) In the given figure AB = 9cm, PA = 7.5cm, and PC = 5cm

Chord AD and BC intersect at P.

(a) Prove that $\triangle$ PAB $\sim \triangle$ PCD

(b) Find the length of CD

(c) Find area of $\triangle$ PAB :area of $\triangle$ PCD   [3]

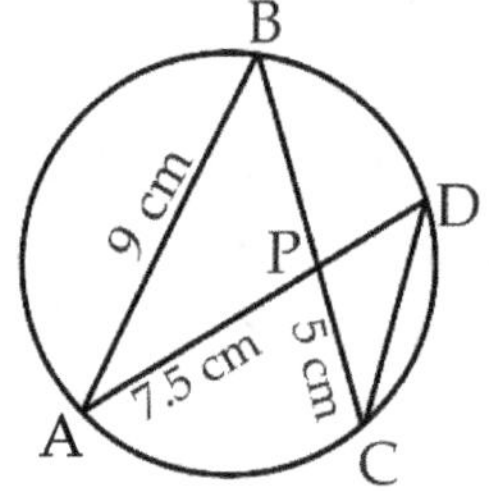

(iii) From the top of a cliff, the angle of depression of the top and bottom of a tower are observed to be 45° and 60° respectively. If the height of the tower is 20m, Find:

(a) The height of the cliff

(b) The distance between the cliff and the tower.   [4]

Solution:

(i) Given

$$A = \begin{bmatrix} 3 & 0 \\ 5 & 1 \end{bmatrix} \quad B = \begin{bmatrix} -4 & 2 \\ 1 & 0 \end{bmatrix}$$

$$A^2 = \begin{bmatrix} 3 & 0 \\ 5 & 1 \end{bmatrix} \times \begin{bmatrix} 3 & 0 \\ 5 & 1 \end{bmatrix} = \begin{bmatrix} 9+0 & 0 \\ 15+5 & 0+1 \end{bmatrix} = \begin{bmatrix} 9 & 0 \\ 20 & 1 \end{bmatrix}$$

$$B^2 = \begin{bmatrix} -4 & 2 \\ 1 & 0 \end{bmatrix} \times \begin{bmatrix} -4 & 2 \\ 1 & 0 \end{bmatrix} - \begin{bmatrix} 16+2 & -8+0 \\ -4+0 & 2+0 \end{bmatrix} = \begin{bmatrix} 18 & -8 \\ -4 & 2 \end{bmatrix}$$

$$AB = \begin{bmatrix} 3 & 0 \\ 5 & 1 \end{bmatrix} \times \begin{bmatrix} -4 & 2 \\ 1 & 0 \end{bmatrix} = \begin{bmatrix} -12+0 & 6+0 \\ -20+1 & 10+0 \end{bmatrix} = \begin{bmatrix} -12 & 6 \\ -19 & 10 \end{bmatrix}$$

$$\therefore A^2 - 2AB + B^2 = \begin{bmatrix} 9 & 0 \\ 20 & 1 \end{bmatrix} - 2\begin{bmatrix} -12 & 6 \\ -19 & 10 \end{bmatrix} + \begin{bmatrix} 18 & -8 \\ -4 & 2 \end{bmatrix} = \begin{bmatrix} 51 & -20 \\ 54 & -17 \end{bmatrix}$$

(ii)

    (a) Consider $\triangle$ PAB and $\triangle$ PCD

        $\angle$BPA = $\angle$DPC (Vertically opposite angles)

        $\angle$ABC = $\angle$ADC (Angles in the same segment are equal)

        $\therefore \triangle$ PAB $\sim \triangle$ PCD (By AA similarity criterion)

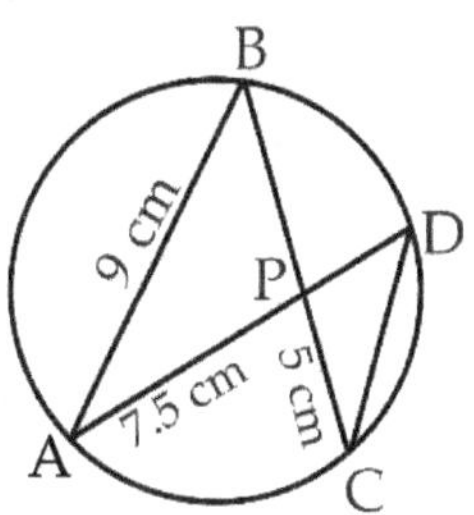

(b) Since $\triangle$ PAB $\sim \triangle$ PCD

$$\Rightarrow \frac{PA}{PC} = \frac{AB}{CD} = \frac{PB}{PD} \text{ (Corresponding sides of similar triangles are proportonal)}$$

$$\Rightarrow \frac{7.5}{5} = \frac{9}{CD}$$

$$\Rightarrow CD = \frac{5 \times 9}{7.5} = 6cm$$

(c) Out of syllabus

(iii)

    In $\triangle$ ABC

$$\tan 60° = \frac{h}{x} \Rightarrow \sqrt{3} = \frac{h}{x} \Rightarrow h = \sqrt{3}x \qquad \qquad ......(i)$$

    In $\triangle$ CDE

$$\tan 45° = \frac{h-20}{x} \Rightarrow 1 = \frac{h_1-20}{x} \Rightarrow x = h - 20 \qquad \qquad .....(ii)$$

Substituting $\quad x = \sqrt{3}x - 20$

$$\Rightarrow \quad (\sqrt{3} - 1)x = 20$$

$$\Rightarrow \qquad \qquad x = \frac{20}{\sqrt{3} - 1} \times \frac{\sqrt{3} + 1}{\sqrt{3} + 1} = 10(1.732 + 1) = 27.32m$$

$$\therefore h = \sqrt{3}x = 1,732 \times 27.32 = 47.32m$$

(a) The height of the cliff = 47.32m

(b) The distance between the cliff and the tower = 27.32m

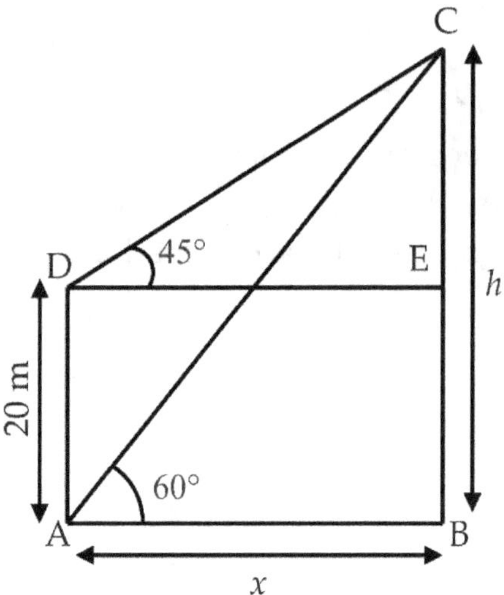

Question 7.

(i) Find the value of $'p'$ is the lines $5x - 3y + 2 = 0$ and $6x - py + 7 = 0$ are perpendicular to each other. Hence find the equation of a line passing through $(-2, -1)$ and parallel to $6x - py + 7 = 0$ **[3]**

(ii) Using properties of proportion find $x{:}y$ given $\dfrac{x^2+2x}{2x+4} = \dfrac{y^2+3y}{3y+9}$ **[3]**

(iii) In the given figure, TP and TQ are two tangents to the circle with center O, touching at A and C respectively. If $\angle BCQ = 55°$ and $\angle BAP = 60°$, find:

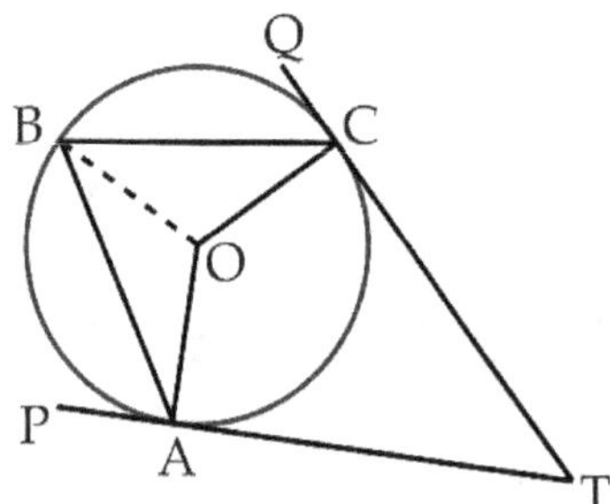

(a) $\angle OBA$ and $\angle OBC$

(b) $\angle AOC$

(c) $\angle ATC$ **[4]**

Solution:

(i) Given $5x - 3y + 2 = 0 \Rightarrow 3y = 5x + 2 \Rightarrow y = \dfrac{5}{3}x + \dfrac{2}{3}$

Therefore slope $m_1 = \dfrac{5}{3}$

Similarly, $6x - py + 7 = 0 \Rightarrow y = 6x + 7 \Rightarrow y = \dfrac{6}{p}x + \dfrac{7}{p}$

Therefore slope $m_2 = \dfrac{6}{p}$

We know $m_1 m_2 = -1$

$$\Leftrightarrow \frac{5}{7} \times \frac{6}{p} = -1 \Rightarrow p = -10$$

Therefore, slope of $6x - py + 7 = 0$ is $m = \frac{6}{p} = -\frac{3}{5}$

Therefore, slope of the required line $= -\frac{3}{5}$ and $(-2, -1)$ as $(x1, y1)$

Using $y - y1 = m(x - x1)s$

$$(y + 1) = -\frac{3}{5}(x + 2)$$

$$\Rightarrow 5y + 5 = -3x - 6$$

$$\Rightarrow 3x + 5y + 11 = 0$$

(ii) $\dfrac{x^2 + 2x}{2x + 4} = \dfrac{y^2 + 3y}{3y + 9}$

Applying componendo and dividendo

$$\frac{^2 + 2x + 2x + 4}{x^3 + 2x - 2x - 4} = \frac{y^2 + 3y + 3y + 9}{y^2 + 3y - 3y - 9}$$

$$\Rightarrow \frac{x^2 + 4x + 4}{x^2 - 4} = \frac{y^2 + 6y + 9}{y^2 - 9}$$

$$\Rightarrow \frac{(x + 2)^2}{(x + 2)(x - 2)} = \frac{(y + 3)^2}{\sqrt{y} + 3)(y - 3)}$$

$$\Rightarrow \frac{x + 2}{x - 2} = \frac{y + 3}{y - 3}$$

Applying componendo and dividendo

$$\frac{x + 2 + x - 2}{x + 2 - x + 2} = \frac{y + 3 + y - 3}{y + 3 - y + 3}$$

$$\Rightarrow \frac{2x}{4} = \frac{2y}{6}$$

$$\Rightarrow \frac{x}{y} = \frac{2}{3}$$

$$\therefore x : y = 2 : 3$$

(iii)

(a) Angle between radius and tangent at the point of contact = 90 degree

$$\angle OAP = 90°$$

$$\therefore \angle OAB = 90° - 60° = 30°$$

As $OA = OB$ (radii)

$$\angle OBA = 30°$$

$$\angle OCQ = 90°$$

$$\therefore \angle OCB = 90° - 55° = 35°$$

Since $OB = OC, \triangle OBC$ is an isosceles triangle

$$\therefore \angle OBC = 35°$$

(b) $\angle ABC = 30° + 35° = 65°$

The angle subtended by an arc at the center is twice that subtended on the circumference.

$$\therefore \angle AOC = 2\angle ABC = 2 \times 65° = 130°$$

(c) AOCT is a quadrilateral. We know that the sum of all the internal angles of a quadrilateral is $360°$

$$\text{Hence, } 90° + 130° + 90° + \angle ATC = 360°$$
$$\Rightarrow \angle ATC = 50°$$

Question 8.

(i) What must be added to the polynomial $2x^3 - 3x^2 - 8x$, so that it leaves a remainder 10 when divided by $2x + 1$? **[3]**

(ii) Mr. Sonu has a recurring deposit account and deposits Rs. 750 per month for 2 years. If he gets Rs. 19125 at the time of maturity, find the rate of interest. **[3]**

(iii) Use a graph paper for this **[4]**

Take 1cm $= 1$ unit on both x and y axes.

(a) Plot the following points on your graph sheet $A(-4,0), B(-3,2), C(0,4), D(4,1)$ and $E(7,3)$

(b) Reflect point B, C, D, and E on the x-axis and name then B', C', D' and E' respectively.

(c) Join the points $A, B, C, D, E, E', D', C', B'$ and A in order. Name the closed figure formed.

Solution:

(i) Let k should be added

Given: $2x^3 - 3x^2 - 8x + k$

When divided by $\quad 2x + 1 \Rightarrow x \ = -\dfrac{1}{2}$

$$f\left(-\frac{1}{2}\right) = 2\left(-\frac{1}{8}\right) - 3\left(\frac{1}{4}\right) - 8\left(-\frac{1}{2}\right) + k$$
$$\Rightarrow 10 = -\frac{1}{4} - \frac{3}{4} + 4 + k$$
$$\Rightarrow 10 = -1 + 4 + k$$
$$\Rightarrow k = 7$$

(ii) Given P $= 750$Rs.

n $= 2$ years $= 24$ months

MV $=$ Rs 19,125

Interest $\quad = $ MV $- $ (P $\times$ n) $= 19125 - 750 \times 24 = 1125$ Rs.

$$\text{Interest} = \frac{p \times n \times (n+1)}{2 \times 12} \times \frac{r}{100}$$

$$1125 = \frac{750 \times 24 \times 25}{2 \times 12} \times \frac{r}{100}$$

$$\Rightarrow r = \frac{1125 \times 100}{750 \times 25} = 6\%$$

(iii) According to the given condition, the figure formed will be of the form as given below

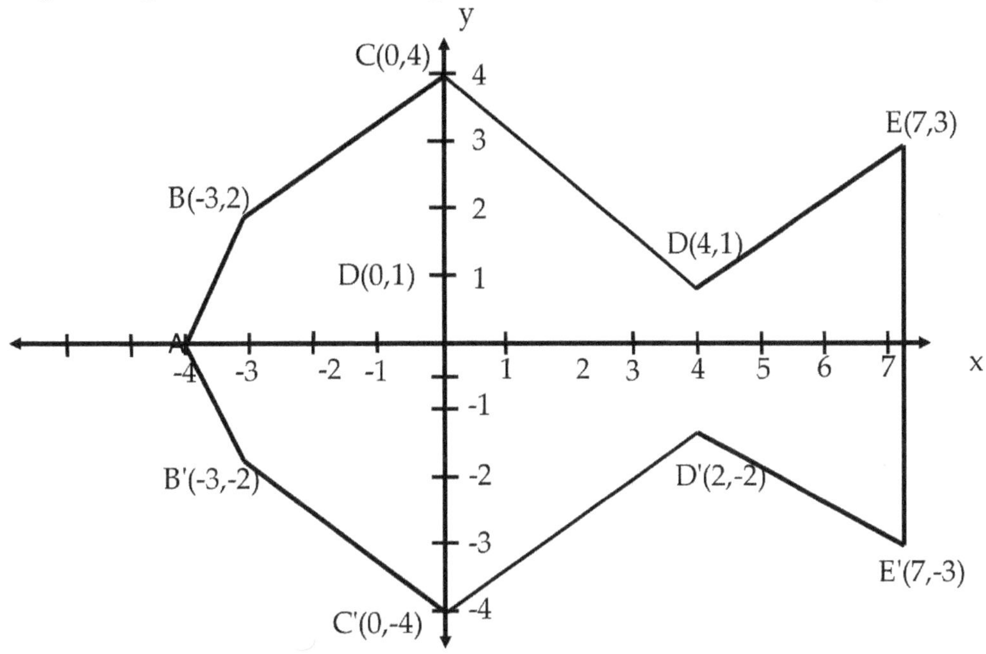

The figure formed is a nonagon (nine edges), It is a FISH.

Question 9.

(i) 4 students enter for a game of shot-put competition. The distance thrown (in meters) is recorded below. **[6]**

Distance in m	$12 - 13$	$13 - 14$	$14 - 15$	$15 - 16$	$16 - 17$	$17 - 18$	$18 - 19$
Number of Students	3	9	12	9	4	2	1

Use graph paper to draw an ogive for the above distribution.
Use a scale of 2cm = 1m on the x-axis and 2cm = 5 students on the other axis.
Hence using your graph paper find:

(a) The median

(b) Upper quartile

(c) Number of students who cover a distance which is above $16\frac{1}{2}$ m

(ii) If $x = \dfrac{\sqrt{2a+1}+\sqrt{2n-1}}{\sqrt{2a+1}-\sqrt{2n-1}}$, prove that $x^2 - 4ax + 1 = 0$ **[4]**

Solution:

(i)

CI	$12 - 13$	$13 - 14$	$14 - 15$	$15 - 16$	$16 - 17$	$17 - 18$	$18 - 19$
f	3	9	12	9	4	2	1
Cf	3	12	24	33	37	39	40

Plot the points, $(13, 3), (14, 12), (15, 24, (16, 33), (17, 37), (18, 39)$ and $(19, 40)$ on the graph paper

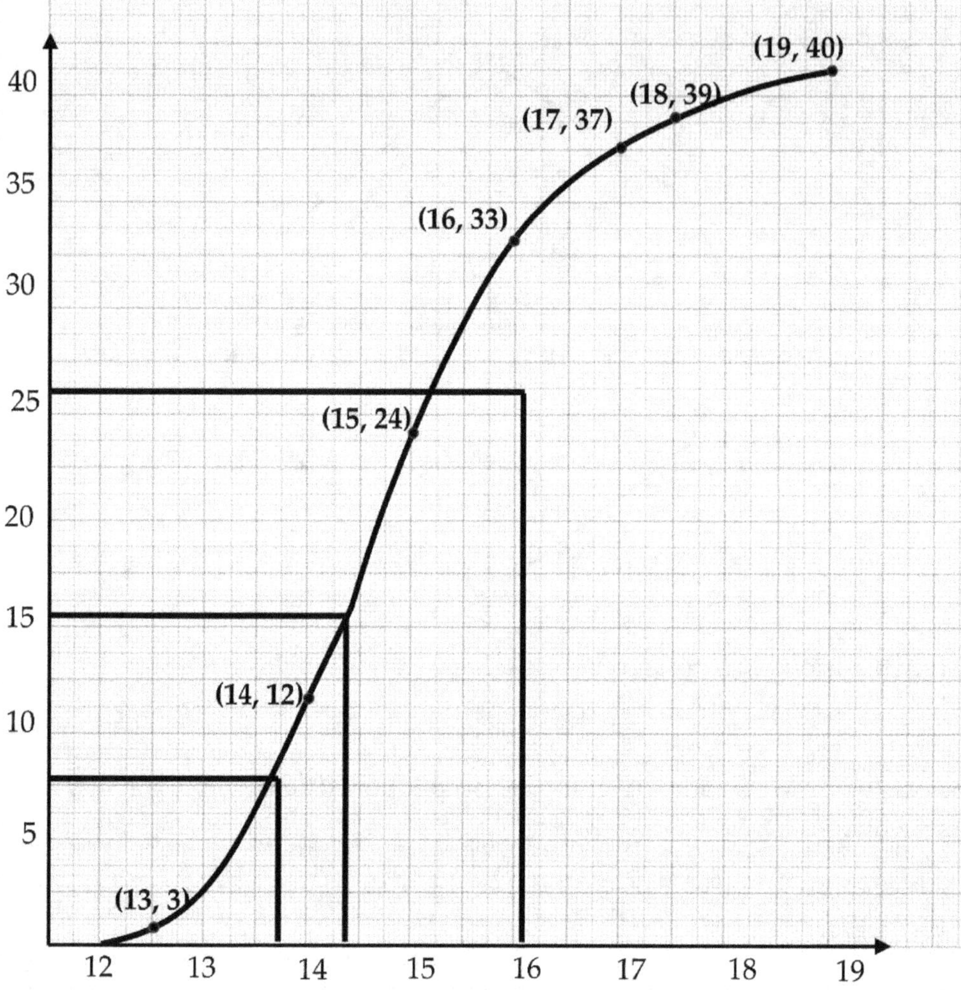

(a) Since N = 40 (even)

Median = $\left(\dfrac{N}{2}\right)$ th observation = 20 th observation = 14.7 m

(b) Upper Quartile = $\left(\dfrac{3}{4}N\right)$ th observation = 30 th observation = 15.6 m

(c) Number of students who cover a distance which is above $16\dfrac{1}{2}$ m = 5 students

(II)

$$x = \frac{\sqrt{2a + 1} + \sqrt{2a - 1}}{\sqrt{2a + 1} - \sqrt{2a - 1}}$$

Applying componendo and dividendo

$$\frac{x+1}{x-1} = \frac{2\sqrt{2a+1}}{2\sqrt{2a-1}} = \frac{\sqrt{2a+1}}{\sqrt{2a-1}}$$

Squaring both sides

$$\frac{(x + 1)^2}{(x - 1)^2} = \frac{2a + 1}{2a - 1}$$

$$\frac{x^2 + 1 + 2x}{x^2 + 1 - 2x} = \frac{2ax + 1}{2a - 1}$$

Applying componendo and dividendo

$$\frac{x^2 + 1 + 2x + x^2 + 1 - 2x}{x^2 + 1 + 2x - x^2 - 1 + 2x} = \frac{2a + 1 + 2a - 1}{2a + 1 - 2a + 1}$$

$$\Rightarrow \frac{2(x^2 + 1)}{4x} = \frac{4a}{2}$$

$$\Rightarrow \frac{x^2 + 1}{2x} = \frac{4a}{2}$$

$$x^2 + 1 = 4ax$$

$x^2 - 4ax + 1 = 0$, Hence proved

Question 10.

(i) If the 6th terms of an AP is equal to four-time its first term and the sum of the first six terms is 75, find the first term and the common difference. **[3]**

(ii) The difference of the two natural numbers of us 7 and their product is 450 Find the numbers **[3]**

(iii) Use ruler and compass for this question. Construct a circle of radius 4.5cm. Draw a chord AB = 6cm.

(a) Find the locus of points equidistant from A and B. Mark the point where it meets the circle as D.

(b) Join AD and find the locus of points that are equidistant from AD and AB. mark the point where it meets the circle as C.

Join BC and CD Measure and write down the length of the side CD of quadrilateral ABCD **[4]**

Solution:

(i) 6th tern = 4a and S_6 = 75

We know that $t_n = a + (n - 1)d$

$$\Rightarrow 4a = a + 5d \Rightarrow 3a = 5d\ldots\ldots.(i)$$

Also $S_n = \frac{n}{2}[2a + (n - 1)d]$

$$\Rightarrow 75 = \frac{6}{2}[2a + 5d] \Rightarrow 75 = 6a + 15d$$

$2a + 5d = 25 \qquad\qquad \ldots\ldots\ldots.(ii)$

Solving (i) and (ii) $\qquad\qquad$ a = 5 and d = 3

Therefore, first term (a) = 3 and common difference (d) = 3

(ii) Let the two natural numbers be x and y

Therefore $x - y = 7$

Also,

$$xy = 450 \Rightarrow y = \frac{450}{x}$$

Substituting $x - \frac{450}{x} = 7$

$$\Rightarrow x^2 - 7x - 450 = 0$$

$\Rightarrow x^2 - 25x + 18x - 450 = 0$

$\Rightarrow x(x - 25) + 18(x - 25) = 0$

$\Rightarrow (x - 25)(x + 18) = 0$

$\Rightarrow x = 25$ or $x = -18$ (not a natural number).

Therefore $x = 25$. Substituting we get $\qquad y = 25 - 7 = 18$

Required numbers are 18 and 25.

(iii) **Step 1**: Draw a circle of radius 3.5cm.

 Step 2: Then take a point A and draw an are 6cm long to intersect the circle at B. Join AB. That is the chord

 Step 3: Locus of equidistant points for AB is the perpendicular bisector. Draw perpendicular bisector.

 Step 4: Mark point D. Join AD.

 Step 5: Draw an angle bisector of angle DAB. This is thelocus for equidistant point for point

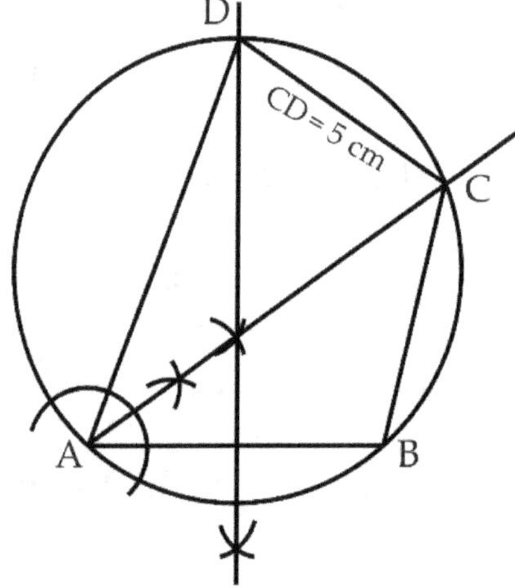

 online AD and AB.

Step 6: Measure CD (5 cm app.)

Question 11.

(i) A model of a high-rise building is made to a scale of $1:50$.

 (a) If the height of the model is 0.8m, find the height of the actual building,

 (b) If the floor area of a flat in the building is $20m^2$. find the floor are of that in the model.

(ii) From a solid wooden cylinder of height 28cm and diameter of 6cm. Two conical cavities are hollowed out. The diameter of the cone is also 6cm and the height is 10.5cm.

 Taking $\pi = \frac{22}{7}$, find the volume of the remaining solid.

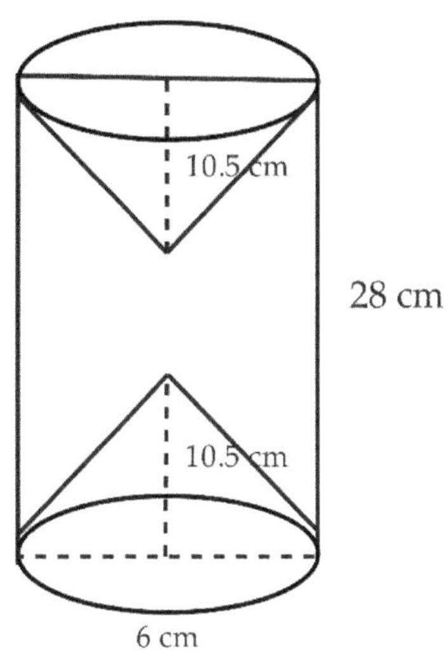

(iii) Prove the identity:
$$\left(\frac{1-\tan\ \theta}{1-\cot\ \theta}\right)^2 = \tan^2\ \theta$$

Solution:
 (i) Out of syllabus
 (ii) Volume of a cylinder $= \pi r^2 H$

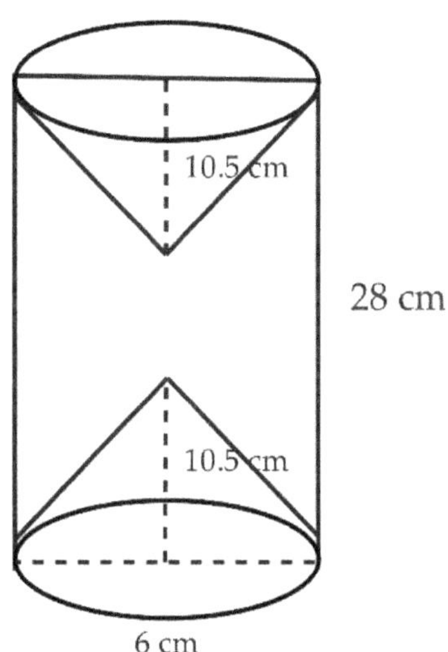

Volume of a cone $\quad = \frac{1}{3}\pi r^2 h$

Given $\qquad : radius\ of\ cylinder\ (r) = 3cm$

$\qquad\qquad Height\ of\ cylinder\ (H) = 28cm$

$\qquad\qquad Height\ of\ cone\ (h) \quad = 10.5cm$

Volume of cylinder $= \pi(3)^2(28) = 252\pi$

Volume of cones $\quad = 2\left[\frac{1}{3}\pi(3)^2(10.5)\right] = 63\pi$

Therefore, Volume of remaining solid $= 252\pi - 63\pi = 189 \times \frac{22}{7} = 594cm^3$

(iii) LHS$= \left(\frac{1-\tan\theta}{1-\cot\theta}\right)^2$

$$= \left(1 - \frac{\sin\,\theta}{\cos\,\theta}\right)^2 \div \left(1 - \frac{\cos\,\theta}{\sin\,\theta}\right)^2$$

$$= \left(\frac{\cos\,\theta - \sin\,\theta}{\cos\,\theta}\right)^2 \div \left(\frac{\sin\,\theta - \cos\,\theta}{\sin\,\theta}\right)^2$$

$$= \frac{(\cos\,\theta - \sin\,\theta)^2}{\cos^2\,\theta} \times \frac{\sin^2\,\theta}{(\cos\,\theta - \sin\,\theta)^2}$$

$$= \frac{\sin^2\,\theta}{\cos^2\,\theta} \quad [\quad \text{as } (a-b)^2 = (b-a)^2]$$

$$= \tan^2\,\theta$$

RHS

Maximum Marks: 40

Time allowed: Two and a half hours

Answers to this Paper must be written on the paper provided separately.

You will not be allowed to write during first 15 minutes.

This time is to be spent in reading the question paper.

The time given at the head of this Paper is the time allowed for writing the answers.

Attempt all questions from Section _A_ and any three questions from Section _B_.

The intended marks for questions or parts of questions are given in brackets [].

Section A

(Attempt all questions from this section)

Question 1.

Choose the correct answers to the questions from the given options. (Do not copy the question. Write the correct answer only. **[10]**

(i) The probability of getting a number divisible by 3 in throwing dice is:

(a) $\frac{1}{6}$

(b) $\frac{1}{3}$

(c) $\frac{1}{2}$

(d) $\frac{2}{3}$

Solution:

In a dice total number are: $1, 2, 3, 4, 5, 6$

divisible by $3 \Rightarrow 3, 6$

$$P(E) = \frac{2}{6} \Rightarrow \frac{1}{3}$$

Answer. (b)

(ii) The volume of a conical tent is 462m^3 and the area of the base is 154m^2. The height of the cone is:

(a) 15m

(b) 12m

(c) 9m

(d) 24m

Solution:

$$\frac{1}{3}\pi r^2 h = 462$$

$$\pi r^2 = 154$$

$$\frac{1}{3} \times 154 \times h = 462$$

$$h = \frac{462 \times 3}{154} = 9m$$

Answer. (c)

(iii) The median class for the given distribution is:

Class Interval	$0 - 10$	$10 - 20$	$20 - 30$	$30 - 40$
Frequency	2	4	3	5

(a) $0 - 10$
(b) $10 - 20$
(c) $20 - 30$
(d) $30 - 40$
Solution:

c.f: 2 $\quad 2 + 4 = 6 \quad 6 + 3 = 9 \quad 9 + 5 = 14$

$$N = 14 \text{ (even)}$$

$$\therefore \text{Median clan} = \left(\frac{14}{2}\right)^{th} = 7th$$
$$= 20 - 30$$

Answer. (c)

(iv) If two lines are perpendicular to one another then the relation between their slopes) m_1 and m_2 is:
(a) $m_1 = m_2$
(b) $m_1 = \dfrac{1}{m_2}$
(c) $m_1 = -m_2$
(d) $m_1 \times m_2 = -1$
Answer. (d)

(v) A lighthouse is 80m high. The angle of elevation of its top from a point 80m away from its foot along the same horizontal line is:
(a) $60°$
(b) $45°$
(c) $30°$
(d) $90°$
Solution:

$$\tan \theta = \frac{80}{80} = 1 \Rightarrow \tan 45°$$
$$\therefore \theta = 45°$$

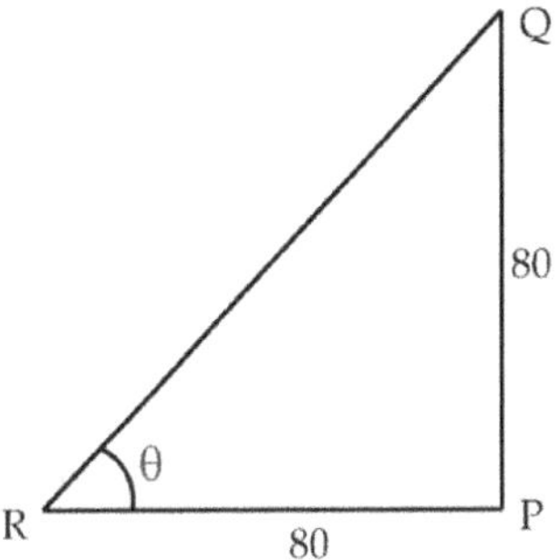

Answer. (b)

(vi) The modal class of a given distribution always corresponds to the:
   (a) Interval with the highest frequency
   (b) Interval with the lowest frequency
   (c) The first interval
   (d) The last interval
   Answer. (a)

(vii) The coordinates of the point $P(-3, 5)$ on reflecting on the x-axis are:
   (a) $(3, 5)$
   (b) $(-3, -5)$
   (c) $(3, -5)$
   (d) $(-3, 5)$
   Solution:

$$p(-3,5) \xrightarrow{x-axis} p'(-3,-5)$$

   Answer. (b)

(viii) ABCD is a cyclic quadrilateral. If $\angle BAD = (2x + 5)^\circ$ and $\angle BCD = (x + 10)^\circ$ then x is equal to:
   (a) 65°
   (b) 45°
   (c) 55°
   (d) 5°

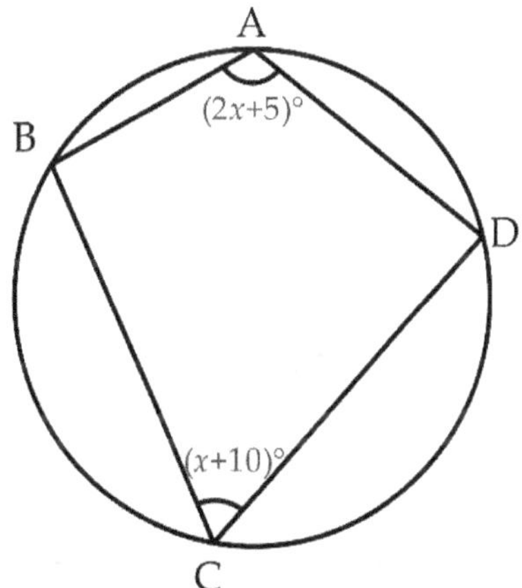

Solution:

∠A+∠C = 180 (Sum of opposite angle of cyclic quadrilateral= 180)

$$2x + 5 + x + 10 = 180$$
$$3x = 180 - 15 \Rightarrow 165$$
$$x = \frac{165}{3} \Rightarrow 55$$

Answer. (c)

(ix) $A(1, 4), B(4,1)$, and $C(x, 4)$ are the vertices of $\triangle$ ABC. If the centroid of the triangle is $G(4,3)$ then x is equal to:

(a) 2

(b) 1

(c) 7

(d) 4

Solution: $(x, y) = \left\{\frac{x_1+x_2+x_3}{3}, \frac{y_1+y_2+y_3}{3}\right\}$

$$4 = \frac{1+4+x}{3}$$
$$x + 5 = 12 \Rightarrow x = 7$$

Answer. (c)

(x) The radius of a roller 100cm long is 14cm. The curved surface area of the roller is:

$\left(\text{Take n} = \frac{22}{7}\right)$

(a) 13200cm^2

(b) 15400cm^2

(c) 4400cm^2

(d) 8800cm^2

Solution:

$$r = 14\text{cm.}$$
$$R = 100\text{cm}$$
$$CSA = 2\pi + h$$
$$= 2 \times \frac{22}{7} \times 14 \times 100$$
$$= 8800\text{cm}^2$$

Answer. (d)

Section – B

(Attempt any four question in this section)

Question 2.

(i) Prove that: [2]

$$\frac{1}{1 + \text{Sin } \theta} + \frac{1}{1 - \text{Sin } \theta} = 2\sec^2 \theta$$

Solution:

L.H.S.

$$= \frac{1 - \sin \theta + 1 + \sin \theta}{(1 + \sin \theta)(1 - \sin \theta)}$$

$$= \frac{2}{1 - \sin^2\theta} \Rightarrow \frac{2x\cos^2\theta}{\cos^2\theta}$$
$$\Rightarrow 2\sec^2\theta\,[\sin^2\theta + \cos^2\theta = 1]$$

(ii) Find 'a', if $A(2a + 2, 3)$, $B(7, 4)$, and $C(2a + 5, 2)$ are collinear. **[2]**

Solution:

Points are collinear

$\therefore$ Slope of AB = slope of BC

$$\text{Slope} = \frac{y_2 - y_1}{x_2 - x_1}$$
$$\frac{4 - 3}{7 - (2a + 2)} = \frac{2 - 4}{2a + 5 - 7}$$
$$\frac{1}{7 - 2a - 2} = \frac{-2}{2a - 2}$$
$$\frac{1}{5 - 2a} = \frac{-2}{2a - 2}$$
$$2a - 2 = -10 + 4a$$
$$2a - 4a = -10 + 2$$
$$-2a = -8$$
$$a = \frac{8}{2}$$
$$a = 4 \text{ **Answer.**}$$

(iii) Calculate the mean of the following frequency distribution. **[3]**

Lass Interval	$5 - 15$	$15 - 25$	$25 - 35$	$35 - 45$	$45 - 55$
Frequency	2	6	4	8	4

Solution:

CI	Class marks(x)	f	fx
$5 - 15$	10	2	20
$15 - 25$	20	6	120
$25 - 35$	30	4	120
$35 - 45$	40	8	320
$45 - 50$	50	4	200
		$\sum f = 24$	$\sum(fx) = 780$

$$\bar{x}(\text{ Mean }) = \frac{\sum fx}{\sum f}$$
$$= \frac{780}{24} \Rightarrow 32.5 \quad \textbf{Ans}$$

(iv) In the given figure O is the center of the circle. PQ and PR are tangents and $\angle QPR = 70°$. Calculate: **[3]**

(a) $\angle QOR$

(b) $\angle QSR$

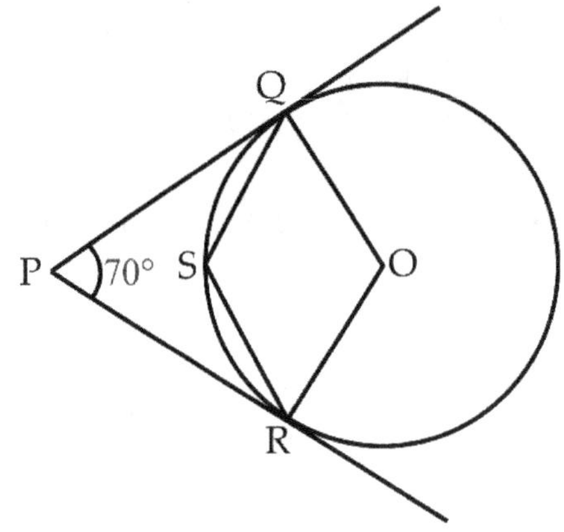

Solution:

$\angle QPR = 70°$

$\angle PQO = \angle PRO = 90°$

(Tangent make 90° with radius at Point of Contact)

$\angle QOR = 360 - (70 + 90 + 90)$

$= 360 - 250 \Rightarrow 110° \text{Ans}$

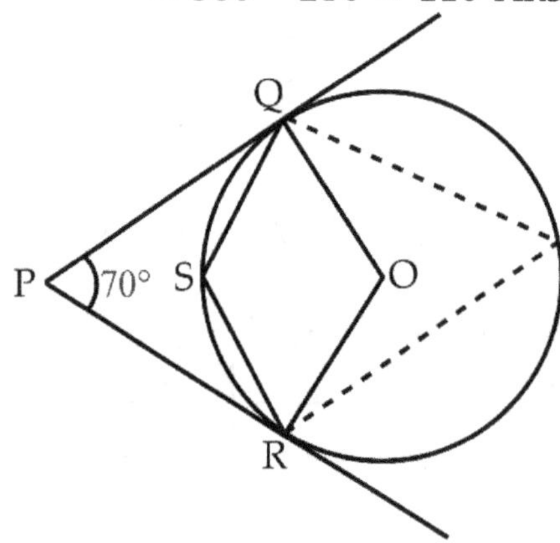

Take a Point T on the circumference, Join QT and RT

$\angle QTR = \frac{1}{2}\angle QOR$ [Angle from an arc at the center is 2 times the angle of the circumference]

$\angle QTR = \frac{1}{2} \times 110 \Rightarrow 55°,$

$\angle QSR = 180 - (55)$ (Opposite angles of cyclic Quadrilateral are supplementary)

$= 125°$ **Answer.**

Question 3.

(i) A bag contains 5 white, 2 red, and 3 black balls. A ball is drawn at random. What is the probability that the ball drawn is a red ball? **[2]**

Solution:

Total ball $= 5 + 2 + 3 \Rightarrow 10$

Red Ball$= 2$

$$\therefore P(E) = \frac{\text{No. of farordble outcomes}}{\text{Total No. of outcomes}}$$

$$= \frac{2}{10} \Rightarrow \frac{1}{5} \qquad \text{**Answer.**}$$

(ii) A solid cone of radius 5cm and height of 9cm is melted and made into small cylinders of a radius of 0.5cm and height 1.5cm. Find the number of cylinders so formed. **[2]**

Solution:

$r = 5$cm

$R = 9$cm.

Volume of cone
$$= \frac{1}{3}\pi r^2 h$$
$$= \frac{1}{3} \times \pi \times 5^2 \times 9$$
$$= 75\pi \, cm^3$$

Volume of cylinder $= \pi r^2 h$
$$= \pi \times (0.5)^2 \times 1.5$$
$$= 0.375\pi \, cm^3$$

No. of cylinder$= \dfrac{\text{Volume of Cone}}{\text{Volume of cylinder}}$
$$= \frac{75\pi}{0.375\pi}$$
$$= 200 \text{ cylinder.} \qquad \textbf{Answer.}$$

(iii) Two lamp posts AB and CD each of height 100m are on either side of the road. P is a point on the road between the two lamp posts. The angles of elevation of the top of the lamp posts from the point P are 60° and 40°. Find the distances PB and PD. **[3]**

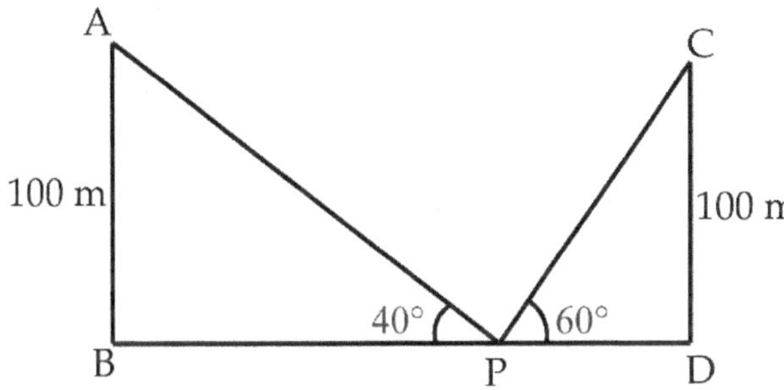

Solution:

In $\triangle$CPD
$$\tan 60^o = \frac{CD}{PD} \qquad\qquad \left[\tan \theta = \frac{P}{B}\right]$$
$$\sqrt{3} = \frac{100}{PD}$$
$$PD = \frac{100}{\sqrt{3}} \Rightarrow \frac{100\sqrt{3}}{3} \, m \qquad\qquad \textbf{Answer.}$$

In $\triangle APB$
$$\tan 40^o = \frac{AB}{BP}$$
$$0.839 = \frac{100}{BP}$$
$$BP = \frac{100}{0.839} \Rightarrow 119.189$$
$$= 119.19m. \qquad\qquad \textbf{Answer.}$$

(iv) Marks obtained by 100 students in an examination are given below

Marks	0 − 10	10 − 20	20 − 30	40 − 40	40 − 50	50 − 61
No. of students	5	15	20	28	20	12

Draw a histogram for the given data using graph paper and find the mode.

Take 2cm = 10 marks along one axis and 2cm = 10 students along the other axis:

Solution: Histogram is pending

Question 4.

(i) Find a point P that divides internally the line segment joining the points $A(-1,0)$ and $B(1,-3)$ in the ratio of $1:3$.

Solution:

let $P(x, y)$ in the Point.

Use section formula

$$A \bullet \underset{(-3, 9)}{} \overset{1}{\underset{}{}} \quad \overset{P}{\underset{(x,\, y)}{\bullet}} \quad \overset{3}{\underset{}{}} \quad \bullet B \underset{(1,\, -3)}{}$$

$$
\begin{aligned}
(x, y) &= \left\{ \frac{m_1 x_2 + m_2 x_1}{r_1 + m_2}, \frac{m_1 y_2 + m_2 y_1}{m_1 + m_2} \right\} \\
&= \left\{ \frac{1 \times 1 + 3(-3)}{1 + 3}, \frac{1(-3) + 3 \times 9}{1 + 3} \right\} \\
&= \left\{ \frac{1 - 9}{4}, \frac{-3 + 27}{4} \right\} \\
&= \left\{ \frac{8}{4}, \frac{24}{4} \right\} \\
&= \{2, 6\} \qquad\qquad \textbf{Answer.}
\end{aligned}
$$

(ii) A letter of the word 'SECONDARY' is selected at random. What is the probability that the letter selected is not a vowel?

Solution:

"SECONDARY"

Not a vowel $= \{S, C, N, D, R, Y\}$

$\qquad\qquad = 6$

total No. of character $= 9$

$$P(E) = \frac{No.\ of\ favorable\ outcome}{total\ no.\ of\ outcome}.$$

$$= \frac{6}{9} \Rightarrow \frac{2}{3} \qquad\qquad \textbf{Answer.}$$

(iii) Use graph paper for this question. Take 2cm = 1 unit along both the axes

(a) Plot the points $A(0, 4), B(2, 2), C(5, 2)$ and $D(4, 0), L(0,0)$ is the origin

(b) Join the points ABCDDC′B′ and A in order and give a geometrical name to the closed figure.

Solution: Graph is pending

(iv) A solid wooden cylinder is of radius 6cm and a height 16cm. Two cones each of radius 2cm and height 6cm are drilled out of the cylinder. Find the volume of the remaining solid. Take $\pi = \dfrac{2\pi}{7}$

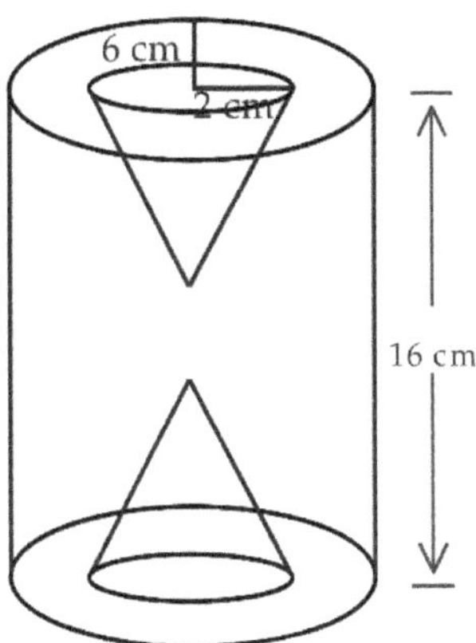

Solution:

Radius (r) of cylinder = 6cm.

height = 16

$$\text{Volume of cylinder} = \pi r^2 h$$
$$= \pi(6)^2 \times 16 \text{cm}^3$$
$$= \frac{22}{7} \times 36 \times 16$$
$$= \frac{12672}{7} \text{cm}^3$$

$$\text{Volume of cone} = \frac{1}{3}\pi r^2 h.$$
$$= \frac{1}{3} \times \pi \times 2^2 \times 6$$
$$= \frac{22}{7} \times 4 \times 2 \Rightarrow \frac{176}{7} \text{cm}^3$$

Volume of Remaining solid = Volume of a cylinder − 2volume of 1 cone

$$= \frac{12672}{7} - \frac{2 \times 176}{7}$$
$$= \frac{12672}{7} - \frac{352}{7}$$
$$= \frac{12320}{7} \Rightarrow 1760 \text{cm}^3 \qquad \textbf{Answer.}$$

Question 5.

(i) Two chords AB and CD of a circle intersect externally at E. If EC = 2cm, EA = 3cm, and AB = 5cm, find the length of CD.

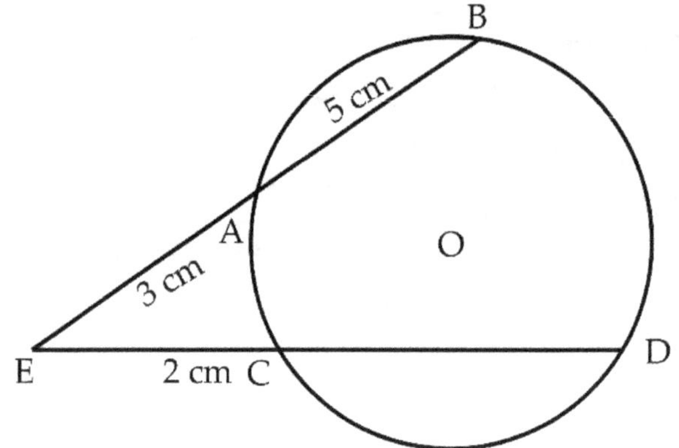

Solution:

$$EA \times EB = EC \times ED$$
$$3 \times (3+5) = 2 \times ED$$
$$\frac{3 \times 8}{2} = ED$$
$$ED = 12\text{cm}$$
$$CD = ED - EC$$
$$= 12 - 2 \Rightarrow 10\text{cm}. \qquad \textbf{Answer.}$$

(ii) Line AB is perpendicular to CD. Coordinates of B, C, and D are respectively $(4, 0)$, $(0, -1)$, and $(4, 3)$

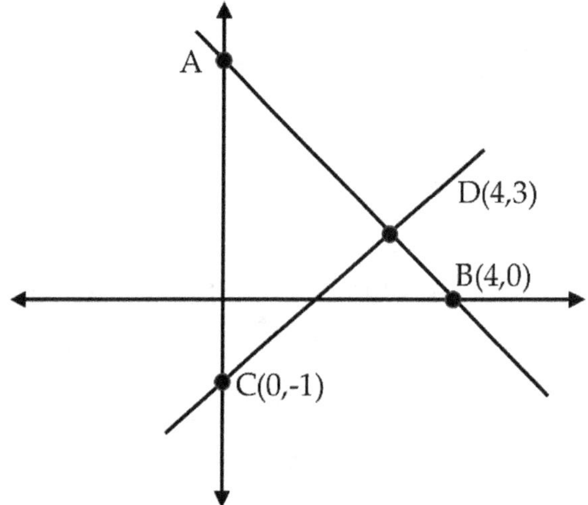

Find:

(a) Slope of CD [2]

(b) Equation of AB

Solution:

(a) Slope of $CD = \frac{y_2 - y_1}{x_2 - x_1}$.

$$= \frac{3 - (-1)}{4 - 0} \Rightarrow \frac{3+1}{4} = 1 \qquad \textbf{Answer.}$$

(b) let $\qquad m_1 = 1$

$\therefore AB$ and CD ax Perpendicular

$$\text{slope}_{(AB)} \times \text{slope}_{(CD)} = -1$$

$$m_2 \times 1 = -1$$
$$m_2 = -1$$

let $B(y_1, 0) \rightarrow (x_1, y_1)$

$\therefore$ equation of
$$AB \Rightarrow y - y_1 = m(x_1 - x_1)$$
$$y - 0 = -1(x - 4)$$
$$y = -x + 4$$
$$x + y - 4 = 0 \qquad\qquad \textbf{Answer.}$$

(iii) Prove that:

$$\frac{(1 + \sin\ \theta)^2 + (1 - \sin\ \theta)^2}{2\cos^2\ \theta} = \sec^2\ \theta + \tan^2\ \theta$$

Solution:

LHS.

$$= \frac{(1 + \sin\ \theta)^2 + (1 - \sin\ \theta)^2}{2\cos^2\ \theta}$$
$$= \frac{1 + \sin^2\ \theta + 2\sin\ \theta + 1 + \sin^2\ \theta - 2\sin\ \theta}{2\cos^2\ \theta}$$
$$= \frac{2 + 2\sin^2\ \theta}{2\cos^2\ \theta} \Rightarrow \frac{2(1 + \sin^2\ \theta)}{2\cos^2\ \theta} \Rightarrow \frac{1 + \sin^2\ \theta}{\cos^2\ \theta}$$
$$= \frac{1}{\cos^2\ \theta} + \frac{\sin^2\ \theta}{\cos^2\ \theta}$$
$$= \sec^2\ \theta + \tan^2\ \theta \qquad \text{RHS}$$

(iv) The mean of the following distribution is 50. Find the unknown frequency,

Class Interval	Frequency
$0 - 20$	6
$20 - 40$	f
$40 - 60$	8
$60 - 80$	12
$80 - 100$	8

Solution:

CI	x	f	fx
$0 - 20$	10	6	60
$20 - 40$	30	f	$30f$
$40 - 60$	50	8	400
$60 - 90$	10	12	840
$80 - 100$	90	8	720
		$\Sigma f = 34$	$\Sigma(fx) = 2020 + 30f$

$$x = \frac{\Sigma fx}{\Sigma f}$$
$$50 = \frac{2020 + 30f}{34 + f}$$
$$1700 + 50f = 2020 + 30f$$
$$50f - 30f = 2020 - 1700$$
$$20f = 320$$

$$f = \frac{320}{20} \Rightarrow 16$$
$$f = 16 \qquad\qquad \textbf{Answer.}$$

Question 6.

(i) Prove that:

$$1 + \frac{\tan^2 \theta}{1+\sec \theta} = \sec \theta$$

Solution:

L.H.S

$$= 1 + \frac{\sec^2 \theta - 1}{1 + \sec \theta} \qquad\qquad (1 + \tan^2 \theta = \sec^2 \theta)$$

$$= 1 + \frac{(\sec \theta + 1)(\sec \theta - 1)}{(1 + \sec \theta)} \qquad [a^2 - b^2 = (a+b)(a-b)]$$

$$= 1 + \sec \theta - 1$$

$$= \sec \theta \qquad\qquad \textbf{Answer.}$$

(ii) In the given figure A, B, C and D are points on the circle with a center O. Given $\angle ABC = 62°$. Find:

(a) $\angle ADC$

(b) $\angle CAB$

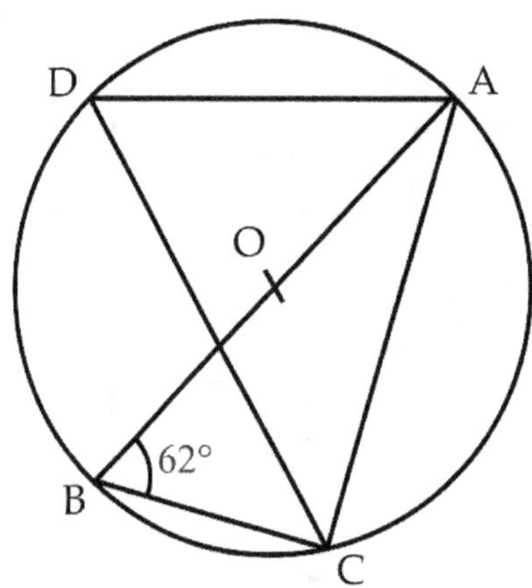

$$\angle ABC = 62°$$
$$\angle ADC = \angle ABC \quad \text{(Angle in same segment)}$$
$$\angle ADC = 62° \qquad\qquad \textbf{Answer.}$$

$$\angle ACB = 90° [\text{Angle on diameter}]$$

In, $\triangle ACB$

$$\angle CAB = 180 - (90 + 62) \quad [\text{Angle Sum prop. of triangle}]$$
$$= 180 - 152$$
$$= 28° \qquad\qquad \textbf{Answer.}$$

(iii) Find the equation of a line parallel to the line $2x + y - 7 = 0$ and pass through the intersection of the lines $x + y - 4 = 0$ and $2x - y = 8$. **[2]**

Solution:

$\because$ line panes through the intersection of $x + y - 4 = 0$ and $2x - y = 8$

let's find the point of intersection

$$x + y = 4 \qquad \text{............(i)}$$
$$2x - y = 8 \qquad \text{............(ii)}$$
$$3x = 12$$
$$x = \frac{12}{3}$$
$$x = 4$$

Put x in (i)

$$y = 4 - 4$$
$$y = 0$$

So, the line panes through $(4,0)$ as (x_1, y_1)

and parallel to $2x + y - 7 = 0$

$\therefore$ Slope of required line = Slope of $2x + y - 7 = 0$

$$y = -2x + 7 \qquad (y = mx + c)$$

(Both parallel)

$\therefore$ Slope of required line $= -2$

$\therefore$ equation of a straight line:

$$y - y_1 = m(x - x_1)$$
$$y - 0 = -2(x - 4)$$
$$y - 0 = -2x + 8$$
$$2x + y - 8 = 0 \qquad \textbf{Answer.}$$

(iv) Marks obtained by 40 students in an examination are given below. **[3]**

Marks	$10 - 20$	$20 - 30$	$30 - 40$	$40 - 50$	$50 - 60$	$60 - 70$
No. of Students	3	8	14	9	4	2

Using graph paper draw an ogive and estimate the median marks. Take 2cm = 10 marks along one axis and 2cm = 5 students along the other axis.

Solution:

C.I	f	C.F
$10 - 20$	3	3
$20 - 30$	8	11
$30 - 40$	14	25
$40 - 50$	9	34
$50 - 60$	4	38
$60 - 70$	2	40
	$N = 40 (even)$	

$$\therefore \text{Median} = \left(\frac{N}{2}\right) \text{th observation}$$
$$= 20 \text{ th}$$
$$= 36 \text{ marks} \qquad \textbf{Answer.}$$

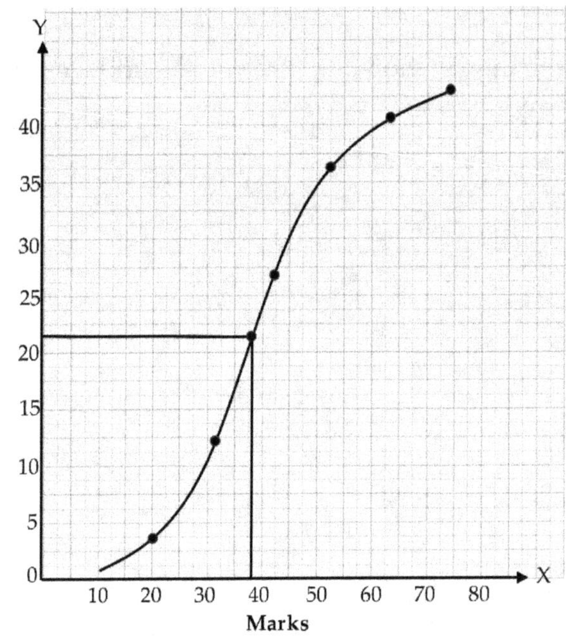

Y
40
35
30
25
20
15
10
5
0
X
10 20 30 40 50 60 70 80
Marks

MOST EXPECTED

QUESTIONS PAPER

Maximum Marks: 80
Time allowed: Two and a half hours
Answers to this Paper must be written on the paper provided separately.
You will not be allowed to write during first 15 minutes.
This time is to be spent in reading the question paper.
The time given at the head of this Paper is the time allowed for writing the answers.

Attempt all questions from Section *A* and any four questions from Section *B*.
The intended marks for questions or parts of questions are given in brackets [].

SECTION – A (40 Marks)
(Attempt all questions from this section)

Question 1. [15]

Chose the correct answers to the questions from the given options:

(i)   The percentage share of CGST of total GST for an Intrastate sale of an article is:
    (a) 100%
    (b) 25%
    (c) 75 %
    (d) 50%

(ii)   A quadratic equation can have:
    (a) At least two roots
    (b) At most two roots
    (c) Always two roots
    (d) Only one root

(iii)   What number must be added to $x^3 - 7x^2 + 14x - 5$ so that the resulting polynomial is exactly divided by $(x - 1)$.
    (a) – 3
    (b) 3
    (c) 2
    (d) – 2

(iv)   If A is a matrix of order 2×1, B is a matrix of order 1×2, so that $A_{2\times1} \times B_{1\times2} = C_{m\times2}$. The value of m is:
    (a) 1
    (b) 2
    (c) 3
    (d) None of the above

(v)   If an AP has $a = 1, t_n = 20$ and $S_n = 399$, then the value of n is:
  (a) 20
  (b) 32
  (c) 38
  (d) 40

(vi) The point $P(2, -4)$ is reflected about the line $x = 0$ to get the image Q. The co-ordinates of Q are:
  (a) $(-2, -4)$
  (b) $(2, 4)$
  (c) $(-2, 4)$
  (d) No change

(vii) Two equilateral triangles are similar by:
  (a) AAA similarity
  (b) SSS similarity
  (c) SAS similarity
  (d) All

(viii) Eight solid spheres of the same size are made by melting a solid metallic cylinder of a base diameter of 6cm and a height of 32cm. The diameter of each sphere is:
  (a) 3cm
  (b) 12cm
  (c) 8cm
  (d) 6cm

(ix) Given $x \in \{1, 2, 3, 4, 5, 6, 7, 8, 9, 10\}$,find the values of x for which: $-3 < 2x - 1 < x + 4$
  (a) $\{0, 1, 2, 3, 4\}$
  (b) $\{0, 1, 2, 3, 4, 5\}$
  (c) $\{1, 2, 3, 4\}$
  (d) None of these

(x)   If a digit is chosen at random from digits $1, 2, 3, 4, 5, 6, 7, 8,$ and $9,$ then the probability that it is odd is
  (a) $\frac{4}{9}$
  (b) $\frac{5}{9}$
  (c) $\frac{1}{9}$
  (d) $\frac{2}{3}$

(xi) The co - ordinates of Q in the following figure:

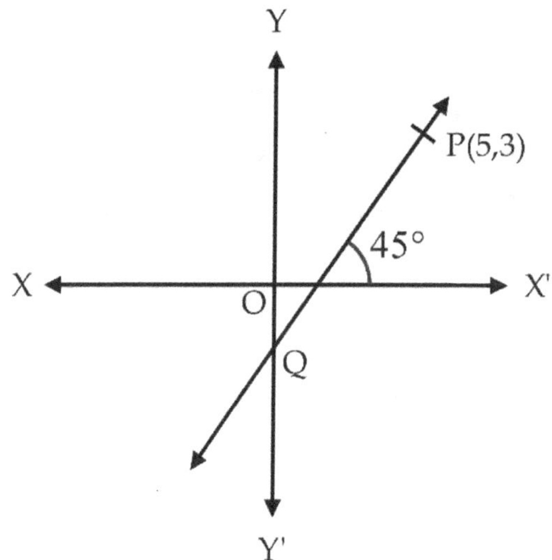

(a) $(-2, 0)$

(b) $(0, -2)$

(c) $(1, -2)$

(d) $\left(0, -\dfrac{3}{2}\right)$

(xii) In the following figures, PAB is secant and PT is tangent to the circle. Find unknown length x in each.

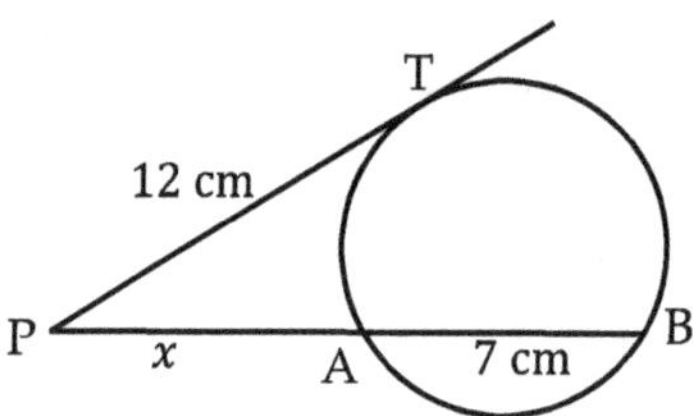

(a) 9 cm

(b) 19cm

(c) 8 cm

(d) 7 cm

(xiii) $9\sec^2 A - 9\tan^2 A$ is equal to:

(a) 1

(b) 9

(c) 8

(d) 0

(xiv) The mode of a frequency distribution can be determined graphically from

(a) Ogive

(b) Histogram

(c) Frequency polygon

(d) Frequency curve

(xv) The sum of the first 10 multiples of 2 is:
   (a) 100
   (b) 110
   (c) 130
   (d) 120

Question 2.

(i)   If show that $\frac{x}{a} = \frac{y}{b} = \frac{z}{c}$, then show that: $\frac{x^3}{a^3} + \frac{y^3}{b^3} + \frac{z^3}{c^3} = \frac{3xyz}{abc}$. [4]

(ii) The maturity value of a R.D. Account is Rs. 21,660. If the monthly installment is Rs. 300 and the rate of interest is 8%; find the time (period) of this R.D. Account. [4]

(iii) Prove the identity:$(\sin A + \cos A)(\tan A + \cot A) = \sec A + \operatorname{cosec} A$ [4]

Question 3.

(i)   The surface area of a solid metallic sphere is $616\,\text{cm}^2$. It is melted and recast into smaller spheres of diameter 3.5cm. How many such spheres can be obtained? [4]

(ii) Given a line segment AB joining the points A (– 4, 6) and B (8, –3). Find:
   (a) The ratio in which AB is divided by the y-axis.
   (b) Find the coordinates of the point of intersection. [4]

(iii) (Use graph paper for this question) [5]
   $A\,(0, 3), B(3, -2),$ and $O(0,0)$ are the vertices of triangle ABO.
   (a) Plot the triangle on a graph sheet taking $2\,cm = 1$unit on both axes.
   (b) Plot D the reflection of B in the Y axis and write its co-ordinates.
   (c) Give the geometrical name of the figure ABOD.

SECTION – B (40 Marks)
(Attempt any four questions from this section)

Question 4.

(i)   A shopkeeper buys an article whose printed price is Rs.4000 from a wholesaler at a discount of 20% and sells it to a consumer at the printed price. If the sales are Intra–state and the rate of GST is 12%, find: [3]

   (a) The price of the article inclusive of GST at which the shopkeeper bought it.

   (b) The amount of tax (under GST) paid by the shopkeeper to the State Government.

   (c) The amount of tax (under GST) received by the Central Government.

(d) The amount which the consumer pays for the article.

(ii) Without solving the following quadratic equation, find the value of ' p ' for which the roots are equal. $px^2 - 4x + 3 = 0$ **[3]**

(iii) Find the mode of the following data: **[4]**

Height (in cm)	$0 - 10$	$10 - 20$	$20 - 30$	$30 - 40$	$40 - 50$
No. of students	6	10	12	32	20

Question 5.

(i) If $A = \begin{bmatrix} 2 & 5 \\ 1 & 3 \end{bmatrix}$, $B = \begin{bmatrix} 4 & -2 \\ -1 & 3 \end{bmatrix}$ and I is the identity matrix of the same order and A^t is the transpose of the matrix of matrix A, find At.B + BI. **[3]**

(ii) In the figure given below, the medians BD and CE of triangle ABC meet at G. Prove that: **[3]**
   (a) $\Delta EGD \sim \Delta CGB$
   (b) $BG = 2\,GD$ from (i) above

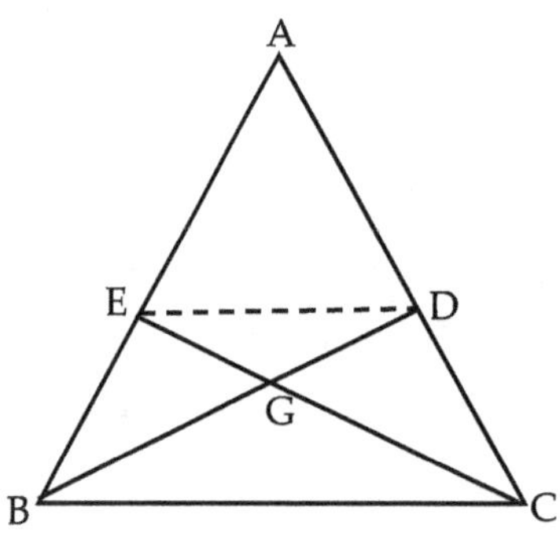

(iii) Use the Remainder Theorem to factorize the following expression:
$2x^3 + x^2 - 13x + 6$. **[4]**

Question 6.

(i) The equation of a line is $3x + 4y - 7 = 0$. Find: **[3]**
   (a) The slope of the line.
   (b) The equation of a line perpendicular to the given line and passing through the intersection of the lines $x - y + 2 = 0$ and $3x + y - 10 = 0$.

(ii) Prove the identity: $\dfrac{1}{\tan A + \cot A} = \cos A \cdot \sin A$ **[3]**

(iii) The third term of an A.P. is 7 and the seventh term exceeds three times the third term by 2. Find the first term, the common difference, and the sum of the first 20 terms. **[4]**

Question 7.

(i) A letter is chosen at random from the letter of the English alphabet. Find the probability that the letter chosen is a **[3]**

(a) Vowel

(b) Consonant

(c) A letter of the word SHUNTED.

(ii) Marbles of diameter 1.4cm are dropped into a cylindrical beaker containing some water and are fully submerged. The diameter of the beaker is 7cm. Find how many marbles have been dropped in it if the water rises by 5.6cm. **[3]**

(iii) In the given figure O is the center of the circle, $\angle BAD = 75°$, and chord BC=chord CD. Find: **[4]**

(a) $\angle BOC$

(b) $\angle OBD$

(c) $\angle BCD$.

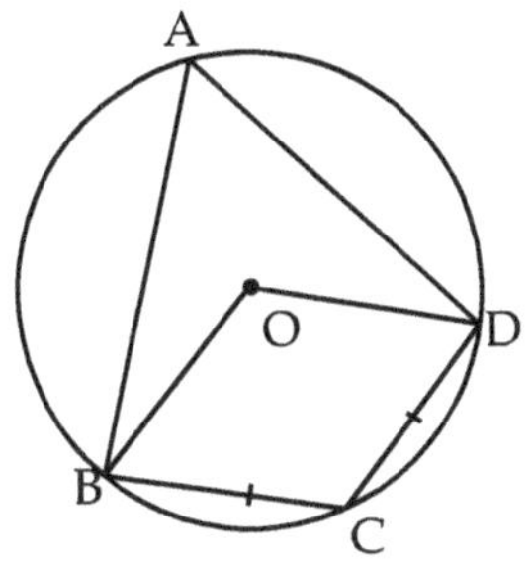

Question 8.

(i) Solve the following inequation and write the solution set: **[3]**

$13x - 5 < 15x + 4 < 7x + 12, x \in$ R, Represent the solution on a real number line.

(ii) Weights of 50 eggs were recorded as given below: **[3]**

Weight in gms	$80 - 84$	$85 - 89$	$90 - 94$	$95 - 99$	$100 - 104$	$105 - 109$	$110 - 114$
No. of eggs	5	10	12	12	8	2	1

Calculate their mean weight to the nearest gram.

(iii) ABC is a right-angled triangle with $\angle ABC = 90°$. D is any point on AB and DE is perpendicular to AC. Prove that: **[4]**

(a) $\triangle ADE \sim \triangle ACB$

(b) If AC $= 13$ cm, BC $= 5$ cm and AE $= 4$ cm. Find DE and AD.

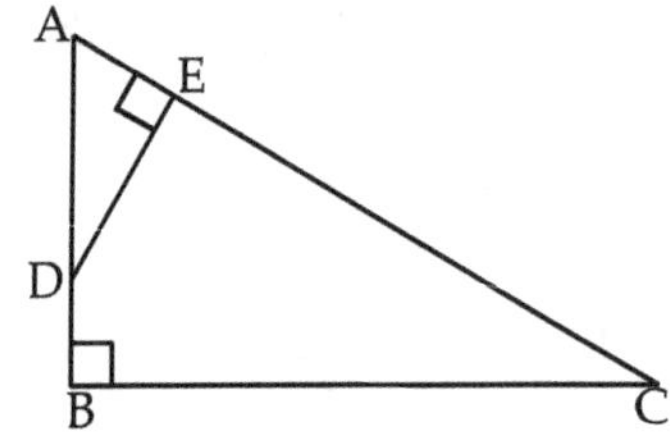

Question 9.

(i)   A boat can go 24 km downstream and 12 km upstream in a total of 4 hours. If speed of boat in still water is 9 km/hr, find the speed of the stream.   **[4]**

(ii) The weights of 60 boys are given in the following distribution table: **[6]**

Weight (kg)	37	38	39	40	41
No. of boys	10	14	18	12	6

Find:

(a) Median

(b) Lower quartile

(c) Upper quartile

(d) Inter-quartile range.

Question 10.

(i)   Using the properties of proportion: If $x = \dfrac{\sqrt{a+1}+\sqrt{a-1}}{\sqrt{a+1}-\sqrt{a-1}}$, prove that $x^2 - 2ax + 1 = 0$ **[3]**

(ii) Using a ruler and compasses only construct a triangle ABC in which BC = 4cm, $\angle ACB = 45°$ and perpendicular from A on BC is 2.5cm. Draw a circle circumscribing the triangle ABC.   **[3]**

(iii) The angle of elevation of the top of the tower from the foot of a building is 60°, and the angle of elevation of the top of the building from the foot of the tower is 30°. If the building is 50 m high, find the height of the tower.   **[4]**

Answers

Question 11.
(i)d ,(ii)b ,(iii)a ,(iv)b ,(v)c ,(vi)a ,(vii)d ,(viii)d ,(ix)c ,(x)b , (xi)b,(xii)a ,(xiii)b ,(xiv)b ,(xv)a
Question 12.
(ii) 5 years
Question 13.
(i) 64 , (ii) (a) 1:2, (b) (0, 3) , (iii) (b) D(-3, -2) (c) Arrow head
Question 14.
(i) (a) Rs. 3584 (b) Rs. 48(c) Rs. 240 (d) Rs. 4480, (ii) $\frac{4}{3}$, (iii) 36.25
Question 15.
(i) $\begin{bmatrix} 11 & -3 \\ 16 & 2 \end{bmatrix}$, (iii) $(x-2)(x+3)(2x-1)$
Question 16.
(i) (a) $-3/4$, (b) $4x-3y+4=0$, (iii) -1, 4, 740
Question 17.
(i) (a) $\frac{5}{26}$ (b) $\frac{21}{26}$ (c) $\frac{7}{26}$, (ii) 150 , (iii) (a) $75°$ (b) $15°$ (c) $105°$
Question 18.
(i) $\{x : x \in R, -4.5 < x < 1\}$ (ii)94 gm, (iii) (a) $DE = 1\frac{2}{3}$ cm, (b) $AD = 4\frac{1}{3}$ cm
Question 19.
(i)3 km/hr , (ii) (a) 39 (b) 38 (c) 40 (d) 2
Question 20.
(iii) 150 m

Maximum Marks: 80

Time allowed: Two and a half hours

Answers to this Paper must be written on the paper provided separately.

You will not be allowed to write during first 15 minutes.

This time is to be spent in reading the question paper.

The time given at the head of this Paper is the time allowed for writing the answers.

Attempt all questions from Section _A_ and any four questions from Section _B_.

The intended marks for questions or parts of questions are given in brackets [].

SECTION – A (40 Marks)

(Attempt all questions from this section)

Question 1. [15]

Chose the correct answers to the questions from the given options:

(i) $\dfrac{1+\tan^2 A}{1+\cot^2 A}$ is equal to:

    (a) $\sec^2 A$

    (b) -1

    (c) $\cot^2 A$

    (d) $\tan^2 A$

(ii) If $(x - k)$ is a factor of $x^3 - kx^2 - 9x + 18$. Find the value of 'k'.

    (a) -2

    (b) 2

    (c) 1

    (d) 3

(iii) Find x and y if $3[4 \quad x] + 2[y \quad -3] = [x \quad 0]$

    (a) $x = 2, y = -5$

    (b) $x = 2, y = 5$

    (c) $x = 3, y = 5$

    (d) $x = 3, y = -5$

(iv) Sum of first n terms of the series $\sqrt{2} + \sqrt{8} + \sqrt{18} + \cdots$ is:

    (a) $\dfrac{n(n+1)}{2}$

    (b) $\sqrt{2}n$

    (c) $\dfrac{n(n+1)}{\sqrt{2}}$

    (d) 1

(v)   A point P is its own image under the reflection in a line l. Describe the position of the point P with respect to the line l.
  (a) On x-axis
  (b) On y-axis
  (c) On line l
  (d) On origin

(vi) If the given figure AB = 24 cm, AC = 18cm, DE = 12 cm DF = 9 cm and$\angle BAC = \angle EDF$. Then $\triangle ABC \sim \triangle DEF$ by the condition.

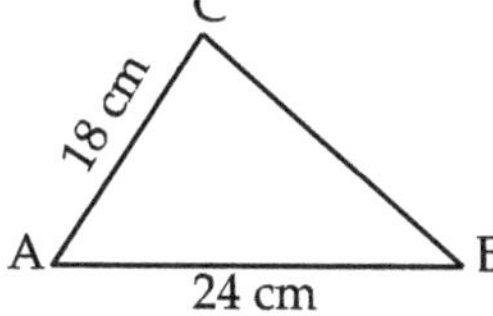

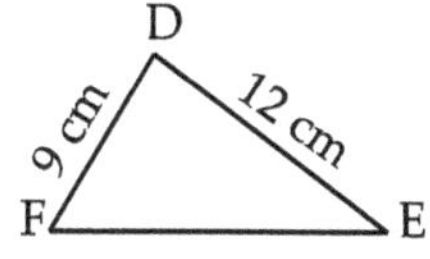

  (a) AAS
  (b) SSS
  (c) AAA
  (d) SAS

(vii) A right triangle with sides of 3cm, 4cm, and 5cm is rotated about the side of 3cm to form a cone. The volume of the cone so formed is
  (a) $22\pi\,\text{cm}^3$
  (b) $16\pi\,\text{cm}^3$
  (c) $15\pi\,\text{cm}^3$
  (d) $17\pi\,\text{cm}^3$

(viii) The solution set representing the following number line is:

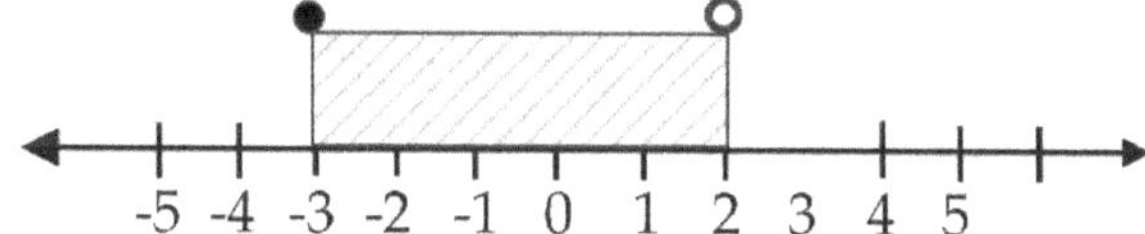

  (a) $\{x: x \in R, -3 \leq x < 2\}$
  (b) $\{x: x \in R, -3 < x < 2\}$
  (c) $\{x: x \in R, -3 < x \leq 2\}$
  (d) $\{x: x \in R, -3 \leq x \leq 2\}$

(ix) The probability of winning a race by a boy is $\frac{x}{12}$. If the probability of not winning the race by the boy is $\frac{2}{3}$, then $x =$
  (a) 2
  (b) 3
  (c) 4
  (d) 6

(x) The value of k for which the lines $kx - 5y + 4 = 0$ and $5x - 2y + 5 = 0$ are perpendicular to each other.
  (a) $k = 1$
  (b) $k = 3$
  (c) $k = 2$
  (d) $k = -2$

(xi) In the given figure AB is the diameter of the circle with center O. If BCD = 120°, find ∠DBA

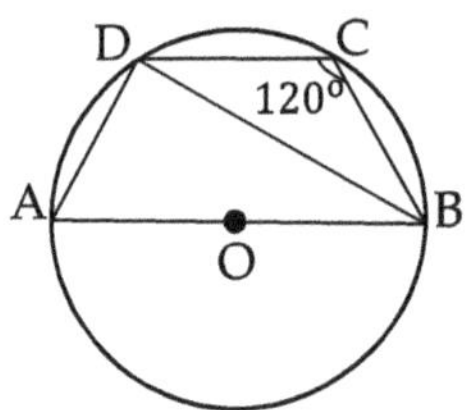

  (a) 25°
  (b) 50°
  (c) 60°
  (d) 30°

(xii) In the class test, the marks scored by 11 students are $13, 17, 20, 5, 3, 19, 7, 6, 11, 15,$ and 17. Find lower quartile:
  (a) 6
  (b) 13
  (c) 17
  (d) None

(xiii) A number of tangents from an external point to a circle:
  (a) 1
  (b) 2
  (c) 3
  (d) Infinitely many

(xiv) The point $(-3, 2)$ lies on the line $ax + 3y + 6 = 0$, calculate the value of 'a'.
  (a) $a = 4$
  (b) $a = 3$
  (c) $a = 2$
  (d) $a = -4$

(xv) State the co-ordinates of the point $(-6, 0)$ under reflection in line $y = 0$.
  (a) $(-6, -4)$
  (b) $(6, \ 4)$
  (c) $(6, -4)$
  (d) No change

Question 2.

(i) Prove the identity: $(\text{cosec}^2\ A - 1)(\sec A + 1)(\sec A - 1) = 1$ **[4]**

(ii) Soumya had a R.D. Account in the Union Bank of India and deposited Rs. 600 per month. If the maturity value of this account was Rs. 34,680 and the rate of interest was 10% per annum; find the time (in years) for which the account was held. **[4]**

(iii) If b is the mean proportion between a and c, then prove that: $\dfrac{a^4+a^2b^2+b^4}{b^4+b^2c^2+c^4} = \dfrac{a^2}{c^2}$

[4]

Question 3.

(i) T is the mid-point of the line segment joining the points $P(0, 5)$ and $Q(4, 0)$. T also divides the line segment OR in the ratio $1 : 2$. Find: **[4]**
  (a) co-ordinates of T
  (b) co-ordinates of R

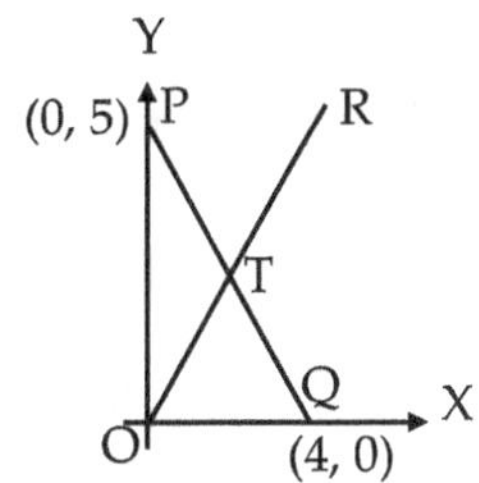

(ii) Attempt this question on graph paper: - **[5]**
  (a) Plot A $(3, 2)$ and B $(5, 4)$ on the graph paper. Take 2 cm = 1 unit on both axes.
  (b) Reflect A and B in the x-axis to the A′, and B′ plot than on the same graph paper.
  (c) Write down:
   i. The geometrical name of the figure ABB′A′
   ii. The image A″ of A, when A is reflected in the origin.
   iii. The single transformation that maps A′ to A″.

(iii) The internal and external diameters of a hollow hemispherical vessel are 21cm and 28cm respectively. Find: **[4]**
  (a) Internal curved surface area,
  (b) External curved surface area,
  (c) Total surface area,
  (d) Volume of material of the vessel.

SECTION – B (40 Marks)
(Attempt any four questions from this section)

Question 4.

(i) Manufacturer A sells a washing machine to dealer B for Rs. 12500. Dealer B sells it to a consumer at a profit of Rs. 1500. If the sales are Intra–state and the rate of GST is 12%. Find: **[3]**

    (a) The amount of tax (under GST) paid by the dealer to the Central Government.

    (b) The amount of tax (under GST) received by State Government.

    (c) The amount that the consumer pays for the machine.

(ii) Without solving the following quadratic equation, find the value of ' m ' for which the given equation has real and equal roots. **[3]**

$$x^2 + 2(m-1)x + (m+5) = 0$$

(iii) For the following frequency distribution draw a histogram. Hence calculate the mode. **[4]**

Class	$0-5$	$5-10$	$10-15$	$15-20$	$20-25$	$25-30$
Frequency	2	7	18	10	8	5

Question 5.

(i) Find x and y, if: $\begin{bmatrix} -2 & 0 \\ 3 & 1 \end{bmatrix}\begin{bmatrix} -1 \\ 2x \end{bmatrix} + 3\begin{bmatrix} -2 \\ 1 \end{bmatrix} = 2\begin{bmatrix} y \\ 3 \end{bmatrix}$ **[3]**

(ii) In the given figure, ABC is a right-angled triangle with$\angle BAC = 90^\circ$ **[3]**
    (a) Prove that: $\triangle ADB \sim \triangle CDA$
    (b) If $BD = 18$ cm and $CD = 8cm$, find AD.

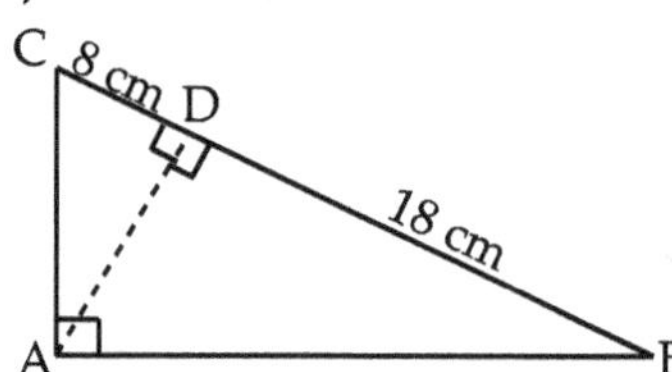

(iii) When $x^3 + 3x^2 - kx + 4$ is divided by $x - 2$, and the remainder is k. Find the value of constant k. **[4]**

Question 6.

(i) In the given figure, write: **[3]**
    (a) The co-ordinates of A, B, and C.

{186}

(b) The equation of the line through A and // to BC.

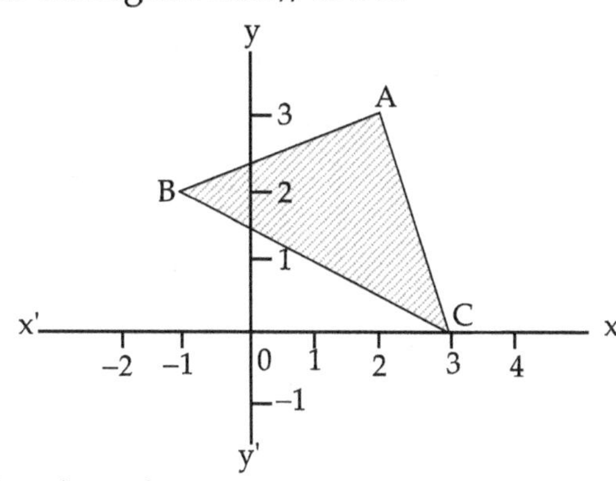

(ii) Prove the identity: $\dfrac{\sec A - 1}{\sec A + 1} = \dfrac{1 - \cos A}{1 + \cos A}$ [3]

(iii) Find the sum of all natural numbers lying between 100 to 200 which are divisible by 4. [4]

Question 7.

(i) Two coins are tossed once. Find the probability of getting: [3]
    (a) 2 heads
    (b) At least 1 tail.
    (c) At most 1 tail

(ii) From a solid cylinder, whose height is 8cm and radius is 6cm, a conical cavity of the height of 8cm and with a base radius of 6cm is hollowed out. Find the volume of the remaining solid. Also, find the total surface area of the remaining solid. [3]

(iii) In the above figure, AB is parallel to DC, $\angle BCE = 80°$, $\angle BAC = 25°$. Find:
    (a) $\angle CAD$
    (b) $\angle CBD$
    (c) $\angle ADC$. [4]

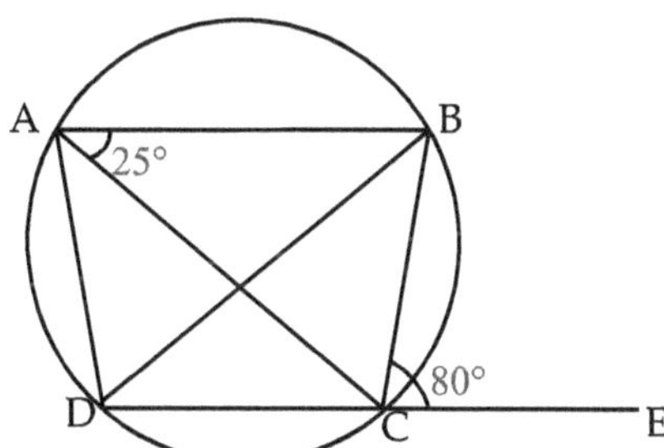

Question 8.

(i) Find the values of x, which satisfy the inequation: [3]
$$-2 \le \frac{1}{2} - \frac{2x}{3} \le 1\frac{5}{6}, x \in \text{N}.$$ Graph the solution on the number line.

(ii) If the mean of the following distribution is 7.5, find the missing frequency f: **[3]**

Variate	5	6	7	8	9	10	11	12
Frequency	20	17	f	10	8	6	7	6

(iii) In the figure given below, QPR is a right-angled triangle, right-angled at Q. XY is parallel to QR, $PQ = 6\,cm$, $PY = 4\,cm$, and $PX : XQ = 1 : 2$. Calculate the lengths of PR and QR. **[4]**

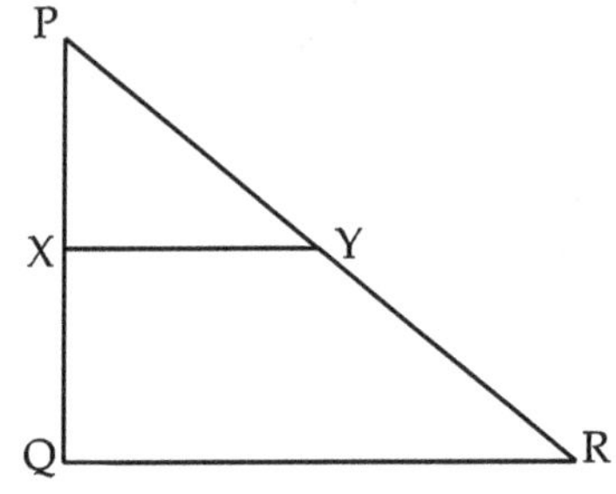

Question 9.

(i) Five years ago, a woman's age was the square of her son's age. Ten years hence her age will be twice that of her son's age. Find: - **[4]**
(a) The age of the son five years ago
(b) The present age of the woman.

(ii) The marks obtained by 100 students in a test are given below: **[3]**

Marks obtained	20	24	28	30	33	38	42	44
No. of students	6	16	22	28	15	4	5	4

Find the median marks.

(iii) In the given figure, DE || BC. **[3]**
(a) Prove that: $\triangle ADE \sim \triangle ABC$
(b) Given that $AD = \frac{1}{2}BD$, calculate DE, if $BC = 4.5$ cm.

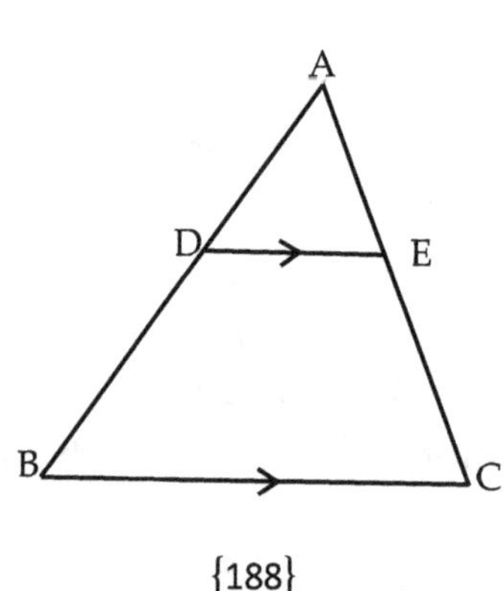

Question 10.

(i) Using the properties of proportion: If $\frac{x^2+y^2}{x^2-y^2} = 2\frac{1}{8}$, find: **[3]**

(a) $\frac{x}{y}$

(b) $\frac{x^3+y^3}{x^3-y^3}$

(ii) Draw a line segment AB of length 8cm. Taking A as the center, draw a circle of radius 4cm, and taking B as the center, draw another circle of radius 3cm. Construct tangents to each circle from the center of the other circle.

[3]

(iii) The angle of elevation of an airplane from a point on the ground is $45°$. After 15 seconds of flight, the angle changes to $30°$. If the plane is flying at a constant height of 2500 m, find the speed of the plane in km/hr. **[4]**

Answers

Question 21.

(i) d , (ii) b , (iii) a , (iv) c , (v) c , (vi) d , (vii) b , (viii) a, (ix) c, (x) d, (xi) d, (xii) a, (xiii) b, (xiv) a, (xv) d

Question 22.

(ii) 4 years

Question 23.

(i) (a) $\left(2, \frac{5}{2}\right)$ (b) $(6, \frac{15}{2})$ (ii) (c) 1. isosceles trapezium 2. (-3, -2) 3. y – axis]
(iii) (a) 693 cm^2 (b) 1232 cm^2 (c) 2194.50 cm^2 (d) 3323.83 cm^3

Question 24.

(i) (a) Rs. 90 (b) Rs. 840 (c) Rs. 15680, (ii) 4, -1, (iii) 12.50

Question 25.

(i) $x = 3, y = -2$, (ii) 12 cm, (iii) $k = 8$

Question 26.

(i) (a) (2,3), (–1,2), (3, 0) (b) $x + 2y - 8 = 0$, (iii) 3900

Question 27.

(i) (a) $\frac{1}{4}$ (b) $\frac{3}{4}$ (c) $\frac{3}{4}$, (ii) $603\frac{3}{7}$ cm^3, $603\frac{3}{7}$ cm^2, (iii) (a) $55°$ (b) $55°$ (c) $100°$

Question 28.

(i) {1, 2, 3} (ii) $x = 16$, (iii) PR = 12 cm, QR = 10.392 cm

Question 29.

(i) (a) 5yrs (b) 30yrs, (ii) 30, (iii) (b) 1.5 cm

Question 30.

(i) (a) $\frac{5}{3}$, (ii) $\frac{76}{49}$, (iii) $600\left(\sqrt{3} - 1\right)$ km/hr